Further Praise for
The Communication Solution

"Planning change is an increasingly important and popular topic across a variety of organizational settings, and nowhere is the need greater than in higher education. *The Communication Solution* helps to address this priority, and it does so in a way that translates theories of organizational change and communication theory into a practical guide for leaders at all levels."

—**Brent Ruben**, PhD, distinguished professor of
communication; founder and senior university fellow,
Center for Organizational Leadership, Rutgers University

"With rapid and uncertain changes in higher education, we need this book now more than ever. Smulowitz uses a storytelling approach to show real-world examples of how to successfully plan and implement change and avoid common pitfalls. Merging theories of leadership and communication, this accessible and engaging text is an essential guide for practitioners, educators, and students."

—**Carolyn Cunningham**, PhD, associate professor,
communication & leadership studies, school of
leadership studies, Gonzaga University, Spokane, WA

"Smulowitz has created a book of incredible value to leaders in higher education. Academics are often asked to 'step up' into administrative roles with little training or experience. Further, they usually find that most books about leadership and change might offer effective advice for managing within corporate cultures but lack relevance for higher education. *The Communication Solution* addresses the unique nature and mission of academic organizations—the diverse range of internal and external stakeholders and their needs, and the critical importance of empowering them—in laying out a roadmap for effective leadership and successful change within our institutions of higher education. Informed by theory and research, but highly accessible and useful for approaching real-world challenges, this book should be required reading for administrators at all levels of our colleges and universities."

—**Jennifer H. Waldeck**, PhD, professor & associate dean,
faculty affairs & academic programming,
Chapman University, Orange, CA

"In a book that is both grounded in theory and immensely practical, Smulowitz has provided an indispensable resource for students and seasoned leaders alike. She writes as a colleague and mentor who understands that the foundational work of self-knowledge and deep listening is as essential to organizational change as the concrete plans to enact it. Her analogies and true-to-life stories breathe context into the data and test it in the real world of organizational leadership."

—**Stephanie Russell**, vice president for mission
integration, Association of Jesuit Colleges and Universities

The Communication Solution

The Communication Solution

Leading Successful Change in Higher Education

Stacy Smulowitz

ROWMAN & LITTLEFIELD
Lanham • Boulder • New York • London

Published by Rowman & Littlefield
An imprint of The Rowman & Littlefield Publishing Group, Inc.
4501 Forbes Boulevard, Suite 200, Lanham, Maryland 20706
www.rowman.com

6 Tinworth Street, London SE11 5AL, United Kingdom

British Library Cataloguing in Publication Information Available

Library of Congress Cataloging-in-Publication Data

Names: Smulowitz, Stacy, 1972- author.
Title: The communication solution : leading successful change in higher education / Stacy Smulowitz.
Description: Lanham, Maryland : Rowman & Littlefield Publishers, 2020. | Includes bibliographical references.
Identifiers: LCCN 2020035079 (print) | LCCN 2020035080 (ebook) | ISBN 9781475854633 (cloth) | ISBN 9781475854640 (paperback) | ISBN 9781475854657 (epub)
Subjects: LCSH: Universities and colleges—United States—Administration. | Communication in higher education—United States. | Educational leadership—United States. | Educational change—United States. | College administrators—Professional relationships—United States.
Classification: LCC LB2341 .S564 2020 (print) | LCC LB2341 (ebook) | DDC 378.00973—dc23
LC record available at https://lccn.loc.gov/2020035079
LC ebook record available at https://lccn.loc.gov/2020035080

♾™ The paper used in this publication meets the minimum requirements of American National Standard for Information Sciences—Permanence of Paper for Printed Library Materials, ANSI/NISO Z39.48-1992.

Contents

Preface   ix

Acknowledgments   xiii

Introduction   1
    How to Use This Book   4
    Summary   4

Part I: Essential Groundwork   5

1 The Nature of Organizational Change   7
    What You Can Expect to Learn in This Chapter   7
    What Is Organizational Change?   7
    The Effect of Planned Organizational Change on Organizations   8
      Resistance   8
    Summary   10
    Notes   11

2 Approaches to the Process of Planned Organizational Change   15
    What You Can Expect to Learn in This Chapter   15
    Strategies for Planned Organizational Change Efforts   15
    Models of Planned Organizational Change Efforts   16
    Top-Level Strategies   17
    Performance Measurement Systems   18
    Summary   20
    Notes   20

3 The Nature of Communication   23
    What You Can Expect to Learn in This Chapter   23

Communication Models   23
    One-Way Communication Flow   24
    Kinetic Flow of Communication   25
    Communication-as-Meaning View   26
The Communication Information Relationship   27
The Inner Workings of Communication   28
    Developing a Sense of Self   28
    Developing Our Own Reality through Perception   29
    Developing Artifacts   30
    Developing an Appreciation of Environmental Threats and
        Negative Feedback   31
    Relying on Our Unconscious Self to Participate in Life 31
    Developing a Way to Organize and Give Meaning to Events
        and People   31
Worldview   34
Summary   35
Notes   35

4 The Nature of Leadership   45
What You Can Expect to Learn in This Chapter   45
What Is Leadership?   45
Why Leadership Is an Important Issue   47
Leadership Approaches   48
Summary   57
Notes   57

Part II: Leadership Practices That Work   **63**

5 Preparing to Lead by Understanding the Higher Education
    Environment   65
What You Can Expect to Learn in This Chapter   65
    External Pressures   66
    Internal Pressures   69
Operational Differences between Higher Education and
    Traditional Industry   70
Systems Thinking   70
Summary   72
Notes   72

6 Leadership Requires Commitment   75
What You Can Expect to Learn in This Chapter   75
Vision   75
Clarity and Reducing Uncertainty   77
Feedback   78
Momentum, Priority, and Urgency   79

Resources 80
Summary 81
Notes 81

7 The Importance of Leading through a Change Agent 85
What You Can Expect to Learn in this Chapter 85
Outlets for Organizational Members to Share 86
Participation, Empowerment, and Involvement 87
Process 88
Summary 90
Notes 90

8 Leaders and the Communication Environment 95
What You Can Expect to Learn in This Chapter 95
Communication and Information 95
Cocreation of Reality 97
Worldview 98
Nonverbal Communication 100
Intentional and Planned versus Unintentional and Unplanned
    Communication 100
Summary 103
Notes 103

9 Organizational Change Buy-In Commitment Loop 107
What You Can Expect to Learn in This Chapter 107
Involving Organizational Members in Decision-Making about
    the Change 109
Voice 110
Why Give Organizational Members Voice? 112
Neglect 113
Buy-In/Commitment Loop 113
Summary 114
Notes 115

Part III: Leadership Toolkit **117**

10 Phase 1: Self Discovery 119
What You Can Expect to Learn in This Chapter 119
It All Begins with You: Becoming Self-Aware 119
Discovering Assumptions and Managing Perceptions 122
    Assumptions 122
    Your Expertise Can Be Limiting 124
Leadership Styles 124
Summary 126
Notes 126

11 Phase 2: Organizational Member Discovery   129
What You Can Expect to Learn in This Chapter   129
   Step 1: Understand Organizational Member's Worldview   130
   Step 2: Create your Main Message to be used Throughout
     the Change Effort   130
   Step 3: Conduct Assessments and Create a Resource List   132
Quick Guide to Steps in the Discovery of Organizational
     Members' Worldview   133
Summary   134
Notes   134

12 Phase 3: Implementation   137
What You Can Expect to Learn in This Chapter   137
Steps to Successful Planned Change Programs   137
   Step 1: Planning   138
   Step 2: Awareness   139
   Step 3: Understanding of and Agreement about
     the Need to Change   142
   Step 4: Involvement   143
   Step 5: Commitment   144
   Step 6: Action   146
   Step 7: Integration   146
   Step 8: Assessment   147
Summary   147
Notes   149

Conclusion   153

References   157

Index   177

About the Author   183

Preface

If you're reading this book, you've probably encountered an organizational change or two. Maybe you've even been asked to lead one—starting tomorrow! I'm sure you've seen successful organizational changes. And, I'm extra sure you've seen some major flops. Sometimes it seems like no matter what you do or how much time and effort you and your team put into the change effort, the old system or ways of doing things keep coming back. Surely, there must be a better way.

You aren't the first person to feel this way, and you won't be the last. There are lots of reasons why planned change efforts fail and lots of reasons why employees revert back to the systems you are trying to change. The key is to learn as much as you can about what works, what doesn't work, and how to best plan for your specific planned organizational change.

But first, a story or two.

MY STORY

My interest in organizational change efforts begins when I was working at a manufacturing organization where I traveled the country with the president, vice president, and director of human resources. As we traveled to each manufacturing plant, the president told employees the story of her resignation from the company when she was chief financial officer and the subsequent appeal from the company's owner to return and save the company.

I grew more and more intrigued each time I heard this story. If things were so bad with the company that she resigned, what would compel her to return? Why did she think she could save the company? What about her message to employees motivated some and detered others? How is our trip to all the manufacturing plants going to change anything? Is there anything I can do that will really make an impact on the company's turnaround?

My job was to implement the first-ever employee opinion survey in all the manufacturing plants across the United States. My favorite memory is from the manufacturing plant in southern California. The plant manager told us that the employees only spoke Spanish, so I brought surveys that were translated into Spanish. An interpreter translated my introduction and explanation for the survey from English to Spanish to the employees. As I watched the employees turn in the survey, I found something really interesting. Almost every survey response was written in English!

Stunned, I asked the interpreter how this happened as I was told that the employees only knew Spanish. I'll never forget his smile when he told me that the employees decided they liked me enough to make it easy for me to read the answers. Then he asked me to keep their knowledge of English a secret from the plant manager. Now I was deeper and deeper into how this process of change works and why people behave the way they do.

THEIR STORY

Years and many organizational change efforts later, I found myself in higher education, observing yet more and more planned organizational changes. These changes had many similarities to the ones I experienced in industry. However, there were some stark differences. These differences, I found out, were because of the nature of the way academic institutions are structured. Again, I watched with curiosity as staff fought over office furniture, had to relocate miles away, and then from their perspective observed the leaders seemingly forget about the whole change effort.

This book tells the story of this change effort and a few other select instances from other academic institutions. This particular change effort is set at a public university in the Northeastern United States. The change was part of a master plan to consolidate several colleges within the university into one cohesive structure. There was much planning that went into the change effort—and much good intention. You'll find that good intentions typically begin most planned change efforts!

With a student focus, the task force recommended changes to the university structure because students applying to and graduating from the university were held to different standards depending on their college within the university. Further, students had access to different benefits, such as career information, depending on their college. The university president decided that the task force recommendations would be implemented during one summer so that the students would not be affected.

Several months later, I interviewed many of the staff, department heads, and senior leaders involved with this planned organizational change effort. In some instances, the stories told from all levels of the organization were similar, while in others, they were very different. One story remained the same. The change occurred. The structure was different. The subsequent reporting system that was to accompany the change, however, had fizzled. The quotes and many of the insights featured throughout this book are taken from this research and is referred to as Case Study Large University throughout the book.[1] Other, smaller anecdotes, will be identified as such and also come from real situations. These are referred to as Case Study Small University throughout the book. Of course, names are changed to protect the guilty as well as the innocent. The story of this larger change effort that you will hear begins with good intentions and ends with frustration, confusion, and relief to have come to the end of the change effort—or did it?

NOTE

1. Smulowitz, S. (2014). Planned organizational change in Higher Education: Dashboard indicators and stakeholder sensemaking—A case study. (Unpublished doctoral dissertation). Rutgers, The State University of New Jersey, New Brunswick, NJ.

Acknowledgments

A project such as this book is not something done in solitude. Many, many thanks to Vicky, Alex, John, Mom, and Dad who provided encouragement, patience, and understanding on countless nights and weekends. This book is dedicated to you.

Many thanks also to Stacey Connaughton who provided unending reviews and advice. And to peer reviewers and other readers: Christina S. Beck, Patty Levan, and Ellen Wilson. Without your thoughtful comments, this book would not be what it is today.

Many special thanks to Tom Koerner, whose positivity, encouragement, and understanding kept me working hard. And, whose enthusiastic support motivated me. And also to Carlie Wall, whose positivity and kindness kept me going. And, whose hard work and dedication helped to make this book be its best.

My unending gratefulness to those whose story is told here and who participated in the research.

Finally, to those who helped me to stick with it, my sincerest appreciation: Angie Gilliland, Susan Jolley, Doreen Rushton, and Kim Strobel.

Introduction

Change is inevitable—especially in higher education, which is faced with pressure of an array of issues from increasing accountability to the rising cost of education, newer and better campus facilities, outstanding foodservice, campus safety, diversity, and inclusion. This pressure comes from a variety of stakeholders such as the following:

- government entities, regulators and figures;
- parents;
- students;
- alumni;
- taxpayers;
- community members;
- donors and funding sources;
- accreditors; and
- boards.

The outlook on education has changed from one where learning is paramount to one where finding a job is the ultimate goal. More and more students are demanding accelerated, online education. Campus-based students compare institutions of higher education not only on academics but also on quality of food and dorm rooms. Donors and politicians are calling for increased accountability of student learning. Parents are concerned about the percentage of students who graduate as well as how long it takes to graduate. And, that's just the beginning.

Higher education leaders not only face these pressing challenges from outside but also face many other challenges from inside the academy. Declining enrollment leads to higher discount rates, which leads to rising costs and

1

budget cuts. Budget cuts affect availability of programming for students, faculty research, and updates to technology and facilities. In some cases, the need to cut budgets leads to less tenure track and more adjunct faculty. A higher percentage of adjunct faculty leads prospective students and their parents to question the quality of education. It's a vicious cycle.

How did this happen? Higher education is organized in silos with many moving parts, both internal and external, that operate on their own. Many leaders in higher education have risen from the academic environment and have not had the opportunity to learn the delicate balance of leading such a diverse entity as they were able to learn the intricacies of their academic discipline. The sheer amount of internal and external issues happening in each silo all at once becomes difficult to handle as priorities overlap. As a result, it is more difficult for leaders in higher education to manage the change process and be successful.

What can the leader do?

1. Self-Discovery—Leaders must step back and objectively assess how they lead and respond to organizational member reactions. Leading change in such a diverse entity requires the skill to manage the communication environment. But first, the leader must have self-awareness of their own beliefs, biases, habits, and vision.
2. Organizational Member Discovery—Especially employees who are being asked to change. Leaders continue to manage the communication environment by being open to learning about concerns from organizational members and the reasons they might resist the change effort. Leaders need to balance what they learn about organizational members with their own self-awareness as well as the vision for the organization.
3. Implement—A Lasting Planned Organizational Change Effort. Managing the communication environment is crucial. The leader must be able to provide organizational members with a clear picture about the ultimate goal of the change effort, its importance to the survival of the organization and where and how organizational members fit in. To be able to do this, the leader must be able to turn silos into collaborative units that recognize and embrace the importance of and lead the change effort for the institution, their department, and most of all for themselves.

Time and time again leaders in higher education—and other industries—make the same mistakes. This book is written to point out how easy it is to make those mistakes, why they happen so often, and how to avoid those mistakes in the future. Using the ideas and concepts in this book can not only help prevent those mistakes but also facilitate lasting planned organizational change to permeate institutional silos and enhance leadership development and overall success.

Employees may expect more out of the planned organizational change effort than you think they do. It's your job as a leader to discover those expectations and to let organizational members drive successful change for your institution. Turn your next planned organizational change effort into a process of collaboration and partnership.

The purpose of this book is to provide a source of advice and direction for current, aspiring, and everyday staff, faculty, and administrative leaders from all disciplines in all varieties of higher education institutions. This book will also provide advice and direction for those who teach practical and theoretical courses on leadership, organizational change, and administration in higher education. Students will learn theory and practical applications and implications of planned organizational change processes. As an added bonus, you can learn more at www.stacysmulowitz.com about the author's views on planned organizational change.

This book provides a practical and theoretical guide based on preexisting and original research data to issues surrounding planned organizational change strategies, core competencies, tools, actions, and an understanding of employee sensemaking of the change process needed for effective leadership in the ever-changing higher education setting.

This book is organized around several themes:

- Part I: Essential Groundwork: Change strategies and performance measurement systems (chapters 1, 2) pinpoint why planned change is important, detail planned organizational change strategies and performance measurement systems, and provide an explanation for the reason that so many organizational members resist change. Communication models, the relationship between communication and information, characteristics of communication, worldviews, the definition of communication, and leadership styles lay the groundwork for understanding their fit to planned organizational change strategies in future chapters (chapters 3, 4).
- Part II: Leadership Practices That Work: An overview of the higher education environment (chapter 5) including the concepts of constant change, silos, systems thinking, diverse array of stakeholders and needs, academic values, and implications for leading change efforts. Proven strategies for leaders to help increase the likelihood of success in change efforts (chapter 6, 7, 8), including commitment, change agents, and the communication environment. The buy-in/commitment loop (chapter 9) ties leadership practices to a fast-track to organizational member buy-in for future change efforts.
- Part III: Leadership Toolkit: A three-phase process for helping leaders and organizational members to drive and succeed at planned change efforts (chapters 10, 11, 12). It details eight steps of successful planned change efforts in higher education.

HOW TO USE THIS BOOK

For the Practitioner: This book contains much useful and practical advice and processes for preparing for and implementing a planned organizational change. You can skip ahead to chapters 5–12 and circle back to the chapters with more theoretical background and information (chapters 1–4). This information will become useful to you to help you understand where the advice is coming from and also the research that supports it.

For the Faculty: For most undergraduate courses and introductory graduate courses, it is helpful for students to read the book from the beginning to be able to grasp the theory behind the processes of planned organizational change. You can supplement this book with a community-based learning project where students are assigned in groups to work with an organization, perhaps on campus or nearby in the community, that is ready to undergo a planned organizational change. Students can act as a consultant group and provide a brief to the client within the organization of a plan to implement the change in their organization.

For the Student: It will be helpful to you, especially if this is the first time you are learning or reading about planned organizational change, to have a thorough understanding of the research. For that reason, it is best that you read the book from beginning to end. Read it, of course, so you can pass your exams. However, it will be most useful to you as a guide for your own change effort. whether you are part of a change effort at work, in a volunteer organizational, or even in your family.

SUMMARY

There are many good books about leading change in academic institutions. Few books reveal the most important part of the change effort journey—how to take into account the cultural conditioning, and the worldview that you and members of your organization have. And how this worldview has limited the thinking, feeling, behaviors, and habits that take place subconsciously throughout every day. The success of your planned change effort rests on your habits. By applying the strategies you learn in this book, you'll have the tools you need to establish and maintain habits for a successful planned change effort at your academic institution.

Part I

Essential Groundwork

As you dig into part I, get ready to immerse yourself in all the nuggets of wisdom about organizational change, leadership, and communication. The information in these chapters lay the groundwork for the decisions and perspectives you need to enact planned organizational change. After reading part I, you will have the necessary understanding of the major components, background, history, and current research into planned organizational change, leadership, and communication. Sit back, devour, and get charged up.

Chapter 1

The Nature of Organizational Change

WHAT YOU CAN EXPECT TO LEARN IN THIS CHAPTER

- What is planned versus unplanned organizational change?
- What are the characteristics of planned organizational change?
- What are some of the effects of planned organizational change on organizations?
- What are some barriers to successful planned organizational change efforts?
- Why do organizational members resist planned organizational change efforts?
- What are some strategies to overcome resistance to planned organizational change efforts?

WHAT IS ORGANIZATIONAL CHANGE?

Being an academic leader requires a basic understanding of the one constant you will endure as a leader in any organization—change. Organizational change is any change that takes place in any organization. One type of change is externally forced, or *unplanned* by organizational members, such as a fire, natural disaster, or even a regulation.[1]

The second type of change is *planned* by organizational members. This type of change can be as simple as using a new colored folder for the same task or something more complex that would change the entire campus. For example, a large, public research university in the Northeastern United States recently underwent a massive planned organizational change. This planned change effort altered the reporting structure for some office staff and required others to move their offices—some up to 50 miles away.

Throughout this book, the concept of planned (as opposed to unplanned) organizational change is used because as leaders we are most often faced with implementing planned change, and it is important to understand the complexities and strategies to do so. A planned organizational change typically occurs because organizational members have determined that this change will improve a shortcoming or impede an anticipated problem.[2] Some leaders design incremental or smaller change to the organization, which leaves the organizational culture in place.[3] Other leaders plan more radical, or revolutionary change which will also change the organization's culture.[4]

Planned organizational change can have a dramatic effect on the organization and its members. Successful implementation can boost employee morale, productivity, and organizational profits.[5] However, some costs associated with planned organizational change include lost time for training, organizational members who resent the changes or leave the organization, uncertainty, and stakeholder weariness.[6]

THE EFFECT OF PLANNED ORGANIZATIONAL CHANGE ON ORGANIZATIONS

Success rates for implementing planned organizational changes are dismal. Some reports show 60–80 percent of change efforts fail to meet their objectives, others in health and social care show that 70 percent fail, and 72 percent fail in IT.[7]

Some change efforts fail because of issues during implementation such as leadership, funding, technology, communication, staffing, and stakeholder reactions.[8] Other reason change efforts fail is a direct result of leaders implementing numerous change efforts over a short duration.[9] As a result, organizational members become burned out, worn out, skeptical, and resistant to future change efforts.[10]

Don't throw in the towel yet! Although most planned organizational changes fail, you can do specific things as a leader to enjoy success. Let's begin with a discussion about resistance to change efforts.

Resistance

Why can't people just go along with the plan? Think about making changes in your life. How did you react the last time your commute to work was rerouted because of a planned construction project or your doctor asked you to eat more veggies and less red meat again? Were you ready to comply without any complaints or trying to figure out a workaround? If so, consider yourself lucky, and rare. The rest of us prefer when things stay the same.[11]

When asked to make changes at work, organizational members become worried or uncertain about their job security, have a lack of trust that things will go as planned, and also have personality conflicts with others.[12] As a result, they tend to resist by doing things like hoard information, lie, become defensive, harbor negative thoughts, and even sabotage plans.[13]

Sometimes, organizational members resist change because they are used to and prefer the status quo, or when things stay the same.[14] Causes of resistance include such issues as lack of trust, threat to job status or security, and personality conflicts, among others.[15]

Ways to look at resistance include behavior, emotion, or cognition. Examples of resistance as behavior include hoarding information, insubordination, and dishonesty.[16] Emotional resistance examples include frustration, aggression, worry, defensiveness, and fear.[17] Examples of cognition resistance include negative thoughts about the change, reluctance, and unreadiness.[18]

Much of the research places blame on employees for resisting change efforts, rather than managers.[19] However, other research points to a manager's lack of communication skills to effectively educate, inform, and persuade organizational members about the change effort.[20] Others point to resistance as an opportunity to take a step back to find areas of improvement in the change effort plan.[21]

When the leader attends to the communication environment of the organization, these would-be resistors can be turned into your biggest champions. Once they understand and are involved in the process, many resistors will go to others and help get them on board.

Some resistors do so because it's the best option for the organization. Leaders need to listen to all resistors and remember that nobody's perfect. Often, employees who work in the trenches and are closest to the situation that needs to change can offer better or just as good alternate change effort solutions. And, more often, these employees will be wondering what took the leader so long to notice that a change had to be made.

A plethora of research shows that leaders have the ability to make the change effort succeed or fail.[22] Some of the ways that leaders can prevent the cause of resistance (worry, fear and uncertainty) rather than address the symptoms (resistance such as defensive, lying saboteurs) include effective communication, specifying a vision for the change effort, ensure stakeholder participation and engagement in the change effort, provide resources, appoint a change agent, provide consistent and timely feedback, and provide visible and consistent support.[23]

Particularly, participation has a large effect on overcoming resistance. Participation allows organizational members to have a say in the change effort, reduces their uncertainty, and helps them to feel that they have more control over the change effort.[24]

Rarely does one see a "significant and successful" large-scale change effort for three reasons.[25] The first reason is that changing the culture of an organization is extremely difficult and this is what's required for deep change efforts.[26] Second, making a case for a change effort is ideal when an organization is at the top of its game. However, this is often a very difficult argument because the organization is so successful.[27] Lastly, there is limited knowledge about planning and implementing organizational change efforts.[28]

Barriers to change effort success include lack of resources (funding, human resources, technological); uncommitted and/or weak leaders; deficient technology; lack of trained staff; ignored or overlooked communication; stakeholder fatigue with too many change programs in a short amount of time; implementation issues; inability to change the culture of the organization to adopt the new change; and unanticipated stakeholder reactions such as resistance or worse.[29] Organizational members are resilient and will find a way to return to previous work habits if culture change does not occur.[30]

Leaders are *the most vital, visible determinant* in the success or failure of planned change efforts.[31] Leaders set the vision and goals for the change effort. They provide the impetus, resources, and ongoing support for change efforts. Leaders of failed change efforts may underestimate one or more of the following: the intricacies of a change effort program; their required dedication and support to the effort; the vision; participation and commitment of the organizational members; the subtleties of organizational culture; the organization's ability to begin and sustain the change effort.[32]

In the end, it is the perception of the organizational members that matters most. If organizational members perceive that the change effort was a success, then it was a success even if the leader perceives the change effort as a failure.[33] Further, the impressions of the organizational members about the current change effort will impact their attitudes about change efforts in the future.[34]

Our perceptions and understanding of the change effort determine our reaction to it. Our understanding is a result of our feelings and thoughts and co-construction, or how we create our view, of reality with others in our organization.[35]

SUMMARY

As a leader of an institution of higher education, it is important to have an understanding of the differences between planned and unplanned organizational change. Most change efforts are planned to improve a shortcoming or anticipated problem. However, success rates for successful planned organizational change are dismal. Often, the change effort itself is blamed. Really, there are a variety of reasons change efforts fail.

While resistance is blamed frequently for failure, listening to reasons that organizational members resist the change effort can be an important step to successful change. Leaders, communication, and participation can have a dramatic effect on the success of the change effort.

NOTES

1. Lewis, L. K. (2011). *Organizational change: Creating change through strategic communication.* Malden, MA: Wiley-Blackwell.

2. Poole, M. S., & Van de Ven, A. H. (2004). *Handbook of organizational change and innovation.* New York: Oxford University Press.

Weick, K. E., & Quinn, R. E. (1999). Organizational change and development. *Annual Review of Psychology, 50,* 361–386.

3. Burke, W. W. (2008). *Organization change: Theory and practice* (2nd ed.). Thousand Oaks, CA: Sage Publishing.

Orlikowski, W. J. (1993). The duality of technology: Rethinking the concept of technology in organizations. *Organization Science, 3*(3), 398–427.

4. Burke, W. W. (2008). *Organization change: Theory and practice* (2nd ed.). Thousand Oaks, CA: Sage Publishing.

Gersick, C. J. G. (1991). Revolutionary change theories: A multilevel exploration of the punctuated equilibrium paradigm. *The Academy of Management Review, 16*(1), 10–36.

Orlikowski, W. J. (1993). The duality of technology: Rethinking the concept of technology in organizations. *Organization Science, 3*(3), 398–427.

5. Klein, K. J., & Sorra, J. S. (1996). The challenge of innovation implementation. *Academy of Management Review, 21*(4), 1055–1080.

6. Lewis, L. K. (2011). *Organizational change: Creating change through strategic communication.* Malden, MA: Wiley-Blackwell.

7. Kee, J. E., & Newcomer, K. E. (2008). Why do change efforts fail?: What can leaders do about it? *The Public Manager, 37*(3), 5–12.

Moullin, M. (2002). *Delivering excellence in health and social care.* Buckingham, UK: Open University Press.

Ruben, B. D. (2009). *Understanding, planning, and leading organizational change: Core concepts and strategies.* Washington, DC: National Association of College and University Business Officers.

Standish Group. (2000). Extreme CHAOS. Retrieved from www.standishgroup.com/sample_research/index.php.

Wheatley, M. J., & Keller-Rogers, M. (1998). Bringing life to organizational change. *Journal of Strategic Performance Measurement* April/May, 6–13.

8. Dent, E. B., & Goldberg, S. G. (1999). Challenging "resistance to change." *Journal of Applied Behavioral Science, 35*(1), 45–47.

Lewis, L. K. (2011). *Organizational change: Creating change through strategic communication.* Malden, MA: Wiley-Blackwell.

9. Zorn, T., Christensen, L. T., & Cheney, G. (1999). *Do we really want constant change? Beyond the bottom line series.* San Francisco, CA: Berrett-Koehler Communications Inc.

10. Zorn, T., Christensen, L. T., & Cheney, G. (1999). *Do we really want constant change? Beyond the bottom line series.* San Francisco, CA: Berrett-Koehler Communications Inc.

11. Piderit, S. K. (2000). Rethinking resistance and recognizing ambivalence: A multidimensional view of attitudes toward an organizational change. *Academy of Management Review, 25*(4), 783–794.

12. Dent, E. B., & Goldberg, S. G. (1999). Challenging "Resistance to change." *Journal of Applied Behavioral Science, 35*(1), 45–47.

13. Argyris, C., & Schon, D. A. (1974). *Theory in practice: Increasing professional effectiveness.* San Francisco, CA: Jossey Bass.

Argyris, C., & Schon, D. A. (1978). *Organizational learning.* Reading, MA: Addison-Wesley.

Ashforth, B. E., & Mael, F. (1989). Social identity theory and the organization. *Academy of Management Review, 12*(1), 20–39.

Brower, R. S., & Abolafia, M. Y. (1995). The structural embeddedness of resistance among public managers. *Group and Organization Management, 20*(2), 149–166.

Coch, L., & French, J. L. P. Jr. (1948). Overcoming resistance to change. *Human Relations, 1*(4), 512–532.

Shapiro, D. L., Lewicki, R. J., & Devine, P. (1995). When do employees choose deceptive tactics to stop unwanted organizational change? *Research on Negotiation in Organizations, 5*, 155–184.

14. Piderit, S. K. (2000). Rethinking resistance and recognizing ambivalence: A multidimensional view of attitudes toward an organizational change. *Academy of Management Review, 25*(4), 783–794.

15. Dent, E. B., & Goldberg, S. G. (1999). Challenging "Resistance to change." *Journal of Applied Behavioral Science, 35*(1), 45–47.

16. Ashforth, B. E., & Mael, F. (1989). Social identity theory and the organization. *Academy of Management Review, 12*(1), 20–39.

Brower, R. S., & Abolafia, M. Y. (1995). The structural embeddedness of resistance among public managers. *Group and Organization Management, 20*(2), 149–166.

Shapiro, D. L., Lewicki, R. J., & Devine, P. (1995). When do employees choose deceptive tactics to stop unwanted organizational change? *Research on Negotiation in Organizations, 5*, 155–184.

17. Argyris, C., & Schon, D. A. (1974). *Theory in practice: Increasing professional effectiveness.* San Francisco, CA: Jossey Bass.

Argyris, C., & Schon, D. A. (1978). *Organizational learning.* Reading, MA: Addison-Wesley.

Coch, L., & French, J. L. P. Jr. (1948). Overcoming resistance to change. *Human Relations, 1*(4), 512–532.

Steigenberger, N. (2015). Emotions in sensemaking: A change management perspective. *Journal of Organizational Change Management, 28*(3), 432–451.

18. Armenakis, A. A., Harris, S. G., & Mossholder, K. W. (1993). Creating readiness for organizational change. *Human Relations, 46*, 681–703.

Piderit, S. K. (2000). Rethinking resistance and recognizing ambivalence: A multidimensional view of attitudes toward an organizational change. *Academy of Management Review, 25*(4), 783–794.

Watson, T. J. (1982). Group ideologies and organizational change. *Journal of Management Studies, 19*(3), 259–275.

19. Dent, E. B., & Goldberg, S. G. (1999). Challenging "Resistance to change." *Journal of Applied Behavioral Science, 35*(1), 45–47.

Piderit, S. K. (2000). Rethinking resistance and recognizing ambivalence: A multidimensional view of attitudes toward an organizational change. *Academy of Management Review, 25*(4), 783–794.

20. Lewis, L. K. (1999). Disseminating information and soliciting input during planned organizational change: Implementers' targets, sources, and channels for communicating. *Management Communication Quarterly, 13*(1), 43–75.

21. Ford, J., & Ford, L. W. (2010). Stop blaming resistance to change and start using it. *Organizational Dynamics, 39*(1), 24–36.

Ford, J. D., Ford, L. W., & D'Amelio, A. (2008). Resistance to change: The rest of the story. *The Academy of Management Review (AMR), 33*(2), 362–377.

22. Kotter, J. P., & Heskett, J. L. (1992). *Corporate culture and performance.* New York, NY: The Free Press.

Schein, E. H. (1985). *Organizational culture and leadership.* San Francisco, CA: Jossey-Bass.

Smulowitz, S. (2014). Planned organizational change in Higher Education: Dashboard indicators and stakeholder sensemaking—A case study (Unpublished doctoral dissertation). Rutgers, The State University of New Jersey, New Brunswick, NJ.

23. Bordia, P., Hobman, E., Jones, E., Gallois, C., & Callan, V. J. (2004). Uncertainty during organizational change: Types, consequences, and management strategies. *Journal of Business and Psychology, 18*(4), 507–532.

Coch, L., & French, J. L. P. Jr. (1948). Overcoming resistance to change. *Human Relations, 1*(4), 512–532.

Dent, E. B., & Goldberg, S. G. (1999). Challenging "Resistance to change." *Journal of Applied Behavioral Science, 35*(1), 45–47.

Lewis, L. K., Schmisseur, A, Stephens, K., & Weir, K. (2006). Advice on communicating during organizational change: The content of popular press books. *Journal of Business Communication, 43*(2), 1–25.

24. Bordia, P., Hobman, E., Jones, E., Gallois, C., & Callan, V. J. (2004). Uncertainty during organizational change: Types, consequences, and management strategies. *Journal of Business and Psychology, 18*(4), 507–532.

25. Burke, W. W. (2008). *Organization change: Theory and practice* (2nd ed.). Thousand Oaks, CA: Sage Publishing.

26. Burke, W. W. (2008). *Organization change: Theory and practice* (2nd ed.). Thousand Oaks, CA: Sage Publishing.

27. Burke, W. W. (2008). *Organization change: Theory and practice* (2nd ed.). Thousand Oaks, CA: Sage Publishing.

28. Burke, W. W. (2008). *Organization change: Theory and practice* (2nd ed.). Thousand Oaks, CA: Sage Publishing.

29. Cameron, K. S., & Quinn, R. E. (2006). *Diagnosing and changing organizational culture.* San Francisco, CA: Jossey-Bass.

Dent, E. B., & Goldberg, S. G. (1999). Challenging "Resistance to change." *Journal of Applied Behavioral Science, 35*(1), 45–47.

Lewis, L. K. (2000). "Blindsided by that on" and "I saw that one coming": The relative anticipation and occurrence of communication problems and other problems in implementer' hindsight. *Journal of Applied Communication Research, 28*(1), 44–67.

Piderit, S. K. (2000). Rethinking resistance and recognizing ambivalence: A multidimensional view of attitudes toward an organizational change. *Academy of Management Review, 25*(4), 783–794.

Zorn, T., Christensen, L. T., & Cheney, G. (1999). *Do we really want constant change? Beyond the bottom line series.* San Francisco, CA: Berrett-Koehler Communications Inc.

30. Cameron, K. S., & Quinn, R. E. (2006). *Diagnosing and changing organizational culture.* San Francisco, CA: Jossey-Bass.

31. Kotter, J. P., & Heskett, J. L. (1992). *Corporate culture and performance.* New York, NY: The Free Press.

32. Fairhurst, G. T. (1993). Echoes of the vision: When the rest of the organizational talks Total Quality. *Management Communication Quarterly, 6,* 331–371.

Kee, J. E., & Newcomer, K. E. (2008). Why do change efforts fail?: What can leaders do about it? *The Public Manager, 37*(3), 5–12.

Lewis, L. K. (2006). Employee perspectives on implementation communication as predictors of perceptions of success and resistance. *Western Journal of Communication, 70*(1), 23–46.

Schein, E. H. (1985). *Organizational culture and leadership.* San Francisco, CA: Jossey-Bass.

33. Lewis, L. K. (2006). Employee perspectives on implementation communication as predictors of perceptions of success and resistance. *Western Journal of Communication, 70*(1), 23–46.

34. Lewis, L. K. (2006). Employee perspectives on implementation communication as predictors of perceptions of success and resistance. *Western Journal of Communication, 70*(1), 23–46.

35. Steigenberger, N. (2015). Emotions in sensemaking: A change management perspective. *Journal of Organizational Change Management, 28*(3), 432–451.

Chapter 2

Approaches to the Process of Planned Organizational Change

WHAT YOU CAN EXPECT TO LEARN IN THIS CHAPTER

- What are the strategies and models of organizational change?
- What are performance measurement systems and why are they important to planned organizational change efforts?

Organizational change is a topic that perplexes many leaders—often before, during, and after they try to accomplish it. Over time, researchers have focused many studies on planned organizational change efforts and as a result our knowledge about these efforts continuously grows. To fully understand the complexities of planned change efforts, let's take a look back in history of some of the strategies, models, and systems.[1]

STRATEGIES FOR PLANNED ORGANIZATIONAL CHANGE EFFORTS

The idea of planned organizational change really took hold around the time of World War II when it became clear that academic research could be applied to industry.[2] Kurt Lewin is credited with the creation of the National Training Laboratories at the Research Center for Group Dynamics at the Massachusetts Institute of Technology (MIT). This is one of the early research studies of team building and group dynamics within organizations.[3] Lewin is also credited with advancing academia so that researchers could integrate their academic knowledge with practitioner needs.[4]

15

Much important research was developed through Lewin's work and the work of other influential researchers who worked with or were influenced by Lewin.[5] Some of these influential researchers include Rensis Likert who developed the Likert Scale.[6] The Likert Scale is still used in survey research today. Survey respondents are asked to choose their agreement or disagreement with a statement on a five or seven-point scale.

Robert Blake and Jane Mouton coauthored *The Managerial Grid*.[7] The managerial grid proposed in this book was created with five different managerial styles in mind. These styles considered leaders with a focus and value on people more so than results, or leaders with a focus on results over people.

Chrys Argyris made applied research a reality for researchers in academia.[8] Prior to this time, academic research was purely seen as an advancement solely for other academics. Argyris brought the spotlight onto research that could help practitioners. It was about this time that the idea of a change agent came to fruition. A change agent is someone internal or external to the organization who creates a vision for change, promotes communication and participation of change efforts, and facilitates the change effort.[9]

Around the time of World War II came the Tavistock Institute of Human Relations and the concept of the Socio-Technical Systems Perspective lead by Eric Trist.[10] Trist and colleagues researched, trained, and consulted with organizational groups. The goal of the Socio-Technical Perspective was to study human and technological integration, looking specifically at quality-of-work-life.

A debate ensued in the coming years whether the purpose of organizational change was to improve organizational performance or the work life of humans.[11] The academic literature still debates whether interpersonal or technological issues are more pressing in change efforts.[12]

MODELS OF PLANNED ORGANIZATIONAL CHANGE EFFORTS

Over the years, scholars have developed many models of organizational change. Much of the research begins with Lewin and so we begin here as well with his three stages of change that many say stand up to the test of time.[13] Stage one is to unfreeze the present state of affairs; stage two is to make the change; and stage three is to freeze when the change and a new state of affairs have become ingrained.

Building off of Lewin's model, Lippitt, Watson, and Westley developed a five-phase model of change.[14] Here scholars propose that consultants establish a reason to change. This is followed by helping employees to view consultants as close enough to the organization to have full understanding of it, yet far enough from the organization to be unbiased. Phase three is where the problem is defined and a solution is implemented. Phase four is proposed to establish the change as the new operating status of the organization. Finally, phase five is where the consultant leaves the organization to work on their own.

In 1987, Weisbord developed four organizational change guidelines.[15] The first guideline was an analysis of the organization's internal capacity for change based on leadership commitment, motivated employees, and a review of the external opportunities available to the organization. Next was participation by everyone in the organization to agree on the change process. The third guideline was to focus on the vision versus the day-to-day, and the fourth guideline was to provide a system to allow for independence within the organization.

Inspired by Lewin, Armenakis and Harris created a readiness model to assess whether or not organizational members perceived that they and the organization were ready for the change effort.[16] In doing so, scholars proposed that leaders must provide recipients of the change effort with a clear vision for the change. Also recipients must agree that there is a discrepancy between the current and desired organizational state. Next, there must be agreement that the type of change effort chosen is appropriate. Efficacy, or the belief that the change effort is doable, must be believed by everyone in the organization. This is supported by the next, principal support, where leaders are viewed as supportive to see the change effort through. Finally, there must be agreement that there is something in the change effort for everyone involved.

Ruben developed the five stages of change model.[17] Stage one shows that there is attention on the change effort and everyone agrees on a need to change. Step two involves and engages everyone in the change effort. Next, there is a commitment to the change effort. Step four is where action or implementation of the change effort occurs. Finally, integration or where the change becomes the new status quo occurs.

TOP-LEVEL STRATEGIES

Throughout these strategies and models, there are a variety of ways the change effort is planned from an overall top-level strategy. Three such strategies to choose from for planning a change effort include empirical-rational, normative-re-educative, and power-coercive.[18] The empirical-rational strategy relies on the change agent understanding and incorporating the desires of organizational members into the messaging about the change effort. The belief is that once organizational members realize that their interests are met (what's in it for me) along with organizational interests, that participation and buy-in will be easier to achieve.

The second strategy is normative re-educative where the change agent first determines the group culture and then works with the group to change the culture to include new rituals and other elements that will make the change effort stick. Throughout this process, the change agents facilitate organizational members' processes to achieve new attitudes, values, and behaviors. Change agents use power-coercive strategies when they leverage the power and influence that some members of the organization have over other members of the organization. In many organizations, this is called "decide and announce—comply or else."

PERFORMANCE MEASUREMENT SYSTEMS

Upon choosing one of these top-level strategies, the change agent then chooses a task-specific strategy for implementation, such as a performance measurement system.[19] Performance measurement aids the leader or change agent with the planned change effort.[20]

The performance measurement system provides continuous data to alert leaders or change agents about inconsistencies, shortcomings, and successes with the change effort. This information is vital to leaders and change agents so that the system or process can be adapted, if needed, to ensure success of the change effort.

There are numerous performance measurement systems that use consistently monitored benchmarks and goals for continuous improvement.[21] The promotion and documentation of change efforts where organizational members and change agents exchange information is also a major function of performance measurement systems.[22] After all, most organizational members—even in higher education these days—are interested in the management of the organization and the value and output to the organizational members or customers.[23]

Over the years, performance measurement has become a staple in industry and increasingly so in higher education since the Spellings Commission report.[24] The industry is flooded with books, workshops, and consultants who prescribe a variety of performance measurement systems. Some of the most popular performance measurement systems include Balanced Scoreboard, ISO, Kaizen, Lean, Malcolm Baldrige National Quality Award Program (MBNQA), Six Sigma, and Total Quality Management (TQM).[25]

Many industries have adopted their own version of performance measurement systems, including the Compstat model in law enforcement and Excellence in Higher Education. Other performance measurement systems to consider include the Dashboard and Performance Prism.

Dashboards, like the name suggests, mimic the dashboard on your car. It shows key performance indicators that light up for critical incidents. For example, if your car overheats, an indicator warning light appears. Similarly, on the Dashboard performance measurement system, key performance indicators will provide warning indicators based on the measurements included. Examples include profit margin, customer satisfaction, or workplace injuries in industry and student learning outcomes in higher education.[26]

An advantage of the Dashboard is that the framework allows any key performance indicator to be measured.[27] A disadvantage of the Dashboard is that the framework solves "something for everyone."[28] If not managed properly, this can lead to a variety of perceptions about the intended outcome of the change effort. And, it may lead some to assume the change effort failed.[29]

The Performance Prism focuses on stakeholders, an important part of the change effort.[30] While the Balanced Scorecard has a more limited focus on stakeholders who are shareholders and customers, the Performance Prism considers additional stakeholders, such as employees.[31] As such they make a good complement to one another. There are five areas of improvement in the Performance Prism[32]:

1. Stakeholder Satisfaction: "Who are the stakeholders and what do they want and need?"
2. Strategies: "What are the strategies we require to ensure the wants and needs of our stakeholders are satisfied?"
3. Processes: "What are the processes we have to put in place to allow our strategies to be delivered?" Processes include developing new products, and services and specific measures that relate with each process should be identified.
4. Capabilities: "What are the capabilities required to operate our processes?" Capabilities are "the combination of people, practices, technology and infrastructure that together enable execution of the organization's business process (both now and in the future)."
5. Stakeholder Contribution: "What contributions does the organization need from its stakeholders to maintain and develop these capabilities?" No other performance measurement system frameworks recognize this back-and-forth rapport between the organization and the employee.

While institutions of higher education are using Dashboards and other types of more popular performance measurement systems, there are some used more often than others. Excellence in Higher Education is built around U.S. higher education accreditation standards and the influential MBNQA program used in industry across the United States. Options for implementation of Excellence in Higher Education are through consultants or with an internally led self-study. Institutions can choose to implement throughout the entire organization or focus on one department or program. Areas of focus include leadership, purposes and plans, beneficiaries and constituencies, programs and services, faculty/staff and workplace, assessment, and information use.[33]

There are seven regional, four faith related, two career related, and fifty-two programmatic accreditation programs nationwide.[34] These accrediting programs consist of somewhat unique and sometimes overlapping criteria to measure performance of the organization or program(s). Institutions of higher education have one regional accreditation program and a variety of faith, career, or programmatic accreditation program criteria to meet.

Regional accreditation programs vary depending on the location of the institution of higher education. For example, an institution of higher education in Pennsylvania reports to the Middle States Commission on Higher Education. They may also report to a faith, career, or several programmatic accreditation programs, depending on the programs available at that institution of higher education.

SUMMARY

Depending on what type of accreditation required for your institution of higher education as well as the criteria set forth in your strategic plan, this chapter provided you with information and resources to be able to determine what top-level and task-specific strategies might work. There is a long history of practitioner-focused academic research to help you in your change effort. Many models of planned organizational change, including Lewin's three stages of change, Lippitt, Watson, and Westley's five-phase model of change, Weisbord's four organizational change guidelines, Armenakis and Harris's Readiness Model and Ruben's five stages of change. Many types of performance measurement systems are mentioned in this chapter. The Dashboard and the Performance Prism performance measurement systems are considered.

NOTES

1. Note that this list is not mean to be exhaustive, rather it provides examples of the history of some of the organizational change literature to provide context.

2. Bennis, W. G. (1966). *Changing organizations.* New York, NY: McGraw-Hill Book Company.

3. Smulowitz, S. (2014). Planned organizational change in Higher Education: Dashboard indicators and stakeholder sensemaking—A case study (Unpublished doctoral dissertation). Rutgers, The State University of New Jersey, New Brunswick, NJ.

4. Bennis, W. G. (1993). *Beyond bureaucracy: Essays on the development and evolution of human organization.* San Fransisco, CA: Jossey-Bass Publishers.

5. Smulowitz, S. (2014). Planned organizational change in Higher Education: Dashboard indicators and stakeholder sensemaking—A case study (Unpublished doctoral dissertation). Rutgers, The State University of New Jersey, New Brunswick, NJ.

6. French, W. L., & Bell, Jr., C. H. (1990). *Organization development: Behavioral science interventions for organization improvement* (4th ed.). Englewood Cliffs, NJ: Prentice-Hall.

7. Blake, R. R., & Mouton, J. S. (1964). *The managerial grid.* Houston, TX: Gulf Publishing Company.

8. French, W. L., & Bell, Jr., C. H. (1990). *Organization development: Behavioral science interventions for organization improvement* (4th ed.). Englewood Cliffs, NJ: Prentice-Hall.

9. Lewis, L. K., Schmisseur, A., Stephens, K., & Weir, K. (2006). Advice on communicating during organizational change: The content of popular press books. *Journal of Business Communication, 43*(2), 1–25.

Smulowitz, S. (2014). Planned organizational change in Higher Education: Dashboard indicators and stakeholder sensemaking—A case study (Unpublished doctoral dissertation). Rutgers, The State University of New Jersey, New Brunswick, NJ.

10. French, W. L., & Bell, Jr., C. H. (1990). *Organization development: Behavioral science interventions for organization improvement* (4th ed.). Englewood Cliffs, NJ: Prentice-Hall.

11. Friedlander, F., & Brown, L. D. (1974). Organization development. *Annual Review of Psychology, 33*, 313–341.

Sashkin, M., & Burke, W. W. (1987). Organization development in the 1980's. *Journal of Management, 13*(2), 393–417.

12. Smulowitz, S. (2014). Planned organizational change in Higher Education: Dashboard indicators and stakeholder sensemaking—A case study (Unpublished doctoral dissertation). Rutgers, The State University of New Jersey, New Brunswick, NJ.

13. Lewin, K. (1951). *Field theory in social science.* New York: Harper & Brothers Publishers.

Weick, K. E., & Quinn, R. E. (1999). Organizational change and development. *Annual Review of Psychology, 50*, 361–386.

14. Lippitt, R., Watson, J., & Westley, B. (1958). *Dynamics of planned change.* New York, NY: Harcourt, Brace.

15. Weisbord, M. R. (1987). Toward third-wave managing and consulting. *Organizational Dynamics, 15*(3), 5–24.

16. Armenakis, A. A., & Harris, S. G. (2009). Reflections: Our journey of organizational change research and practice. *Journal of Change Management, 9*(2), 127–142.

17. Ruben, B. D. (2009). *Understanding, planning, and leading organizational change: Core concepts and strategies.* Washington, DC: National Association of College and University Business Officers.

18. Chin, R., & Benne, K. D. (1985). General strategies for effecting change in human systems. In W. G. Bennis, K. D. Benne, & R. Chin (Eds.), *The planning of change* (4th ed.). New York, NY: Holt, Rinehart & Winston.

19. Smulowitz, S. (2014). Planned organizational change in Higher Education: Dashboard indicators and stakeholder sensemaking—A case study (Unpublished

doctoral dissertation). Rutgers, The State University of New Jersey, New Brunswick, NJ.

20. Smulowitz, S. (2014). Planned organizational change in Higher Education: Dashboard indicators and stakeholder sensemaking—A case study (Unpublished doctoral dissertation). Rutgers, The State University of New Jersey, New Brunswick, NJ.

21. Eckerson, W. (2011). *Performance dashboards: Measuring, monitoring and managing your business* (2nd ed.). Hoboken, NJ: John Wiley & Sons.

Smulowitz, S. (2014). Planned organizational change in Higher Education: Dashboard indicators and stakeholder sensemaking—A case study (Unpublished doctoral dissertation). Rutgers, The State University of New Jersey, New Brunswick, NJ.

22. Smulowitz, S. (2014). Planned organizational change in Higher Education: Dashboard indicators and stakeholder sensemaking—A case study (Unpublished doctoral dissertation). Rutgers, The State University of New Jersey, New Brunswick, NJ.

23. Moullin, M. (2002). *Delivering excellence in health and social care.* Buckingham, UK: Open University Press.

24. U.S. Department of Education. (2006). *The Spellings Commission report.* Washington, DC: Department of Education.

25. Smulowitz, S. (2014). Planned organizational change in Higher Education: Dashboard indicators and stakeholder sensemaking—A case study (Unpublished doctoral dissertation). Rutgers, The State University of New Jersey, New Brunswick, NJ.

26. Smulowitz, S. (2014). Planned organizational change in Higher Education: Dashboard indicators and stakeholder sensemaking—A case study (Unpublished doctoral dissertation). Rutgers, The State University of New Jersey, New Brunswick, NJ.

27. Smulowitz, S. (2014). Planned organizational change in Higher Education: Dashboard indicators and stakeholder sensemaking—A case study (Unpublished doctoral dissertation). Rutgers, The State University of New Jersey, New Brunswick, NJ.

28. Lunger, K. (2006). Why you need more than a dashboard to manage your strategy. *Business Intelligence Journal, 11*(4), 8–17. Quote from p. 6.

29. Smulowitz, S. (2014). Planned organizational change in Higher Education: Dashboard indicators and stakeholder sensemaking—A case study (Unpublished doctoral dissertation). Rutgers, The State University of New Jersey, New Brunswick, NJ.

30. Neely, A., Adams, C., & Crowe, P. (2001). The Performance Prism in practice. *The Academy of Management Review, 5*(2), 6–12.

31. Adams, C., & Neely, A. (2000). The Performance Prism to boost M&A success. *Measuring Business Excellence, 4*(3), 19–23.

Kaplan, R. S., & Norton, D. P. (1996). *The balanced scorecard: Translating strategy into action.* Boston, MA: Harvard Business School Press.

32. Neely, A., Adams, C., & Crowe, P. (2001). The Performance Prism in practice. *The Academy of Management Review, 5*(2), 6–12. Quotes from pp. 6–7.

33. Ruben, B. D. (2009). *Excellence in Higher Education Guide 2009: An integrated approach to assessment, planning and improvement in colleges and universities.* Washington, DC: National Association of College and University Business Officers.

34. CHEA (2019). *2019-202 Director of CHEA-Recognized Organizations.* Washington, DC: Council for Higher Education Accreditation.

Chapter 3

The Nature of Communication

WHAT YOU CAN EXPECT TO LEARN IN THIS CHAPTER

- How are communication models similar and different?
- What is the difference between information and communication?
- What are the six characteristics of the inner workings of communication?
- What is communication?

The widespread familiarity of the term "communication" provides no assurance that people who use the term have a thorough understanding of the actual process and system that makes it work. In fact, as the term has becomes more and more a part of everyday language, the risk of misuse and overuse increases.[1]

What is communication? Communication is like love. Everyone knows what it is until they are pressed to provide a definition. Go ahead, define love. Now, define communication. Next, ask a friend to define both. Did your friend say something different from your definition? They are not so easy to define. Why is that? Let's unpack the concept of communication to find out. (You're on your own with love!)

COMMUNICATION MODELS

Regardless of your role, communication can be perplexing. Over time, researchers have focused much attention on communication, and especially its role in organizational change. There are a variety of approaches to

understand the phenomenon of communication.[2] These approaches have been
built upon over the years.

One-Way Communication Flow

Source – Message – Receiver: Those who view communication as a one-
way flow find that the message is the information. This view dates back to
Aristotle where he believed that there was a source that sent a persuasive
message to a receiver.[3] The main purpose behind Aristotle's approach was to
persuade the listeners, or receivers, to buy into and accept, the speakers, or
senders, message.[4]

Source – Message – Channel – Receiver – Effect: Aristotle's view of communication persisted into the 1940s and heavily influenced the update by
Lasswell.[5] Communication is still viewed as a one-way flow where the source
sends a persuasive message to a receiver. The difference is that the medium,
or channel, by which the message is sent to the receiver now includes mass
media. In addition to Aristotle's view of communication as persuading the
receiver to adopt the sender's message, Lasswell added other outcomes,
effects, such as entertaining and informational.[6]

Source – Encoded Message – Channel – Noise – Receiver (Decodes Message):
Scholars Shannon and Weaver created a further extension to this one-way flow
model the following year by incorporating new components.[7] In this model, a
source creates a message that is transmitted as an encoded message through a
channel to the receiver that decodes the message for the final destination. Noise,
or a disturbance, can affect the way the message travels through the channel,
and thus disrupts the message from being received as it was originally sent by
the sender.

For example, if a sender is communicating through a mobile phone, the
channel is the signal that travels from one cellular tower to another. Noise is
considered any "breaking up" of the sound, or the call being dropped. The
call is transmitted from the sender's mobile phone and the receiver is the
other phone or device that receives the call. The person on the receiving end
is the final destination for the message. It's easy to see how "noise" can affect
the way the person on the receiving end can come to a different understanding
of the message than how it was sent.

*Source – Message – Channel (Mass Media) – Receiver (Via Opinion Leader) –
Receiver*: A few years later, in 1955, Katz & Lazarsfeld further developed
this model to include the influence of opinion leaders in what they term a

"Two-Step Flow."[8] The main idea behind this inclusion is that the message is transmitted through mass media to opinion leaders who interpret and disseminate the message to subsets of the public that mass media outlets don't necessarily reach.[9] These subsets of the public are influenced by the opinion leaders.

It becomes obvious that the one-way flow of communication is transmission-oriented and quite linear in scope. This approach to communication served scholars well to advance the field. Although it is still highly referenced as the prevailing communication approach, it is outdated with the exception of computer-mediated-communication activities such as text messaging and email. Just think about the issues you have had to get the person you've sent a text message or email to understand your intent.

Kinetic Flow of Communication

In this approach, shapes represent kinetic energy or constant change to illustrate the continuous loop of the communication process.

Environment – Receiver A – Receiver B – Receiver C (and so on) – Feedback: The approach was developed by scholars Westley and MacLean in 1957.[10] Communication begins when the receiver receives the message. The focus is on the way the receiver interprets the message from their environment rather than how the message is sent. Westley and MacLean described an environment where there are a number of messages that are interpreted and then passed along to others.[11] This approach also includes a method for the receiver to provide feedback.

Thayer, in 1968, viewed the communication process as a circular shape in which there is a continuous development to the way individuals create and interpret messages leaving participants curious as to whether they are acting as sender or receiver at any given moment. In doing so, the receiver encodes and decodes messages based on things they "take-into-account" and therefore may find more receptive.[12] This helps explain why some messages resonate more and are acted upon with greater intensity for certain people and not others.

Fred Dance viewed the communication process in the shape of a helical-spiral as an illustration of the social interaction implications of the communication process.[13] Dance introduced the dimension of marking the particular time each person was involved at a specific point on the spiral.[14] In Dance's view, the interactions will double back on itself as depicted by the points marked on the spiral. This was an early attempt to frame communication as "circular and progressive."[15]

The key difference between the kinetic approach and the one-way flow of communication is that there is constant change via interaction between sender and receiver in the kinetic approach. The one-way view is static without inter-action between sender and receiver.

Communication-as-Meaning View

Newer research shows that the process of communication provides a mutual understanding of the meaning of a message between the sender and the receiver. There is generally a back and forth between the sender and the receiver until the meaning of the message is negotiated and understood simi-larly by both. In part, this mutual understanding relies on similar experiences and perspectives.[16] And, the sender and receiver are purposefully engaged in the process, as opposed to the one-way flow where the receiver is in a pas-sive role.

In 1967, Watzlawick, Beavin and Jackson developed a two-way model of communication where the key lies in the meaning and relationship that is negotiated between the sender and the receiver as they go back and forth with messages to each other.[17] Of course, in this approach, the meaning the receiver places upon the message and what the receiver actually understands may be quite different from what the sender intended due to differences in reality and previous experiences for each.[18]

More recently, this idea of meaning is shaped by the concept of sense-making. Sensemaking is when humans take a retrospective look to better understand what's going on in their environment.[19] Often, sensemaking occurs when there is a discrepancy between what is and what was.[20] During these times, humans look within and to others to make sense of their environment.[21]

The key differences between this perspective and the other views of communication are that in the communication-as-meaning view, there is negotiated meaning of messages between sender and receiver. This is often associated with sensemaking. The kinetic view is constant change via interac-tion of sender and receiver and the one-way view is static without interaction between sender and receiver.

The perspectives offered in this section provide a range of contexts begin-ning with Aristotle, a one-way theorist, who spoke of public, face-to-face speeches from one person to a group; and continuing with the addition of a communication channel—possibly mass media (television, radio, print) or mediated—in the sense of the use of telephones (both landlines and mobiles), video conferencing, and computer (email, instant messaging, blogs, and so on).

In these latter instances, such communication could take place either from one person to another individual or from one person to a group of people. Depending on the situation, one can view this as either one or two-way communication. For example, two individuals may speak to each other face-to-face (two-way) while in another instance one person may be conducting a seminar for hundreds of viewers spanning the globe via video conferencing (one-way).

In addition, some of these approaches show how communication and information function in these various contexts. For some, such as Aristotle, the message is information. Here a speaker provides information to a gathering of town citizens, for example. For others, such as Watzlawick, Beavin, and Jackson, we look at how information is transmitted to a receiver who may only understand the message if they negotiate the meaning. In grasping this model, one can appreciate the difficulties an administrator might have in working with a faculty member, as they will both approach a task from a different perspective and possibly with a different goal in mind.

THE COMMUNICATION INFORMATION RELATIONSHIP

The relationship between information and communication is complex. The focus of communication is on meaning construction, interaction, and behavior.[22] It is how social interactions occur.[23] The focus of information is on documents, systems, and its transmission.[24]

Communication and information are interdependent.[25] It is through information processing that communication is possible, yet communication produces information.[26]

Borrowing from biology, matter-energy and information processing are both a necessity for living systems.[27] Living or open systems "exist only through continual exchanges with the environment.[28] And, it is through information processing that communication—"the process by which living systems interact with their environment and other systems"—is possible.[29]

At the same time, "*information arises out of communication: it is the product of communication* . . . process and product are inseparable . . . and interdependent."[30] There is no occasion where information may be viewed independently of communication.[31]

It is through these continual give-and-take exchanges, or negotiated meaning of messages, that humans seek to make sense of information.[32]

Humans also seek to recreate relationships with the environment and reestablish boundaries to create harmony once again through these social systems.[33]

THE INNER WORKINGS OF COMMUNICATION

Taking a broad, yet complex perspective to answer the question, "What is communication?" one can say that it is one of two (the other being matter-energy) fundamental biological processes for all living systems.[34] But leaving the answer at that stage also misses much of the inner workings of communication.

The following section reviews six characteristics of the inner workings of communication. They all presuppose that communication and information are indeed separate entities, and they all overlap rather than appear as distinct and individual characteristics.

Several characteristics appear in the literature about the inner workings of communication. They all rest on the assumption that communication is the primary way we as a human system—be it a system of an organization or a family—create and maintain relationships with the environment and the people in it.[35] Even more so, communication assists in this creation and maintenance of relationships by the following six characteristics: developing a sense of self; developing our own reality through perception; developing artifacts; developing an appreciation of environmental threats/negative feed-back; relying on our unconscious self to participate in life; and developing a way to organize and give meaning to events. What follows will go in-depth into these characteristics. However, they are not meant to stand entirely on their own, as they are interrelated with each other.

Developing a Sense of Self

From birth to one-year of age humans develop at an incredible rate.[36] When we are first born, simply opening our eyes to the environment of bright lights and all the sounds and noises around us are most likely overwhelming. After time we become used to all that noise and then little by little develop the ability to uncurl from the fetal position, smile, burp, eat, sit up, and eventually walk. In another year or so we begin to talk, first using a few words, and then finally develop the ability to speak in sentences.

As we progress through these stages, we also develop our identity, individuality, and worldview, or perspective about how things "are." In this same sense, the experiences with communication that we have help us to develop our sense of self.[37] No one else can duplicate exactly our experiences, just as no two children—even twins—are the same. No two pets are the same, and no two organizations or groups are the same.[38]

For example, let's assume there are two small children both age two and both learning to speak. In one household, there is a black cat and in the other household, there are no pets. It is very likely that the child in the house with the cat will be able to say cat and possibly black and the cat's name at a faster pace than the child without pets. The cat has been a part of this child's experience growing up.

Now let's assume that both children grew up with a cat. The ability to say "cat" as well as the cat's name and color may be a part of the child's ability at an early age the determination of every cat being equal is not so.[39] It is also possible to emulate someone or benchmark and replicate a program another organization has in place, but it will never be exactly the same.

For example, an alumni office in one university may request information from another alumni office about the way in which they plan, coordinate, and implement a mentoring program for undergraduate students. Even if the alumni office plans, coordinates, and implements in the same manner as the office they received the information from, their experiences will still differ. This is because the people who are responsible for the plans, coordination, and implementation are different and bring with them their own life experiences.

Finally, in developing a sense of self, credit is due to one's family, friends, and social groups (e.g., schools and religious affiliations) for socializing us into our culture. This socialization occurs through communication and is a necessity to "participation in social reality."[40]

Developing Our Own Reality through Perception

The way we understand things (or not), construct information, and act in response to others actions and words is wholly dependent upon our "cognitive map." This "map" is developed from previous experiences, genetics, memories, assumptions, beliefs, attitudes, biases, history, and values.[41]

This ability to see things comes to us through the use of words, but the same word doesn't always mean the same thing to everybody.[42] The words we choose to use symbolize a combination of reality and self.[43]

For example, a fact might be that we saw two children running from the kitchen. Our "cognitive map" tells us that these children took a cookie from the cookie jar without asking. This is based on our perceptions of what's going on, the context within which it takes place, and therefore the meanings they hold for us.[44] Keep in mind that as we observe what's happening in our environment:

- Context provides meaning[45]
- Our perception is our reality[46]
- Objective versus internal realities are different[47]
- Intentions aren't always what occurs[48]

In this example, then, from previous experience when these children were running from the kitchen in this manner, the last five times they had taken a cookie from the cookie jar without asking. We observed the children running in a particular manner and could describe what we saw.[49] From that we could draw inferences about what we saw and make decisions.[50]

The purpose behind this is not to catch a juvenile thief. It is to preserve the children's hunger for dinner that consists of foods that are more nutritious than a cookie. Based on our perception we know that these children prefer the taste of a cookie to that of dinner (except maybe pizza) and that their purpose is to feel full while eating food that tastes good. Our reality is that filling up on a cookie rather than more nutritious food is a waste of calories. Most children find cookies for dinner to be adequate.

From this example, we can see that reality is determined for each individual based on their "purposes, perspectives, capabilities, and competencies" and are "temporary, communicationally created assumptions subject to continuous revision."[51] In much this same way, we tend to selectively participate in new experiences and events in which we are familiar with the topic or origin.[52] One can also see the relationship and meaning socialization has on helping us to develop our own reality.

Developing Artifacts

Artifacts aid human beings in performing their activities.[53] Most children would certainly take part in the cookie heist. However, the sight of a chair placed strategically in a corner might compel the children to go without stealing the cookie. Here the "timeout" chair is considered an artifact for punishment of a bad deed or simply as a visual reminder to the child of the penalty that awaits a bad deed. Conversely, the children might perceive the absence of a chair that's typically present as a symbol to steal cookies.

In another example, symbols from the nonprofit group Mothers against Drunk Driving (MADD) become artifacts to the person who sees and recognizes them as such.[54] Other artifacts of our time are the mobile phone, tablet, and computer. The telephone was originally meant for short conversations and now can be used as a source of entertainment, navigation, encyclopedia, and more.[55] Similarly, sitting at the head of the conference table can be understood as a symbol of power.

Developing an Appreciation of Environmental Threats and Negative Feedback

We learn from prior experiences and memories of previous events.[56] We also learn what works and what doesn't work based on negative feedback or gaps remaining between the status quo and a goal.[57] As we go about our daily lives, we take into account those experiences, memories, and gaps when we encounter threats from the environment.[58]

The way in which we as living systems respond to those threats is based on what we've learned from our past, the context within which they take place, our perceptions of reality, and who we are.[59] "Communication is the process by which living systems interact with their environment and other systems through information processing."[60]

Relying on Our Unconscious Self to Participate in Life

Part of what separates humans from other living systems is the ability to rely on our unconscious self to participate in the activities of life without the need to think about the process of communication.[61] It would be cumbersome to go through a mental thought process of communicating (listen to what he just said, now interpret what he just said in a way that is meaningful to me given my past experiences, values, culture, memories, and so on) just as it would be to drink from a cup (pick up cup with hand, place to mouth, open mouth, and so on).

However, it is just this unconscious ability that allows us to drink from a cup and hold a conversation at the same time without needing to think about the intricacies of doing so. Similarly, the learning process of socialization teaches us from an early age important cultural habits and taboos such as taking turns when you speak and not spitting at or hitting one another.[62] Alternatively, these unconscious realities of self allow us to become rigid in our thinking which can lead to misunderstandings and conflict.[63]

Developing a Way to Organize and Give Meaning to Events and People

As we take into account our previous experiences, perceptions of reality, and who we are, we continually add new experiences, which change and recreate our perceptions of reality and possibly who we are. In doing so our mind helps us to organize our thoughts, perceptions, and experiences so that we can better understand and give meaning to them as we try to understand events in our life.[64]

In this same way, our mind helps us to interact with others to create and maintain significances within our relationships, make sense of our own reality, and develop meaning along with them.[65] The concepts of self-reference and self-reflexivity are appropriate here.[66] Self-reference, the things we see and say about others, says as much about ourselves as it does about others. Self-reflexivity is our ability to see what's inside ourselves, what makes us tick.

It is in this same way—through communication—that we as human beings develop social systems.[67] For example, after the untimely death of her daughter to a drunk driver, Candy Lightner formed MADD. As MADD grew from an idea held by its founder to a nationwide phenomenon the goals of the organization evolved. Lightner withdrew from the organization because its goals no longer aligned with her original intent. Over time the group developed its own culture full of recognizable symbols, activities, and communication patterns.[68] This happened as organizational members communicated with each other to create and recreate their social system.

To take yet a deeper look into these six characteristics let us consider the following example. There are two people Sally and Henry. Sally is a professor at West Lake University and Henry is a senior in her research methods course. During his time in the course, Henry was extremely negative toward both the course and Sally. The only reason he took the course was because it was a requirement to graduate.

As a result, his attitude was to do only what he needed to do to get by with a minimal passing grade. This included missing as many classes as permitted and doing the least amount of work in all the projects. It had worked for him before with other classes.

Sally was new to both the university and the course. She has just completed her doctoral program and was juggling four new course preparations, continuing her research and networking in a new university and geographic region. Throughout college, she was always interested in putting forth her best effort, even in courses with which she had no interest.

Mid-way through the semester, Sally announced that there would be extra credit opportunities. She urged Henry and a few others to complete them as their mid-term grades were barely passing. Sally asked Henry and a few others to stay after class several times and spoke with them about their grades and abilities to do a better job with projects. She also offered to help them along the way by reviewing their work before it was submitted.

Henry would listen half-heartedly, thank Sally for her interest, and go away seemingly uninterested. All of the others completed the extra credit assignments and improved on their work in the class. The end of the semester came and Henry's grade had slipped to failing.

Sally agonized over whether or not to give him the three extra points he needed to pass the course. Ultimately, Sally decided to report the failing grade Henry earned, especially since he was given the same opportunities as others and he did not act upon them.

Upon receipt of his end of semester grades, Henry called Sally in a panic to find out what he could do to pass the course. He remembered that she had offered him help before and was hopeful that she would again. When Henry found out that Sally would not work with him to change his grade he became furious and ended up appealing his grade and complaining to the department Chairperson and Dean about Sally.

What happened here? One could easily say that Henry didn't deserve to pass the course because he simply didn't do the work that was required. And that would be correct from one perspective. Burrowing deeper we can find other pieces to the inner workings of communication within this example.

1. Henry and Sally are at quite different life stages. Given their differences in past experiences, both in and out of the classroom, they each bring with them different perspectives and expectations for the same research methods course. Sally brings with her the perspective of excelling in her academic work regardless of the obstacles. She also brings with her the assumption that everyone else shares that same work ethic "reality." In addition Sally brings the perspective of a faculty member who is responsible for students learning in a structured and fair environment. Henry is a senior who just wants to graduate.

   Both Sally and Henry are unconsciously creating information and responding to situations based on their own previous experiences, assumptions, memories, beliefs, attitudes, and values.[69] They have developed their own reality through their individual perceptions about what's happening in their environment. Further, Sally and Henry's reality was shaped by their sense of self. Their socialization played a large role in the way they participated in their social reality.

2. At one point, Sally offered her help to Henry and other students. Unfortunately, for Henry, he sought out that offer for help after it was not available anymore. Sally made a genuine offer for help. However, her unstated definition of help in this situation was to include happenings prior to the final exam period. Henry simply recalled her offer for help and was hopeful that Sally would comply.

   Sally and Henry understood different meanings to the offer of "help." Each interpreted the timeframe for the offer differently.[70] The grade, or artifact, symbolized the significance of these differences.

3. Henry was upset with his experience with the research methods course, and specifically, Sally. He couldn't figure out why she refused to help him in the end. The only reason that made sense to him was that Sally just disliked him. When, in fact, Sally agonized over giving Henry a failing

grade. Henry, wanting to graduate, responded in a negative manner by appealing the grade and complaining to the Chairperson and Dean about Sally.

Context plays a big role, because without passing the course, Henry cannot graduate and is required to retake the course.[71] In an attempt to avoid this unpleasant outcome, Henry responded in a manner in which his cognitive map in this context told him to, albeit unconsciously.[72] Henry tried to appeal the grade.

4. As it turns out the reality that Henry perceived during the course where he could miss many classes and turn in work that was on the verge of being unacceptable to get by was not the same reality as Sally's.[73]

These realities are determined for each of us based on our individual perspectives and are "temporary, communicationally created assumptions subject to continuous revision."[74] As we rely on our unconscious self to participate in life, sometimes we become rigid in our thinking. We rely too much on previous experiences and this causes conflict. In this example, Henry relied on his previous experience of doing the minimum in other classes. Unfortunately, this caused conflict with his ultimate goal of graduating on time.

5. In the end we find that Henry did ultimately live in the reality of Sally's world because she controlled the course grade. He did end up taking the course again the semester after he would have graduated. But this time, he was better able to scan his environment. Henry was able to recall the threats from his previous experience and recognize the rather large gap that his previous reality left in his plans for graduation.[75]

Possibly more important is that Henry was able to find meaning and give significance to this learning experience.[76] This experience helped Harry throughout the remainder of his life. He became conscious of what was expected of him and what the gaps or negative feedback might be if he didn't meet those expectations.

WORLDVIEW

As we unravel the inner workings of communication, it becomes clear that we really know less about what we think we know. What we inherently believe and think, our reality and what things mean to us, that we know is really a manifestation of our total experiences to-date. Similar to the adage of "older and wiser," as we age we gain experiences, both positive and negative, which shape our beliefs, actions, meanings, and reality. These inner workings of communication manifest in our worldview, our rules for how life "ought to" or "should" be.

Knowing that no two people share the exact same experiences will only help us as we communicate. The meanings each of us hold for one word or concept is not the same as another holds. And for that matter, the meaning of a word or concept we have today will most likely change on another day. Depending on the context in which the word or concept is used it might hold different meanings to the same person and most definitely to different people.

For these reasons, it is essential to use a communication model with a focus on the relationship and sensemaking between the sender and the receiver rather than the intentions of the sender alone. With this in mind the following definition of human communication is offered: Human communication is the process by which we impose our meanings upon messages that we receive and send. These meanings are based on previous experiences, values, and beliefs and are typically taken for granted by us. They vary and change based on context and further experiences and help form our individual realities and sense of self.

SUMMARY

Communication and information have a complex relationship. They are interdependent. It is through information processing that communication is possible. At the same time, communication produces information.

Over time many communication models have been developed. Today we use the model of the relationship and sensemaking between the sender and receiver. Communication is the way we create and maintain relationships with the environment and the people in it. We do so using these six characteristics: developing a sense of self; developing our own reality through perception; developing artifacts; developing an appreciation of environmental threats/negative feedback; relying on our unconscious self to participate in life; and developing a way to organize and give meaning to events. These six characteristics manifest our worldview, or the rules we develop over time for the way things "ought" to be.

NOTES

1. Peters, J. D. (1999). Introduction: The problem of communication. In J. D. Peters (Ed.), *Speaking into the air: A history of the idea of communication* (pp. 1–31). Chicago: University of Chicago.

2. Note that this is not an exhaustive explanation of each approach to communication, rather it provides examples and a brief overview to help provide context.

3. Ruben, B. D., & Stewart, L. P. (2006). *Communication and human behavior* (5th ed.). Boston, MA: Pearson Education.

4. Ruben, B. D., & Stewart, L. P. (2006). *Communication and human behavior* (5th ed.). Boston, MA: Pearson Education.

5. Lasswell, H. D. (1948). The structure and function of communication in society. In L. Bryson (Ed.), *The communication of ideas: A series of addresses* (pp. 37–51). New York, NY: Institute for Religious and Social Studies.

6. Ruben, B. D., & Stewart, L. P. (2006). *Communication and human behavior* (5th ed.). Boston, MA: Pearson Education.

7. Ruben, B. D., & Stewart, L. P. (2006). *Communication and human behavior* (5th ed.). Boston, MA: Pearson Education.

Shannon, C. E., & Weaver, W. (1949). *The mathematical theory of communication.* Urbana, IL: University of Illinois Press.

8. Katz, E., & Lazarsfeld, P. F. (1955). *Personal influence.* New York, NY: The Free Press.

Ruben, B. D., & Stewart, L. P. (2006). *Communication and human behavior* (5th ed.). Boston, MA: Pearson Education.

9. Ruben, B. D., & Stewart, L. P. (2006). *Communication and human behavior* (5th ed.). Boston, MA: Pearson Education.

10. Westley, B. H., & MacLean, M. S. (1957). A conceptual model for communications research. *Journalism Quarterly, 34*(1), 31–38.

11. Ruben, B. D., & Stewart, L. P. (2006). *Communication and human behavior* (5th ed.). Boston, MA: Pearson Education.

12. Ruben, B. D., & Stewart, L. P. (2006). *Communication and human behavior* (5th ed.). Boston, MA: Pearson Education.

Thayer, L. (1968). *Communication and communication systems.* Homewood, IL: Irwin.

13. Dance, F. (1967). *Human communication theory.* New York: Holt, Rinehart & Winston.

Rafaeli, S. (1988). From new media to communication. *Sage Annual Review of Communication Research: Advancing Communication Science, 16,* 110–134.

14. Ruben, B. D., & Stewart, L. P. (2006). *Communication and human behavior* (5th ed.). Boston, MA: Pearson Education.

15. Rafaeli, S. (1988). From new media to communication. *Sage Annual Review of Communication Research: Advancing Communication Science, 16,* 110–134. Quote on p. 113.

16. Halloran, J. D. (1985). Information and communication: Information is the answer, but what is the question? In B. D. Ruben (Ed.), *Information & behavior: Vol. 1* (pp. 27–39). New Brunswick: Transaction Books.

17. Watzlawick, B., Beavin, J., & Jackson, D. (1967). *Pragmatics of human communication.* London: Faber & Faber.

Ruben, B. D., & Stewart, L. P. (2006). *Communication and human behavior* (5th ed.). Boston, MA: Pearson Education.

18. Halloran, J. D. (1985). Information and communication: Information is the answer, but what is the question? In B. D. Ruben (Ed.), *Information & behavior: Vol. 1* (pp. 27–39). New Brunswick: Transaction Books.

19. Weick, K. E. (1995). *Sensemaking in organizations.* Thousand Oaks, CA: Sage. Weick, K. E. (2001). *Making sense of the organization.* Malden, MA: Blackwell Publishing.

20. Weick, K. E. (1995). *Sensemaking in organizations.* Thousand Oaks, CA: Sage. Weick, K. E. (2001). *Making sense of the organization.* Malden, MA: Blackwell Publishing.

21. Weick, K. E. (1995). *Sensemaking in organizations.* Thousand Oaks, CA: Sage. Weick, K. E. (2001). *Making sense of the organization.* Malden, MA: Blackwell Publishing.

22. Ruben, B. D. (1992). The communication-information relationship in system-theoretic perspective. *Journal of the American Society for Information Science, 43*(1), 15–27.

23. Berger, P. L., & Luckmann, T. (1967). *The social construction of reality: A treatise in the sociology of knowledge.* Garden City, NY: Doubleday.

24. Ruben, B. D. (1992). The communication-information relationship in system-theoretic perspective. *Journal of the American Society for Information Science, 43*(1), 15–27.

25. Ruben, B. D. (1992). The communication-information relationship in system-theoretic perspective. *Journal of the American Society for Information Science, 43*(1), 15–27.

26. Ruben, B. D. (1992). The communication-information relationship in system-theoretic perspective. *Journal of the American Society for Information Science, 43*(1), 15–27.

27. Miller, J. G. (1965). Living systems: Basic concepts. *Behavioral Science, 10*(3), 193–237.
Ruben, B. D. (1972). General system theory: An approach to human communication. In R. W. Budd & B. D. Ruben (Eds.), *Approaches to human communication* (pp. 120–144). New York, NY: Spartan.
Thayer, L. (1968). *Communication and communication systems.* Homewood, IL: Irwin.

28. von Bertalanffy, L. (1968). General system theory: Foundations. In *Development Applications* (p. 3). New York, NY: George Braziller, Inc. Quote p. 32.

29. Ruben, B. D. (1992). The communication-information relationship in system-theoretic perspective. *Journal of the American Society for Information Science, 43*(1), 15–27. Quote p. 21.

30. Ruben, B. D. (1992). The communication-information relationship in system-theoretic perspective. *Journal of the American Society for Information Science, 43*(1), 15–27. Quote p. 22.

31. Mokros, H. B., & Ruben, B. D. (1991). Understanding the communication-information relationship: Levels of information and contexts of availabilities. *Knowledge: Creation, Diffusion, Utilization, 12*(4), 373–388. Quote p. 378.

32. Ruben, B. D., & Stewart, L. P. (2006). *Communication and human behavior* (5th ed.). Boston, MA: Pearson Education.

Weick, K. E. (2001). *Making sense of the organization.* Malden, MA: Blackwell Publishing.

Weick, K. E. (1979). *The social psychology of organizing* (2nd ed.). Malden, MA: Blackwell Publishing.

Westley, B. H., & MacLean, M. S. (1970). A conceptual model for communications research. In K. K. Sereno & C. D. Mortensen (Eds.), *Foundations of communication theory* (pp. 103–107). New York, NY: Harper and Row Publishers.

33. Berger, P. L., & Luckmann, T. (1967). *The social construction of reality: A treatise in the sociology of knowledge.* Garden City, NY: Doubleday.

Burr, V. (2003). *Social constructionism* (2nd ed.). New York, NY: Routledge.

34. Miller, J. G. (1965). Living systems: Basic concepts. *Behavioral Science, 10*(3), 193–237.

Ruben, B. D. (1992). The communication-information relationship in system-theoretic perspective. *Journal of the American Society for Information Science, 43*(1), 15–27. Quote p. 22.

35. Ruben, B. D. (1979). General system theory. In R. W. Budd & B. D. Ruben (Eds.), *Interdisciplinary approaches to human communication* (pp. 95–118). Rochelle Park, NJ: Hayden Book Company, Inc.

Ruben, B. D. (1992). The communication-information relationship in system-theoretic perspective. *Journal of the American Society for Information Science, 43*(1), 15–27. Quote p. 22.

Ruben, B. D., & Stewart, L. P. (2006). *Communication and human behavior* (5th ed.). Boston, MA: Pearson Education.

36. Ruben, B. D., & Stewart, L. P. (2006). *Communication and human behavior* (5th ed.). Boston, MA: Pearson Education.

37. Peters, J. D. (1999). Introduction: The problem of communication. In J. D. Peters (Ed.), *Speaking into the air: A history of the idea of communication* (pp. 1–31). Chicago: University of Chicago.

Ruben, B. D., & Stewart, L. P. (2006). *Communication and human behavior* (5th ed.). Boston, MA: Pearson Education.

Thayer, L. (1979). Communication: Sine qua non of the behavioral sciences. In R. W. Budd & B. D. Ruben (Eds.), *Interdisciplinary approaches to human communication* (pp. 7–31). Rochelle Park, New Jersey: Hayden Book Company, Inc.

38. Delgado, J. M. R. (1979). Neurophysiology. In R. W. Budd & B. D. Ruben (Eds.), *Interdisciplinary approaches to human communication* (pp. 119–134). Rochelle Park, NJ: Hayden Book Company, Inc.

Dervin, B. (1977). Useful theory for librarianship: Communication, not information. *Drexel Library Quarterly, 13*(3), 16–32.

Ruben, B. D. (1979). General system theory. In R. W. Budd & B. D. Ruben (Eds.), *Interdisciplinary approaches to human communication* (pp. 95–118). Rochelle Park, NJ: Hayden Book Company, Inc.

Smith, A. G. (1979). Anthropology. In R. W. Budd & B. D. Ruben (Eds.), *Interdisciplinary approaches to human communication* (pp. 57–70). Rochelle Park, NJ: Hayden Book Company, Inc.

Thayer, L. (1979). Communication: Sine qua non of the behavioral sciences. In R. W. Budd & B. D. Ruben (Eds.), *Interdisciplinary approaches to human communication* (pp. 7–31). Rochelle Park, New Jersey: Hayden Book Company, Inc.

39. Mokros, H. B., & Ruben, B. D. (1991). Understanding the communication-information relationship: Levels of information and contexts of availabilities. *Knowledge: Creation, Diffusion, Utilization, 12*(4), 373–388. Quote p. 378.

40. Mokros, H. B., & Ruben, B. D. (1991). Understanding the communication-information relationship: Levels of information and contexts of availabilities. *Knowledge: Creation, Diffusion, Utilization, 12*(4), 373–388. Quote p. 378.

41. Craig, R. T. (1999). Communication theory as a field. *Communication Theory, 9*(2), 119–161.

Delgado, J. M. R. (1979). Neurophysiology. In R. W. Budd & B. D. Ruben (Eds.), *Interdisciplinary approaches to human communication* (pp. 119–134). Rochelle Park, NJ: Hayden Book Company, Inc.

Miller, J. G. (1965). Living systems: Basic concepts. *Behavioral Science, 10*(3), 193–237.

Ruben, B. D. (1979). General system theory. In R. W. Budd & B. D. Ruben (Eds.), *Interdisciplinary approaches to human communication* (pp. 95–118). Rochelle Park, NJ: Hayden Book Company, Inc.

Smith, A. G. (1979). Anthropology. In R. W. Budd & B. D. Ruben (Eds.), *Interdisciplinary approaches to human communication* (pp. 57–70). Rochelle Park, NJ: Hayden Book Company, Inc.

Thayer, L. (1979). Communication: Sine qua non of the behavioral sciences. In R. W. Budd & B. D. Ruben (Eds.), *Interdisciplinary approaches to human communication* (pp. 7–31). Rochelle Park, New Jersey: Hayden Book Company, Inc.

42. Ruben, B. D. (1992). The communication-information relationship in system-theoretic perspective. *Journal of the American Society for Information Science, 43*(1), 15–27. Quote p. 22.

Smith, A. G. (1979). Anthropology. In R. W. Budd & B. D. Ruben (Eds.), *Interdisciplinary approaches to human communication* (pp. 57–70). Rochelle Park, NJ: Hayden Book Company, Inc.

43. Halloran, J. D. (1985). Information and communication: Information is the answer, but what is the question? In B. D. Ruben (Ed.), *Information & behavior: Vol. 1* (pp. 27–39). New Brunswick: Transaction Books.

44. Blumer, H. (1979). Symbolic interaction. In R. W. Budd & B. D. Ruben (Eds.), *Interdisciplinary approaches to human communication* (pp. 135–153). Rochelle Park, New Jersey: Hayden Book Company, Inc.

Delgado, J. M. R. (1979). Neurophysiology. In R. W. Budd & B. D. Ruben (Eds.), *Interdisciplinary approaches to human communication* (pp. 119–134). Rochelle Park, NJ: Hayden Book Company, Inc.

Halloran, J. D. (1985). Information and communication: Information is the answer, but what is the question? In B. D. Ruben (Ed.), *Information & behavior: Vol. 1* (pp. 27–39). New Brunswick: Transaction Books.

Ruben, B. D., & Stewart, L. P. (2006). *Communication and human behavior* (5th ed.). Boston, MA: Pearson Education.

Smith, A. G. (1979). Anthropology. In R. W. Budd & B. D. Ruben (Eds.), *Interdisciplinary approaches to human communication* (pp. 57–70). Rochelle Park, NJ: Hayden Book Company, Inc.

Thayer, L. (1979). Communication: Sine qua non of the behavioral sciences. In R. W. Budd & B. D. Ruben (Eds.), *Interdisciplinary approaches to human communication* (pp. 7–31). Rochelle Park, New Jersey: Hayden Book Company, Inc.

45. Smith, A. G. (1979). Anthropology. In R. W. Budd & B. D. Ruben (Eds.), *Interdisciplinary approaches to human communication* (pp. 57–70). Rochelle Park, NJ: Hayden Book Company, Inc.

46. Thayer, L. (1979). Communication: Sine qua non of the behavioral sciences. In R. W. Budd & B. D. Ruben (Eds.), *Interdisciplinary approaches to human communication* (pp. 7–31). Rochelle Park, New Jersey: Hayden Book Company, Inc.

47. Dervin, B. (1977). Useful theory for librarianship: Communication, not information. *Drexel Library Quarterly, 13*(3), 16–32.

48. Halloran, J. D. (1985). Information and communication: Information is the answer, but what is the question? In B. D. Ruben (Ed.), *Information & behavior: Vol. 1* (pp. 27–39). New Brunswick: Transaction Books.

49. Smith, A. G. (1979). Anthropology. In R. W. Budd & B. D. Ruben (Eds.), *Interdisciplinary approaches to human communication* (pp. 57–70). Rochelle Park, NJ: Hayden Book Company, Inc.

50. Smith, A. G. (1979). Anthropology. In R. W. Budd & B. D. Ruben (Eds.), *Interdisciplinary approaches to human communication* (pp. 57–70). Rochelle Park, NJ: Hayden Book Company, Inc.

Dervin, B. (1977). Useful theory for librarianship: Communication, not information. *Drexel Library Quarterly, 13*(3), 16–32.

51. Smith, A. G. (1979). Anthropology. In R. W. Budd & B. D. Ruben (Eds.), *Interdisciplinary approaches to human communication* (pp. 57–70). Rochelle Park, NJ: Hayden Book Company, Inc. Quotes p. 86, 89.

52. Ruben, B. D., & Stewart, L. P. (2006). *Communication and human behavior* (5th ed.). Boston, MA: Pearson Education.

53. Miller, J. G. (1965). Living systems: Basic concepts. *Behavioral Science, 10*(3), 193–237.

54. Mokros, H. B., & Ruben, B. D. (1991). Understanding the communication-information relationship: Levels of information and contexts of availabilities. *Knowledge: Creation, Diffusion, Utilization, 12*(4), 373–388. Quote p. 378.

55. Ruben, B. D., & Stewart, L. P. (2006). *Communication and human behavior* (5th ed.). Boston, MA: Pearson Education.

56. Miller, J. G. (1965). Living systems: Basic concepts. *Behavioral Science, 10*(3), 193–237.

57. Belkin, N. J., & Robertson, S. E. (1976). Information science and the phenomenon of information. *Journal of the American Society for Information Science, 27*(4), 197–204.

Ruben, B. D. (1979). General system theory. In R. W. Budd & B. D. Ruben (Eds.), *Interdisciplinary approaches to human communication* (pp. 95–118). Rochelle Park, NJ: Hayden Book Company, Inc.

Wiener, N. (1966). Cybernetics. In A. G. Smith (Ed.), *Communication and culture: Readings in the codes of human interaction* (pp. 25–35). New York: Holt, Rinehart and Winston.

58. Thayer, L. (1979). Communication: Sine qua non of the behavioral sciences. In R. W. Budd & B. D. Ruben (Eds.), *Interdisciplinary approaches to human communication* (pp. 7–31). Rochelle Park, New Jersey: Hayden Book Company, Inc.

59. Ruben, B. D., & Stewart, L. P. (2006). *Communication and human behavior* (5th ed.). Boston, MA: Pearson Education.

60. Ruben, B. D. (1992). The communication-information relationship in system-theoretic perspective. *Journal of the American Society for Information Science, 43*(1), 15–27. Quote p. 21.

61. Bateson, G. (1996). Communication. In H. B. Mokros (Ed.), *Interaction and identity: Information and behaviour: Vol. 5* (pp. 45–70). New Brunswick, NJ: Transaction Publishers.

Frings, H. (1979). Zoology. In R. W. Budd & B. D. Ruben (Eds.), *Interdisciplinary approaches to human communication* (pp. 33–55). Rochelle Park, New Jersey: Hayden Book Company, Inc.

Miller, J. G. (1965). Living systems: Basic concepts. *Behavioral Science, 10*(3), 193–237.

Mokros, H. B., & Ruben, B. D. (1991). Understanding the communication-information relationship: Levels of information and contexts of availabilities. *Knowledge: Creation, Diffusion, Utilization, 12*(4), 373–388. Quote p. 378.

Ruben, B. D. (1979). General system theory. In R. W. Budd & B. D. Ruben (Eds.), *Interdisciplinary approaches to human communication* (pp. 95–118). Rochelle Park, NJ: Hayden Book Company, Inc.

Thayer, L. (1979). Communication: Sine qua non of the behavioral sciences. In R. W. Budd & B. D. Ruben (Eds.), *Interdisciplinary approaches to human communication* (pp. 7–31). Rochelle Park, New Jersey: Hayden Book Company, Inc.

62. Mokros, H. B., & Ruben, B. D. (1991). Understanding the communication-information relationship: Levels of information and contexts of availabilities. *Knowledge: Creation, Diffusion, Utilization, 12*(4), 373–388. Quote p. 378.

63. Ruben, B. D., & Stewart, L. P. (2006). *Communication and human behavior* (5th ed.). Boston, MA: Pearson Education.

64. Ruben, B. D. (1979). General system theory. In R. W. Budd & B. D. Ruben (Eds.), *Interdisciplinary approaches to human communication* (pp. 95–118). Rochelle Park, NJ: Hayden Book Company, Inc.

65. Blumer, H. (1979). Symbolic interaction. In R. W. Budd & B. D. Ruben (Eds.), *Interdisciplinary approaches to human communication* (pp. 135–153). Rochelle Park, New Jersey: Hayden Book Company, Inc.

Dervin, B. (1977). Useful theory for librarianship: Communication, not information. *Drexel Library Quarterly, 13*(3), 16–32.

Ruben, B. D. (1979). General system theory. In R. W. Budd & B. D. Ruben (Eds.), *Interdisciplinary approaches to human communication* (pp. 95–118). Rochelle Park, NJ: Hayden Book Company, Inc.

66. Ruben, B. D., & Stewart, L. P. (2006). *Communication and human behavior* (5th ed.). Boston, MA: Pearson Education.

67. Mokros, H. B., & Ruben, B. D. (1991). Understanding the communication-information relationship: Levels of information and contexts of availabilities. *Knowledge: Creation, Diffusion, Utilization, 12*(4), 373–388. Quote p. 378.

68. Mokros, H. B., & Ruben, B. D. (1991). Understanding the communication-information relationship: Levels of information and contexts of availabilities. *Knowledge: Creation, Diffusion, Utilization, 12*(4), 373–388. Quote p. 378.

69. Delgado, J. M. R. (1979). Neurophysiology. In R. W. Budd & B. D. Ruben (Eds.), *Interdisciplinary approaches to human communication* (pp. 119–134). Rochelle Park, NJ: Hayden Book Company, Inc.

Miller, J. G. (1965). Living systems: Basic concepts. *Behavioral Science, 10*(3), 193–237.

Ruben, B. D. (1979). General system theory. In R. W. Budd & B. D. Ruben (Eds.), *Interdisciplinary approaches to human communication* (pp. 95–118). Rochelle Park, NJ: Hayden Book Company, Inc.

Ruben, B. D., & Stewart, L. P. (2006). *Communication and human behavior* (5th ed.). Boston, MA: Pearson Education.

Smith, A. G. (1979). Anthropology. In R. W. Budd & B. D. Ruben (Eds.), *Interdisciplinary approaches to human communication* (pp. 57–70). Rochelle Park, NJ: Hayden Book Company, Inc. Quotes p. 86, 89.

Thayer, L. (1979). Communication: Sine qua non of the behavioral sciences. In R. W. Budd & B. D. Ruben (Eds.), *Interdisciplinary approaches to human communication* (pp. 7–31). Rochelle Park, New Jersey: Hayden Book Company, Inc.

70. Ruben, B. D., & Stewart, L. P. (2006). *Communication and human behavior* (5th ed.). Boston, MA: Pearson Education.

Smith, A. G. (1979). Anthropology. In R. W. Budd & B. D. Ruben (Eds.), *Interdisciplinary approaches to human communication* (pp. 57–70). Rochelle Park, NJ: Hayden Book Company, Inc. Quotes p. 86, 89.

71. Ruben, B. D., & Stewart, L. P. (2006). *Communication and human behavior* (5th ed.). Boston, MA: Pearson Education.

Smith, A. G. (1979). Anthropology. In R. W. Budd & B. D. Ruben (Eds.), *Interdisciplinary approaches to human communication* (pp. 57–70). Rochelle Park, NJ: Hayden Book Company, Inc. Quotes p. 86, 89.

72. Delgado, J. M. R. (1979). Neurophysiology. In R. W. Budd & B. D. Ruben (Eds.), *Interdisciplinary approaches to human communication* (pp. 119–134). Rochelle Park, NJ: Hayden Book Company, Inc.

Ruben, B. D., & Stewart, L. P. (2006). *Communication and human behavior* (5th ed.). Boston, MA: Pearson Education.

Smith, A. G. (1979). Anthropology. In R. W. Budd & B. D. Ruben (Eds.), *Interdisciplinary approaches to human communication* (pp. 57–70). Rochelle Park, NJ: Hayden Book Company, Inc.

Thayer, L. (1979). Communication: Sine qua non of the behavioral sciences. In R. W. Budd & B. D. Ruben (Eds.), *Interdisciplinary approaches to human communication* (pp. 7–31). Rochelle Park, New Jersey: Hayden Book Company, Inc.

73. Thayer, L. (1979). Communication: Sine qua non of the behavioral sciences. In R. W. Budd & B. D. Ruben (Eds.), *Interdisciplinary approaches to human communication* (pp. 7–31). Rochelle Park, New Jersey: Hayden Book Company, Inc.

74. Smith, A. G. (1979). Anthropology. In R. W. Budd & B. D. Ruben (Eds.), *Interdisciplinary approaches to human communication* (pp. 57–70). Rochelle Park, NJ: Hayden Book Company, Inc. Quote p. 89.

75. Miller, J. G. (1965). Living systems: Basic concepts. *Behavioral Science, 10*(3), 193–237.

Ruben, B. D. (1979). General system theory. In R. W. Budd & B. D. Ruben (Eds.), *Interdisciplinary approaches to human communication* (pp. 95–118). Rochelle Park, NJ: Hayden Book Company, Inc.

76. Ruben, B. D. (1979). General system theory. In R. W. Budd & B. D. Ruben (Eds.), *Interdisciplinary approaches to human communication* (pp. 95–118). Rochelle Park, NJ: Hayden Book Company, Inc.

Ruben, B. D., & Stewart, L. P. (2006). *Communication and human behavior* (5th ed.). Boston, MA: Pearson Education.

Chapter 4

The Nature of Leadership

WHAT YOU CAN EXPECT TO LEARN IN THIS CHAPTER

- What is a leader?
- Why is leadership important?
- What are the key components of leadership?
- What are some approaches to leadership?

WHAT IS LEADERSHIP?

No matter who you talk to or what you read, you will find a different definition of leadership. Certainly, the way leadership is described, researched, and thought about is different depending on that person's perspective and background. Some agree that a kindergarten-aged child exhibits behavioral leadership at home by taking care of her pet. Others agree that leaders are born, not made. Many view leadership as possessing certain characteristics, traits, or skills.[1] And, many believe that if you have a title, such as president, chairperson, or manager that you are a leader.

The perspective taken in this book certainly agrees that there are many characteristics, traits, and skills that leaders possess. However, it would be difficult to pinpoint specifically which one(s) makes a leader. The perspective in this book also agrees that the kindergartener is a leader. By consistently feeding, watering, walking, brushing, and caring for her pet, she is influencing her family that she can lead that "project."

The perspective in this book does not agree that one has to be born with leadership ability. In fact, the perspective here is that anyone can be a leader.

Finally, we've all had a manager who couldn't lead their way out of a cubicle. Just because someone has a title doesn't mean they are a leader. In fact, many people who don't have a title emerge as a leader. How many times have you heard someone say, "Well, he's the boss, but SHE really runs the show?"

If there are leaders, there must be followers. Leadership is defined by the way the leader and followers create their reality together. They do so by the way they interact and communicate with each other. At times, then, one could argue that the leadership role is actually fulfilled by the followers and at other times, by the leader. Given this idea, at times it is hard to distinguish who is leading and who is following.

Many leadership actions occur unintentionally and unplanned.[2] What a leader does and says in informal situations is often much more important than what they say at a formal event where they have prepared a speech. For example, the department chairperson in Case Study Small University delivered a prepared statement about his leadership philosophy to the faculty. In this statement, he spoke about how he values everyone's thoughts and opinions. Yet at faculty department meetings during the first year as chairperson, he repeatedly blocked nearly all ideas and gave reasons why faculty member's opinions were wrong. As the chairperson listened to others' ideas, he folded his arms and wrinkled his face.

The chairperson really thought that he was holding up his leadership philosophy. However, his actions communicated something entirely different to the department members—that their thoughts and opinions didn't matter. Between meetings, faculty began to discuss this disparity and to express their dissatisfaction with his leadership to each other. After a few months, faculty began to lose respect for him. Yes, his title was one of a leader, but the followers (the faculty) no longer considered him to be a leader. Needless to say, after his first term ended, he was not reelected as chairperson and faculty continue to have a very different relationship with him than they did before he was chairperson.

Two key components of leadership from this example include the ability to be consistent with planned and unplanned, and intentional and unintentional actions.[3] The chairperson never considered that he would be contested for a second term and couldn't figure out what went wrong. He planned and was intentional about his words in his formal speech, but during unplanned and with unintentional actions, he undermined those words.

A third key component of leadership is that to be a leader, there must be followers.[4] In this example, faculty became so disenfranchised with the chairperson that they ended up going to department meetings and simply agreeing with the chairperson because they knew it was futile to even suggest an alternative. Some faculty even stopped attending department meetings. Other faculty went rogue and just did whatever they wanted without consulting the chairperson. At times, this rogue action led to a reversal of a process the chairperson had set in place. This, in turn, led other faculty to follow the new, rogue, process.

A fourth key component of leadership is the chairperson's nonverbal cues.[5] As he listened to the other faculty member's ideas, he scowled his face and crossed his arms giving them the impression that he was not happy with their ideas. This added to faculty perceptions that no matter what the chairperson said, he was going against faculty desires.

A fifth key component of leadership is the ability to pay attention to and work with different cultures and worldviews.[6] In this example, the chairperson, consumed with administrative duties, forgot what it was like to be faculty. He entered the discussions with blinders on to others' points of view. Rather, the chairperson was so caught up in his role and tasks that he neglected to think about the impact of processes and decisions on the faculty in his own department.

One of the most frequent definitions of leadership states that it is "a process whereby an individual influences a group of individuals to achieve a common goal."[7] However, this definition seems incomplete, given the social nature of leadership.[8] Just as the previous example showed, members of the department cocreated their experience as they discussed the actions of the chairperson and concluded that the only way to correct the problem was to elect a new chairperson.[9]

WHY LEADERSHIP IS AN IMPORTANT ISSUE

Leadership is a hot topic today. In fact, the topic of leadership ranks among the top issues in studies about planned organizational change.[10] Over time, leadership has become a primary area of research seen to influence superior/subordinate effectiveness—such as satisfaction, productivity, and team building—in change programs and in business overall.[11]

Much of the early leadership literature is dominated by Chris Argyris who argued that the individual and the organization are in direct conflict because individuals are expected to lose their independence while assuming a dependent role upon the organization.[12] Argyris developed the concept of participative management, where organizational members are involved with decision-making. Organizational member participation in decision-making turns the "cog in the wheel" employee into one who is connected and committed to the organization.[13]

In the following years, a set of learning theories for organizations was developed.[14] The intent was for the leader to exhibit model behavior for their employees in the expectation that they would be emulated. Further, that learning and change would occur through these leadership practices. It was around this time that we learned that leader's experiences and background, as well as the organization's environment, can influence the performance of their employees.[15]

Later, others discovered that before change can occur through leadership practices, leaders must first understand that employees must feel the need to change, not be told to change.[16] The way leadership is approached in these and other studies varies based on characteristics, behaviors, competencies, and more.

LEADERSHIP APPROACHES

A number of leadership approaches have been developed over the years. Some have become more popular than others, and there is ongoing debate about which is the best approach, if any. This summary of leadership approaches is not meant to be exhaustive by any means.[17] Its purpose is to provide you with a brief understanding of several leadership approaches to help you discover where you have similarities and perhaps differences.

First, let's take a look at leadership *traits and characteristics*. The big idea in this early stage of leadership research was that one could learn what traits and characteristics the great leaders of the world possessed.[18] This is where the idea that leaders were born, not made, originated.[19] Throughout the 1900s research focused on the idea that traits and characteristics, such as intelligence, self-confidence, determination, integrity and sociability, separated leaders from non-leaders.[20]

As the research progressed, it was evident that traits and characteristics were not the holy grail of leadership. There is no evidence that any one trait or characteristic makes a leader.[21] However, this type of research has continued over the years and many studies and leadership trait assessments have resulted. These assessments made determining leaders versus non-leaders effortless for organizations and self-discovery. There was also a resurgence of the trait and characteristic method in 2006 with the concept of charismatic leadership.[22]

The next mindset of leadership is based on skills. Rather than figuring out which traits or characteristics were more prevalent of leaders versus non-leaders, this mindset looked at the skills that were needed to be considered a leader.[23] A considerable difference between the skills and the trait mindset is that the *skills mindset* says that leadership can be learned, whereas the trait mindset says leaders are born (see table 4.1). Two major streams of thought identify this mindset. The first is the Three-Skills Approach.[24] This approach consists of technical skills, or skills specialized in a field; human skills, or skills working with people; and conceptual skills, or skills working with ideas.[25]

Table 4.1 Leadership Approaches

Leadership Approaches	Emphasis	Slogan	Examples	Point Of View	Researchers
Trait/ Characteristic	Leader personality	Leaders are born, not made	Charisma Intelligence Self-confidence Determination Integrity Sociability	Leader	Kirkpatrick & Locke, 1991; Lord, DeVader, & Alliger, 1986; Mann, 1959; Stogdill, 1948; 1974; Zaccaro, Kemp & Bader, 2004
Skills	Leader skills	Leadership can be learned	Three-Skills Approach (technical, human, conceptual) Skills Model (capabilities: knowledge, skills)	Leader	Katz, 1955; Mumford, Zaccaro, Harding, Jacobs & Fleishmam, 2000
Behavior	Leader behavior	What leaders "do" and how they "act" has an impact on their employees	Task behavior Relationship behavior	Leader	Blake & Mouton, 1964, 1978, 1985; Blake & McCanse 1991
Situational	Leadership in different situations	Leaders match style to followers' skills and motivation for each situation	Directive behaviors Supportive behaviors	Follower and context	Hersey & Blanchard, (1969)
Path-Goal	Leaders behavior complements or supplements follower needs	How leaders motivate followers to complete tasks	Leaders define goals, clarify path, remove obstacles, and provide support to followers.	Follower and context	Evans, 1970; House, 1971; House & Dessler, 1974; House & Mitchell, 1974

(Continued)

Table 4.1 Leadership Approaches (*Continued*)

Leadership Approaches	Emphasis	Slogan	Examples	Point Of View	Researchers
Leader-Member Exchange Theory	A leadership process with a focus on the dyadic relationship between the leader and the followers.	Leaders engage followers to become part of the in-group, which ultimately leads to achieving goals for the follower, leader, and organization.	In-group Out-group Leadership making: phase 1 stranger, phase 2 acquaintance, phase 3 mature partnership	Interactions between leader and followers	Graen & Uhi-Bien, 1991, 1995
Transformational	A leadership process that inspires followers to make exceptional changes.	Leaders motivate followers to do more than what is expected.	Charisma Vision	Process between followers & leaders	Avolio, 1999; Bass, 1985, 1998; Bass & Avolio, 1990; Burns, 1978
Authentic	A leader who is genuine, or authentic.	We need an honest and credible leader.	Authenticity	Intrapersonal focus on leader Interpersonal focus on interactions between leader and follower Developmental focus on leader	Avolio & Gardner, 2005; Eagly, 2005; Shamir & Eilam, 2005; George, 2003; Walumbwa, Avolio, Gardner, Wernsing & Peterson, 2008
Servant	Leaders have a desire to serve. They empower and help followers develop and grow, which, in turn, promotes organization, leader, and societal growth.	Care for others	Conceptualizing Emotional healing Putting followers first Helping followers grow and succeed Behaving ethically Empowering Creating value for the community	Leader and leader behaviors	Greenleaf, 1970, Liden, Wayne, Zhao & Henderson, 2008

Adaptive	Leaders provide support to followers so they can work on implementing and adapting to a change given their situation.	Change and adjust	Technical challenges Technical and adaptive challenges Adaptive challenges	Follower centered	Heifetz, 1994; Heifetz, Grashow & Linsky, 2009
Psychodynamic	Leaders must first understand their behavior, then what motivates followers.	Self-understanding is key.	Socialization and relationship themes Leader-follower relationship Narcissism	Leader	Kets de Vries, 2005; Kets de Vries & Miller, 1984
Everyday	Nontraditional leaders who tune into issues and improvise to get things done.	Anyone can lead at any time.	Interpretation Constant adjustment Formulations of temporary solutions Sensemaking	Leader Event-driven	Holmberg, Tyrstrup, 2010
Team	Leaders help the team to accomplish goals by monitoring and diagnosing issues and taking action.	Do whatever it takes for the team to succeed.	Leader decisions Leader actions: internal and external Team effectiveness	Focus on leader's understanding of team needs	Hill, 2016

Source: Northouse, P. G. (2016). *Leadership: Theory and practice.* (7th Ed.) Los Angeles: Sage Publications, Inc.
Note: Adapted from original source to highlight differences between leadership approaches.

The second skills mindset is the Skills Model.[26] This model incorporates competencies such as problem-solving skills with individual attributes such as motivation to determine leadership outcomes such as performance. Similar to the trait model, this model has also been developed into an assessment tool that can be used by organizations or for self-discovery, which adds to its appeal.

While there are many models for leadership *competencies*, one, in particular, presents a comprehensive view looking at categories of competencies including analytic, personal, communication, positional, and organizational (see table 4.2). Some critics claim that many components are trait oriented and that there are too many parts to the model.[27] However, practitioners often find these types of models helpful to determine areas of strength and improvement.

Another approach to leadership is based on the *behavior* of the leader.[28] This approach focuses on what leaders "do" and how they "act" by assessing their task and relationship behaviors.[29] One of the most popular results of this approach is the Managerial Grid, now the Leadership Grid.[30] This grid evaluates leaders on their focus on work and people. For example, some leaders value people (relationships) more than they do work and vice versa. However, the approach also takes into consideration that there may be times where either relationship or task focus should be implemented. Either way, this is a good exercise for leaders to understand their normal area of focus and whether or not that area of focus serves them well in all situations.

The *Situational Approach* is one of the most used approaches in leadership application.[31] Leaders need to be either directive or supportive, depending on the followers' skills and motivations and on the situation.[32] Directive leaders set goals and deadlines, and supportive leaders encourage participation and praise followers among other forms of help.[33] It is up to the leader to determine whether followers need to have a supportive or directive leader depending on the situation and the followers' skill level and motivation.

Path-Goal Theory is another leadership approach. This approach focuses on how the leader defines goals, clarifies the path, removes obstacles, provides support, and rewards to the followers appropriate for the situation and followers' needs.[34] It is based on the expectancy theory of motivation and path-goal hypothesis and takes into account leader behaviors, characteristics of followers, and task and follower motivation.[35] The leader chooses a style (directive, supportive, participative, or achievement-oriented) to fill the gap between the task and the follower's needs. The theory is complete with predictions about which leadership style to adopt to different types of tasks.[36]

A change in the approach from leader-focused to a focus on the interaction between leaders and followers is central to the *leader-member exchange theory.*[37] The inspiration behind this theory is that the more high-quality partnership the leader can develop with followers, the more benefit there is for the organization, the follower, and the leader.[38] Those followers with the highest-quality partnership with the leader are part of an in-group network with increased access to support and engagement with the leader. Those followers with low-quality partnership with the leader are part of an out-group network treated fairly by leaders, but not given special attention. In-group followers put forth extra effort beyond their job description, while out-group followers tend to have a "punch the clock" attitude. Leaders are encouraged to include all followers into the in-group and to be mindful about how each follower wants to be included.[39]

Transformational leadership has become one of the more popular leadership approaches over the years.[40] This approach emphasizes that some leaders have more charisma and vision than others. Therefore, these leaders are more easily able to inspire followers to look beyond self-interest to the interests of the organization as a whole.[41] Overall, transformational leaders are trusted, serve as role models, and inspire change.

One of the most modern leadership approaches is that of the *authentic leader.*[42] Authentic leaders are seen as genuine to followers. There are five characteristics, or traits of authentic leaders: understand their purpose, possess and act on their good values, involved in trusted and open relationships with followers, maintain consistent and steady self-discipline, and show compassion to followers.[43] Authentic leadership develops over time and through life experiences.[44]

The desire to serve gets our *servant leader* started. Servant leaders channel this inner desire to serve by empowering their followers to be able to maximize their potential. In turn, the organization, leader, and society as a whole also see improvements.[45] The servant leader will be influenced by the context and culture of their organization; their own attributes, traits, and ideologies; and follower receptivity to the idea of a servant leader.[46]

Seven core behaviors constitute the servant leaders process.[47] Conceptualizing, or the ability to truly know the organization, permits servant leaders to be able to tell when things go awry, focus on, and creatively solve the issue.[48] The second behavior is emotional healing where the servant leader shows empathy and attends to the personal well-being of followers. The third behavior is putting followers before those of the servant leader.

Knowing followers' desires and helping them grow and be successful is the fourth behavior of the servant leader. Being fair, honest and ethical is the next behavior. Empowering followers builds their confidence and self-efficacy. This is the sixth behavior of servant leaders. Finally, servant leaders give back to the community and inspire others to do the same. The ultimate

Table 4.2   **Competencies Framework**

Analytic Competencies	Personal Competencies	Communication Competencies	Positional Competencies	Organizational Competencies
Self-assessment	Character, personal values, & ethics	Credibility & charisma	Education	Vision-setting
Problem definition	Cognitive ability, & creativity	Influence & persuasion	Experience	Management & supervision
Stakeholder analysis	Enthusiasm	Interpersonal & group orientation	Expertise	Information & knowledge management
Systems/Organization Analysis	High standards	Listening, attention, question-asking, & learning	Knowledge of sector	Technical capability
Analysis of technology to support leadership	Personal conviction & persistence	Public speaking, presentation skills, debate, & discussion	Knowledge of organization	Empowerment & supportiveness
Problem solving	Self-discipline& self-confidence	Diversity & intercultural orientation	Familiarity with task type	Teaching & coaching
Review and analysis of results	Tolerance for uncertainty & risk taking	Role modeling	Language & vocabulary	Facilitation & negotiation

Source: Gigliotti, R. A. (2019). *Competencies for effective leadership: A framework for assessment, education and research.* Emerald Publishing Limited.

outcomes of the servant leader are to spur follower performance and growth, organizational performance and positively impact society.[49]

Adaptive leaders focus on supporting stakeholders need to adapt and change to different situations.[50] Adaptive leaders use six key behaviors to facilitate the change process with stakeholders.[51] The first key behavior is "getting on the balcony" or taking a step back to see the big picture of what's happening in the organization. This includes looking at organizational processes and personalities and how they affect one another from a systems perspective.

The second behavior is identifying adaptive challenges. Leaders need to be adept at determining which types of challenges are technical versus adaptive so that they know if they can solve the challenge or if they need to involve the stakeholders. There are three possibilities. Some situations present simple technical challenges, which are easily accomplished by the leader.

The second situation is a combination of technical and adaptive challenges, which is accomplished by stakeholders with resources from the leader. The last type of situation presents adaptive challenges, where the leader serves as a source of strength to stakeholders who may need to reframe the situation and view it from a different perspective.[52] Adaptive challenges are typically those that trigger an emotional response because they hit a value or worldview.

Regulating the distress that accompanies change for stakeholders is a third behavior of adaptive leaders.[53] Change efforts produce uncertainty for stakeholders and can cause distress. Adaptive leaders need to be sure to monitor the stress levels of stakeholders and to be able to provide some relief so that it does not cripple the change effort.[54]

The fourth behavior of adaptive leaders is to ensure stakeholders maintain disciplined attention. At times, some stakeholders will resist or avoid the change. Leaders need to encourage their stakeholders and help them to get through the hard work to realize the benefits of the change.[55]

While leaders need to be able to direct stakeholder's actions, they also need to be able to assess when it's time to let them do the work on their own. This is the challenge of the fourth behavior of adaptive leadership. The fifth behavior of adaptive leaders is to ensure that all voices are heard even if some of those voices come from stakeholders who may be marginalized and considered lower-status.

The *psychodynamic approach* to leadership begins with a self-reflexive examination of the leader.[56] How was the leader socialized? What major events impacted the leader's childhood? What is the leader's worldview? How do these connections impact the way the leader behaves and acts with their stakeholders? Based on the Clinical Paradigm, this approach posits that the subconscious provides a rationale for everyday actions and behaviors.

Much of the history of this approach is rooted in the works of Freud, and of the Tavistock Institute.

Key concepts include a focus on the way the leader is socialized and relationship themes that develop over time; leader-follower relationships such as dependency, flight-fight, and pairing; social defense mechanisms, mirroring, idealizing, identification with aggressor, "shared madness," and leader narcissism.[57] This approach emphasizes the reflective leader first understanding themselves and then understanding others in the organization. These understandings can bring change within the leader and ultimately show increased organizational relationships and effectiveness.[58]

A nontraditional leadership phenomenon, *everyday leadership*, is becoming more popular. This type of leadership is fairly new. No matter the context, everyday leadership is viewed as leadership that anyone can do. Moms, kids, the bank teller, and even the neighbor can be an everyday leader.[59] Some of the research states that this type of leadership is event driven.[60]

There are three ways that everyday leaders act: (1) interpret the situation to understand what happened and why the expected outcome didn't happen; (2) constantly adjust their decisions because either there were many ways to solve the issue or the situation is in constant change; and (3) developing solutions that are usually temporary stop-gap measures.[61] Underlying these actions is the way the everyday leaders make sense of the situation based on their worldview.[62] There is much research needed to determine more about everyday leaders, their characteristics, how they work, how they are perceived, and how effective they are.

Team leadership can be formal or informal.[63] At times teams use shared leadership between formal and informal leaders or distributed leadership where all team members share the leadership responsibility using their strengths.[64] Team leaders face three important decisions. The first decision is whether to continue to monitor the team's progress or to take action to assist the team.

If the leader decides that action is needed, then the leader's next decision is to determine whether the assistance required involves the task, or relationships. Examples of task situations include goal focusing, facilitating decisions, and training. Examples of relational situations include coaching, collaborating, managing conflict, and modeling principles.

The final decision is whether the assistance required involves an internal or external environmental situation to the team. Examples of environmental situations include networking, advocating, assessing, and sharing information. Once the leader determines the outcomes of these three decisions, then they need to determine how to assist the groups. The leader needs to do whatever is needed to make the team successful.[65]

SUMMARY

This chapter provided an understanding of what it means to be a leader and why leadership is important. There are many approaches to leadership. This chapter provides a brief summary of a number of leadership approaches to consider as you determine your leadership style and approach for your planned organizational change effort.

NOTES

1. Brubaker, D. L. (2006). *The charismatic leader: The presentation of self and the creation of educational settings*. Thousand Oaks, CA: Corwin Press.

Conger, J., & Kanungo, R. (1987). Toward a behavioral theory of charismatic leadership in organizational settings. *The Academy of Management Review, 12*(4), 637–647.

Kirkpatrick, S. A., & Locke, E. A. (1991). Leadership: Do traits matter? *Academy of Management Executive, 5*(2), 48–60.

Nadler, D. A., & Tushman, M. L. (1990). Beyond the charismatic leader: Leadership and organizational change. *California Management Review, 32*(2), 77–97.

Ruben, B. D. (2006). *What leaders need to know and do: A leadership competencies scorecard*. Washington, DC: NACUBO.

2. Ruben, B. D., DeLisi, R., & Gigliotti, R. A. (2017). *A guide for leaders in higher education: Core concepts, competencies and tools*. Sterling, VA: Stylus Publishing.

3. Ruben, B. D., DeLisi, R., & Gigliotti, R. A. (2017). *A guide for leaders in higher education: Core concepts, competencies and tools*. Sterling, VA: Stylus Publishing.

4. Barge, J. K., & Fairhurst, G. (2008). Living leadership: A systemic constructionist approach. *Leadership Quarterly, 4*(3), 227–251.

Ruben, B. D. (2006). *What leaders need to know and do: A leadership competencies scorecard*. Washington, DC: NACUBO.

5. Ruben, B. D., DeLisi, R., & Gigliotti, R. A. (2017). *A guide for leaders in higher education: Core concepts, competencies and tools*. Sterling, VA: Stylus Publishing.

6. Ruben, B. D., DeLisi, R., & Gigliotti, R. A. (2017). *A guide for leaders in higher education: Core concepts, competencies and tools*. Sterling, VA: Stylus Publishing.

7. Northouse, P. G. (2016). *Leadership: Theory and practice* (7th ed.). Los Angeles: Sage Publications, Inc. Quote p. 6.

8. Barge, J. K., & Fairhurst, G. (2008). Living leadership: A systemic constructionist approach. *Leadership Quarterly, 4*(3), 227–251.

Ruben, B. D., DeLisi, R., & Gigliotti, R. A. (2017). *A guide for leaders in higher education: Core concepts, competencies and tools*. Sterling, VA: Stylus Publishing.

9. Barge, J. K., & Fairhurst, G. (2008). Living leadership: A systemic constructionist approach. *Leadership Quarterly, 4*(3), 227–251.

10. Smulowitz, S. (2014). Planned organizational change in Higher Education: Dashboard indicators and stakeholder sensemaking—A case study (Unpublished doctoral dissertation). Rutgers, The State University of New Jersey, New Brunswick, NJ.

11. Bennis, W. G. (1959). Leadership theory and administrative behavior: The problem of authority. *Administrative Science Quarterly, 4*, 259–301.

Cobb, A. T., & Margulies, N. (1981). Organization development: A political perspective. *The Academy of Management Review, 6*(1), 49–59.

Porras, J. I., & Berg, P. O. (1978). The impact of organization development. *Academy of Management Review, 3*, 249–266.

Porras, J. I., & Silvers, R. C. (1991). Organization development and transformation. *Annual Review of Psychology, 42*, 51–78.

Sashkin, M., & Burke, W. W. (1987). Organization development in the 1980's. *Journal of Management, 13*(2), 393–417.

12. Argyris, C. (1955). Organizational leadership and participative management. *The Journal of Business, 28*(1), 1–7.

13. Argyris, C. (1955). Organizational leadership and participative management. *The Journal of Business, 28*(1), 1–7.

14. Argyris, C., & Schon, D. A. (1978). *Organizational learning.* Reading, MA: Addison-Wesley.

15. Lieberson, S., & O'Connor, J. F. (1972). Leadership and organizational performance: A study of large corporations. *American Sociological Review, 37*(2), 117–130.

16. Labianca, G., Gray, B., & Brass, D. J. (2000). A grounded model of organizational schema change during empowerment. *Organization Science, 11*(2), 235–257.

17. Note that the purpose of this book does not capture leadership styles in-depth. For a rather full account of these, please see: Northouse, P. G. (2016). *Leadership: Theory and practice* (7th ed.). Los Angeles: Sage Publications, Inc.

Information from this source was used as a reference and summary for the content in this chapter.

18. Northouse, P. G. (2016). *Leadership: Theory and practice* (7th ed.). Los Angeles: Sage Publications, Inc.

19. Northouse, P. G. (2016). *Leadership: Theory and practice* (7th ed.). Los Angeles: Sage Publications, Inc.

20. Conger, J., & Kanungo, R. (1987). Toward a behavioral theory of charismatic leadership in organizational settings. *The Academy of Management Review, 12*(4), 637–647.

House, R. J. (1977). A 1976 theory of charismatic leadership. In J. G. Hunt & L. L. Larson (Eds.), *Leadership: The cutting edge* (pp. 199–272). Carbondale: Southern Illinois University Press.

Kirkpatrick, S. A., & Locke, E. A. (1991). Leadership: Do traits matter? *Academy of Management Executive, 5*(2), 48–60.

Nadler, D. A., & Tushman, M. L. (1990). Beyond the charismatic leader: Leadership and organizational change. *California Management Review, 32*(2), 77–97.

Northouse, P. G. (2016). *Leadership: Theory and practice* (7th ed.). Los Angeles: Sage Publications, Inc.

21. Northouse, P. G. (2016). *Leadership: Theory and practice* (7th ed.). Los Angeles: Sage Publications, Inc.

Stogdill, R. M. (1948). Personal factors associated with leadership: A survey of the literature. *Journal of Psychology, 25, 35–71.*

22. Jung, D., & Sosik, J. J. (2006). Who are the spellbinders? Identifying personal attributes of charismatic leaders. *Journal of Leadership & Organizational Studies, 12,* 12–27.

Northouse, P. G. (2016). *Leadership: Theory and practice* (7th ed.). Los Angeles: Sage Publications, Inc.

23. Northouse, P. G. (2016). *Leadership: Theory and practice* (7th ed.). Los Angeles: Sage Publications, Inc.

Ruben, B. D. (2006). *What leaders need to know and do: A leadership competencies scorecard.* Washington, DC: NACUBO.

24. Katz, R. L. (1955). Skills of an effective administrator. *Harvard Business Review, 33*(1), 33–42.

25. Katz, R. L. (1955). Skills of an effective administrator. *Harvard Business Review, 33*(1), 33–42.

26. Mumford, M. D., Zacaro, S. J., Harding, F. D., Jacobs, T. O., & Fleishman, E. A. (2000). Leadership skills for a changing world: Solving complex social problems. *Leadership Quarterly, 11*(1), 11–35.

27. Northouse, P. G. (2016). *Leadership: Theory and practice* (7th ed.). Los Angeles: Sage Publications, Inc.

28. Northouse, P. G. (2016). *Leadership: Theory and practice* (7th ed.). Los Angeles: Sage Publications, Inc.

29. Northouse, P. G. (2016). *Leadership: Theory and practice* (7th ed.). Los Angeles: Sage Publications, Inc. Quote p. 71.

30. Blake, R. R., & McCanse, A. A. (1991). *Leadership dilemmas: Grid solutions.* Houston, TX: Gulf Publishing Company.

Blake, R. R., & Mouton, J. S. (1964). *The managerial grid.* Houston, TX: Gulf Publishing Company.

Blake, R. R., & Mouton, J. S. (1978). *The new managerial grid.* Houston, TX: Gulf Publishing Company.

Blake, R. R., & Mouton, J. S. (1985). *The managerial grid III.* Houston, TX: Gulf Publishing Company.

Northouse, P. G. (2016). *Leadership: Theory and practice* (7th ed.). Los Angeles: Sage Publications, Inc.

31. Blanchard, K., Zigarmi, D., & Nelson, R. (1993). Situational Leadership® after 25 years: A retrospective. *Journal of Leadership Studies, 1*(1), 22–36.

Blanchard, K., Zigarmi, D., & Zigarmi, D. (2013). *Leadership and the one minute manager: Increasing effectiveness through Situational Leadership® II.* New York: William Morrow.

Hersey, P., & Blanchard, K. H. (1969). Life-cycle theory of leadership. *Training and Development Journal, 23,* 26–34.

Northouse, P. G. (2016). *Leadership: Theory and practice* (7th ed.). Los Angeles: Sage Publications, Inc.

32. Northouse, P. G. (2016). *Leadership: Theory and practice* (7th ed.). Los Angeles: Sage Publications, Inc.

33. Northouse, P. G. (2016). *Leadership: Theory and practice* (7th ed.). Los Angeles: Sage Publications, Inc.

34. Northouse, P. G. (2016). *Leadership: Theory and practice* (7th ed.). Los Angeles: Sage Publications, Inc.

35. Georgopoulous, B. S., Mahoney, G. M., & Jones, Jr., N. W. (1957). A path-goal approach to productivity. *Journal of Applied Psychology, 41*, 345–353.

House, R. (1971). A path goal theory of leader effectiveness. *Administrative Science Quarterly, 16*(3), 321–339.

Northouse, P. G. (2016). *Leadership: Theory and practice* (7th ed.). Los Angeles: Sage Publications, Inc.

Vroom, V. H. (1964). *Work and motivation.* New York: McGraw Hill.

36. Northouse, P. G. (2016). *Leadership: Theory and practice* (7th ed.). Los Angeles: Sage Publications, Inc.

37. Graen, G. B., & Uhi-Bien, M. (1995). Relationship-based approach to leadership: Development of leader-member exchange (LMX) theory of leadership over 25 years: Applying a multi-level, multi-domain perspective. *Leadership Quarterly, 6*(2), 219–247.

38. Northouse, P. G. (2016). *Leadership: Theory and practice* (7th ed.). Los Angeles: Sage Publications, Inc.

39. Northouse, P. G. (2016). *Leadership: Theory and practice* (7th ed.). Los Angeles: Sage Publications, Inc.

40. Northouse, P. G. (2016). *Leadership: Theory and practice* (7th ed.). Los Angeles: Sage Publications, Inc.

41. Bass, B. M. (1985). Leadership and performance beyond expectations. New York: Free Press.

Achor, S. (2010). *The happiness advantage: How a positive brain fuels success in work and life.* New York, NY: CURRENCY.

Northouse, P. G. (2016). *Leadership: Theory and practice* (7th ed.). Los Angeles: Sage Publications, Inc.

42. Northouse, P. G. (2016). *Leadership: Theory and practice* (7th ed.). Los Angeles: Sage Publications, Inc.

43. George, B. (2003). *Authentic leadership: Rediscovering the secrets to creating lasting value.* San Francisco: Jossey-Bass.

44. Northouse, P. G. (2016). *Leadership: Theory and practice* (7th ed.). Los Angeles: Sage Publications, Inc.

45. Northouse, P. G. (2016). *Leadership: Theory and practice* (7th ed.). Los Angeles: Sage Publications, Inc.

46. Liden, R. C., Wayne, S. J., Zhao, H., & Henderson, D. (2008). Servant leadership: Development of a multidimensional measure and multi-level assessment. *Leadership Quarterly, 19*, 161–177.

47. Liden, R. C., Wayne, S. J., Zhao, H., & Henderson, D. (2008). Servant leadership: Development of a multidimensional measure and multi-level assessment. *Leadership Quarterly, 19*, 161–177.

48. Liden, R. C., Wayne, S. J., Zhao, H., & Henderson, D. (2008). Servant leadership: Development of a multidimensional measure and multi-level assessment. *Leadership Quarterly, 19*, 161–177.

49. Liden, R. C., Wayne, S. J., Zhao, H., & Henderson, D. (2008). Servant leadership: Development of a multidimensional measure and multi-level assessment. *Leadership Quarterly, 19*, 161–177.

50. Northouse, P. G. (2016). *Leadership: Theory and practice* (7th ed.). Los Angeles: Sage Publications, Inc.

51. Heifetz, R. A. (1994). *Leadership without easy answers.* Cambridge, MA: Belknap Press.

Heifetz, R. A., & Laurie, D. L. (1997). The work of leadership. *Harvard Business Review, 7*(1), 124–134.

52. Northouse, P. G. (2016). *Leadership: Theory and practice* (7th ed.). Los Angeles: Sage Publications, Inc.

53. Northouse, P. G. (2016). *Leadership: Theory and practice* (7th ed.). Los Angeles: Sage Publications, Inc.

54. Northouse, P. G. (2016). *Leadership: Theory and practice* (7th ed.). Los Angeles: Sage Publications, Inc.

55. Northouse, P. G. (2016). *Leadership: Theory and practice* (7th ed.). Los Angeles: Sage Publications, Inc.

56. Northouse, P. G. (2016). *Leadership: Theory and practice* (7th ed.). Los Angeles: Sage Publications, Inc.

57. Bion, W. R. (1961). *Experiences in groups.* London: Tavistock.

Kets de Vries, M. F. R. (1979, July/August). Managers can drive their subordinates mad. *Harvard Business Review,* 125–134.

Kets de Vries, M. F. R. (1989). Leaders who self-destruct: The causes and cures. *Organizational Dynamics, 17*(4), 4–17.

Kets de Vries, M. F. R. (2009). *Reflections on leadership and character.* London: Wiley.

Kets de Vries, M. F. R. (2011). *Reflections on groups and organizations: On the couch with Manfred Kets de Vries.* London: Wiley.

McDougall, J. (1985). *Theater of the mind.* New York: Basic Books.

Northouse, P. G. (2016). *Leadership: Theory and practice* (7th ed.). Los Angeles: Sage Publications, Inc.

Paulhus, D. L., & John, O. P. (1998). Egoistic and moralistic biases in self-perception: The interplay of self-deceptive styles with basic traits and motives. *Journal of Personality, 66*(6), 1025–1060.

58. Northouse, P. G. (2016). *Leadership: Theory and practice* (7th ed.). Los Angeles: Sage Publications, Inc.

59. Martin, A. (2007). *Everyday leadership.* Center for Creative Leadership https ://www.ccl.org/articles/white-papers/everyday-leadership/.

60. Holmberg, I., & Tyrstrup, M. (2010). Well then—What now? An everyday approach to managerial leadership. *Leadership, 6*(4), 353–372.

61. Holmberg, I., & Tyrstrup, M. (2010). Well then—What now? An everyday approach to managerial leadership. *Leadership, 6*(4), 353–372.

62. Holmberg, I., & Tyrstrup, M. (2010). Well then—What now? An everyday approach to managerial leadership. *Leadership, 6*(4), 353–372.

Weick, K. E. (1995). *Sensemaking in organizations.* Thousand Oaks, CA: Sage.

63. Northouse, P. G. (2016). *Leadership: Theory and practice* (7th ed.). Los Angeles: Sage Publications, Inc.

64. Northouse, P. G. (2016). *Leadership: Theory and practice* (7th ed.). Los Angeles: Sage Publications, Inc.

65. Northouse, P. G. (2016). *Leadership: Theory and practice* (7th ed.). Los Angeles: Sage Publications, Inc.

Part II

Leadership Practices That Work

What you really want to know are the key leadership practices that work to ensure a successful planned organizational change effort in higher education. That, my friend, is the "Holy Grail" of change programs. While no book can tell you exactly what will work successfully each time, there are several leadership practices that are more impactful than others. The chapters in part II provide you with an overview of each of these leadership practices.

Chapter 5

Preparing to Lead by Understanding the Higher Education Environment

WHAT YOU CAN EXPECT TO LEARN IN THIS CHAPTER

- What types of internal and external issues are pressing for institutions of higher education?
- What are the differences that exist between institutions of higher education and traditional organizations?
- What are some operational differences between institutions of higher education and traditional organizations?
- What is systems thinking?

Close your eyes. Imagine yourself walking around an office in a traditional organization. Next, imagine yourself walking around a college campus. Can you feel the difference between the two? Which one has more energy and excitement? The college campus, of course! Why do you think that is?

From the moment you take your first step onto a college campus, you can feel the difference from being in a traditional organizational office setting. Perhaps it is the energy of students dashing from class to class chattering about their life plans, or the faculty discussing their latest research, or the IT staff trying to figure out how to update the computer labs. Whatever the difference is, you can be sure it is deeper than what you first see and feel.

As leaders of an institution of higher education, you should be keenly aware of the deeper differences between higher education and traditional organizations. These differences increase in intensity when organizational changes take place.

As you move forward through this and the chapters that follow, keep in mind that the only guarantee is that change is constant. New forces and trends will develop and pressure higher education to change with them. However, while the pressure to change may come from a variety of sources, the underlying planned organizational change processes remain the same. With that in mind, this chapter will help you understand two types of pressures facing leaders of higher education: internal and external. Following is a discussion of each topic.

What pressures keeps leaders of institutions of higher education awake at night? The list is extensive with topics such as COVID-19, race, safe spaces and LGBTQ+, sexual harassment and assault, binge drinking, faculty and staff unions, social media, diversity and inclusion, protests, security, international students, admissions rates, the rising costs of education, research funding, infrastructure upkeep, new technology, and, for some, the weather. And, that's just for starters.

These pressures come from a multitude of stakeholders, such as government entities, regulators, parents, students, alumni, taxpayers, community members, donors and funding sources, accreditors, and boards. Let's first examine some external pressures that keep leaders of institutions of higher education awake at night.

External Pressures

Pick up any higher education-related publication and you will find persistent concerns about the constant change that government, society, and stakeholders require, expect, and sometimes demand from institutions of higher education. Increasingly, higher education has come under scrutiny by many external stakeholders.

Over the past decade or so, a dramatic area of change, spurred by the government, focused on the assessment of performance and outcomes and how this information is used to document, report, and improve effectiveness of institutions of higher education. The 2006 Spellings Commission Report brought higher education into the national spotlight by challenging these institutions to use consistent assessment measures, show accountability and provide continuous improvement.[1]

This report spurred a major change in the way regional accrediting agencies evaluate institutions of higher education. As a result, institutions of higher education were forced to implement assessment, accountability, and continuous improvement programs. Many institutions of higher education created assessment offices, hired consultants, and used measurement-based strategies to help facilitate this government-forced planned organizational change effort.

The effects of the COVID-19 pandemic have touched every person on the planet. Higher education was quick to react by sending students home and transitioning to online learning during the spring, 2020 semester. The consequences of this decision were enormous. Some of the obstacles for students, staff, and faculty included internet access and speed, a safe and quiet home environment and time restrictions. Many faculty, staff, and students were caring for or mourning sick or deceased family members, required to work as an essential employee or became a "teacher" for their children also at home and learning online.

The summer of 2020 brought other obstacles as campus leaders felt pressure to announce decisions about the fall 2020 semester schedule and in-person versus online class format. This decision includes the knowledge that a sudden increase in infections will occur. However, the timing and severity of that increase is unclear as of this writing. Most campuses are preparing facilities for social distancing and other safety measures. Faculty, students, parents, and other constituents debate the pros and cons of returning to campus face-to-face.

The #BlackLivesMatter and #MeToo movements are sweeping the nation with implications for every industry, including colleges and universities. Campuses across the United States are revising nondiscrimination and anti-harassment policies, ensuring offices of equity and diversity directly report to the president, vowing to hire more diverse faculty and staff, and including more courses that represent racism and discrimination.[2]

Visit the compliance office in any institution of higher education and you will find a newly minted version of a policy on sexual harassment and sexual assault. Many now place a ban on romantic relationships between faculty and students and have restated measures taken to review policing tactics and training and their ban on the use of choke holds.[3]

According to the 2019 Inside Higher Education Survey of Chief Academic Officers, "nearly half (46 percent) of provosts of American colleges and universities report that at least one faculty member at their institution has faced allegations of sexual harassment in the last year. The percentage was highest (90 percent) at public doctoral institutions and lower in other sectors."[4] Many institutions are involved with some of the following societal-forced planned organizational changes such as dismissing faculty and staff, attending conferences to discuss how to handle these issues, rewriting policies, and training employees.

Similar to government and society, many other stakeholders have needs and demands for higher education. For example, employers would like institutions of higher education to provide greater "soft skills" such as leadership, communication, and teamwork to students, in addition to "hard skills" such as accounting and science.[5] These softer skills provide employers with a more effective employee team. In addition, employers can teach specifics of hard skills to employees easier than they can teach employees how to communicate, write, and work in teams effectively.

Institutions of higher education participate in their communities in a variety of ways, yet some communities expect more. Some of these expectations include, but are not limited to, using the expertise of faculty and students to serve the community, attracting families with students attending the institution, as well as families of student athletes from other institutions to spend money in the community on food, hotels, personal shopping, and so on.[6]

Property tax exemption is controversial in some communities. Community members feel it is unfair for institutions of higher education to be exempt from paying property tax, especially in those areas where financial and physical decay are rampant.[7] Many universities publicly post information about activities such as number of community service hours, economic output, job support, student dollars spent on community dining, and more on their website to help the community see some of the work they contribute annually and to help combat negative perceptions about their tax-exempt status.[8] Others voluntarily contribute funding to help the economic development of their communities.

Parents, guardians, and the public are concerned with the rising costs of higher education as well as the increases in student debt.[9] A recent conversation with a director in a physical rehabilitation center stated her concern about the rise in student debt compared with the entry-level salary in the field. She strongly feels this might contribute to a shortage of therapists in the near future, as they weigh the costs and benefits, and perhaps decide to choose an alternate career.

Institutions of higher education rely on the government, individuals, and a variety of other funding groups for grants and funding for research projects, capital investments, community investments, faculty and student travel to conferences, and more. Much of this funding goes to the hard sciences, but some also goes to the humanities.

While funding increased considerably from 1997 to 2007 by approximately $11.7 billion, funding from 2007 to 2017 increased by much less, approximately $2 billion.[10] The dip in funding over the past decade causes concern that funding will continue to dip. If this comes to fruition, then institutions of higher education will need to rely more heavily on funding from individuals and corporations. These considerations don't even take into account the economic impact of COVID-19 pandemic.

As the threat of massive open online courses (MOOCs) may be diminishing,[11] institutions of higher education are increasingly pursuing more and more online course and degree opportunities.[12] This pursuit of potential new students is viewed as a rare opportunity to tap into an unmet need in the marketplace by administrators. Yet, many faculty are resistant to online courses because they feel in-person courses are a much better learning experience for students.

New tax laws may also provide changes to the way individuals and corporations contribute to higher education as well as other charities. All this equals uncertainty for leaders of higher education as they budget and plan for the future.

Internal Pressures

It used to be that full-time, tenure-track faculty taught college and university students. It was a rare occasion that an adjunct faculty member had an opportunity to teach at an institution of higher education. Most adjunct faculty who taught at that time had a specialization in healthcare law or retail buying and they could provide more timely and hands-on information to students. Very few adjunct faculty at that time had a PhD.

Walk into any institution of higher education today and you will see something concerning. The ratio of adjunct faculty to full-time, tenure-track faculty has been reversing in some institutions of higher education.[13] While many adjunct faculty still have a specialization, many hold a PhD.

Why aren't these PhDs on a tenure-track, full-time teaching line? Adjunct faculty cost significantly less and do not require benefits or membership in the faculty union. These reduced costs are attractive to institutions of higher education looking to cut costs. However, at some institutions of higher education, full-time, tenure-track faculty and associations such as the American Association of University Professors (AAUP) are fighting for adjunct rights and the hiring of more full-time, tenure-track faculty.

Full-time, tenure-track faculty tend to have a better idea of student needs and concerns at their institution of higher education while adjunct faculty tend to come and go based on the class(es) they teach. Many adjunct faculty make a living by traveling from one institution of higher education to another to make ends meet. This limits the time they can invest in getting to know students, faculty, and the culture of each institution.

It also limits their input about issues of curriculum and other department management and prevents them from contributing to the institution as a whole unlike full-time, tenure-track faculty. As you can imagine, this also affects the amount of input faculty have toward the governance, policies, and procedures of the university because more adjunct faculty means less faculty able to voice their concerns and ideas to the administration.

Some of the other internal pressures include increasing demands for a focus on issues of diversity and inclusion, safety and security, declining population and admissions rates, publishing demands, and infrastructure, among others. The list of pressures on leaders of institutions of higher education is growing. To be able to confront these challenges, one of the first factors to consider is the way that higher education differs from traditional industry.

OPERATIONAL DIFFERENCES BETWEEN HIGHER EDUCATION AND TRADITIONAL INDUSTRY

As a leader in higher education, you surely are aware of the silos that exist in your institution. While the administrative group in an institution of higher education operates with a similar hierarchical structure to many traditional organizations, the academic group has a very different structure. Looking at the higher education administrative group and traditional organizations, you will find each have a similar hierarchy of president, chief financial officer, vice presidents, directors and staff. The academic group is loosely led by the chief academic officer, or provost, along with associate provosts, deans, department chairpersons, and faculty. Other differences are possible across community colleges, teaching institutions, and research institutions.

While the reporting lines are different in the administrative and academic groups within institutions of higher education, the true difference is really much deeper and correlates to their different mission and roles.[14] Faculty focus on scholarship, teaching, and service. Anything that falls outside of these areas are considered less important to the mission and roles of most faculty as they are granted tenure and promoted solely on those three areas. Once you, as a leader of higher education, understand the mission and role of the faculty, you will learn that the decision-making of faculty is a direct result of this focus.

Further, the administration has little to do with the promotion of the faculty as they operate independently with a rank and tenure board that reviews faculty applications for promotion. This board in most institutions of higher education consists of tenured faculty and the chief academic officer. Hopefully you are beginning to see that this unique academic structure consists of many independent elements, or silos, that are loosely tied together because of their ultimate interdependence.[15]

SYSTEMS THINKING

Think about the way your body parts function independently, yet interdependently, to keep you alive. Your heart needs to be able to function as a heart while your liver functions as a liver. Without either, you cannot survive. The same systems thinking can be applied to institutions of higher education.[16]

The admissions office, an administrative office, functions on its own, as does the academic department of Science. However, neither of them can survive without each other. They are both independent and interdependent.

The admissions office has certain goals, agreed upon within their administrative division, to bring a certain number of new students into the university each year. The Science department faculty also have individual goals—research, teaching, and service. In addition, the faculty might have departmental goals that fit mostly into teaching and service. However, faculty cannot teach students who are not in their classes. Similarly, the admissions department cannot attract new students interested in science to a university without a Science department.

To help understand this a bit more, we need to rely on the biology field and general systems thinking. Systems thinking is particularly ideal to understand the relationship between planned organizational change, human change, and communication. Humans go about their daily lives using communication as an essential life process. Communication enables humans to make, get, alter, and apply information to go about their daily lives.[17]

The complex relationship of the independent, yet interdependent admission and Science departments described earlier provides an example of systems theory, in particular, open systems. Open systems do not exist in isolation. They are "required" to have exchanges with their environment but also to function independently and have their own boundaries. These exchanges of information about each system's operation and boundaries are produced and reproduced through communication and also created within the system through disruption and restoration.[18]

Overlooking the interdependence of the larger system can have catastrophic results to the smaller and larger systems, or divisions and departments in a university. Going back to the example, if faculty in the Science department do not help the admission department at university events such as Open House, then there may be less science students admitted and so on until there is no need for a Science department anymore. Not only will faculty be dismissed, but the university overall suffers because it can no longer compete in the science field.

However, when the science and admissions departments get together and discuss their respective operations, they are more likely to figure out how they can best work together to attract more students to the Science program. Through communication, members from both departments can cocreate their reality of what it is like to work with each other. Organizational members will determine what they can do to collaborate and where boundaries are drawn. For example, some admissions departments are excited to bring faculty to high schools and others are not.

In an ideal world, this collaboration would culminate in a plan to recruit new students together. Perhaps, the faculty and admissions staff will decide that they have found an enthusiastic partner and develop a new joint recruiting program. In some instances, this happens and in others, organizational members can't seem to get past their differences. No one said it was going to be easy.

Making this new joint recruiting program a reality will cause some disruption to the way things normally occur. Inevitably, someone's feathers will be ruffled. There will be squawking. Perhaps feathers might even fly about. Eventually, there will be a restoration where either the new joint recruiting program will come together and become the new norm or the program will fade away and become one of those stories about how the admissions and science departments tried to work together. Either way, welcome to higher education.

As you read this book, consider your institution of higher education. Keep in mind that looking at the different levels within a system is key because individuals working together from all these levels can accomplish much more than any one going it alone.[19] Therefore, examples throughout this book examine communication and information processing at the individual, group, organizational, and across the organization levels as well as the interaction between those levels.[20]

SUMMARY

Leaders in higher education face a multitude of pressures both internal and external. This chapter provided you with details about many of those issues. In addition, this chapter provided you with an understanding of the inherent silos that exist in institutions of higher education. It's important to understand the way your organization functions both independently and interdependently—through systems thinking. This knowledge will serve you well as you lead and interact with stakeholders from across your institution of higher education.

NOTES

1. U.S. Department of Education. (2006). *The Spellings Commission report.* Washington, DC: Department of Education.

2. Pilarz, S. R., S. J. (2020, Jun. 11). Actions to combat racism and discrimination. *Royal News.* Scranton, PA: The University of Scranton. https://news.scranton .edu/articles/2020/06/news-president-actions-to-combat-racism.shtml.

3. Jaschik, S. (2019, Jan. 23). For Provosts, more pressure on tough issues. *Inside Higher Education.* Retrieved from: https://www.insidehighered.com/news/survey/20 19-inside-higher-ed-survey-chief-academic-officers.

Pilarz, S. R., S. J. (2020, Jun. 11). Actions to combat racism and discrimination. *Royal News.* Scranton, PA: The University of Scranton. https://news.scranton .edu/articles/2020/06/news-president-actions-to-combat-racism.shtml.

4. Jaschik, S. (2019, Jan. 23). For Provosts, more pressure on tough issues. *Inside Higher Education.* Retrieved from: https://www.insidehighered.com/news/survey/20 19-inside-higher-ed-survey-chief-academic-officers.

5. Andrews, M. (2015, June 30). What do employers want? *Inside Higher Education.* Retrieved from: https://www.insidehighered.com/blogs/stratedgy/what-do-employers-want.

6. Bienen, H. (2017, Jan. 24). The role of major Universities in their local communities. *The Evolution.* Retrieved from: https://evolllution.com/revenue-streams/market_opportunities/the-role-of-major-universities-in-their-local-communities/.

7. Robinson, J. A. (2017, Oct. 16). Should all university property be tax exempt? *The James G. Martin Center for Academic Renewal.* Retrieved from: https://www.jamesgmartin.center/2017/10/university-property-tax-exempt/.

Schneider, M., & Klor de Alva, J. (2016, July 8). Why should rich universities get huge property tax exemptions? *The Washington Post.* Retrieved from: https://www.washingtonpost.com/news/grade-point/wp/2016/07/08/why-should-rich-universities-get-huge-property-tax-exemptions/?noredirect=on&utm_term=.280ff6ca324e.

8. Community Relations. (2018). *Economic and community impact.* Scranton, PA: The University of Scranton. Retrieved from: https://www.scranton.edu/about/community-relations/economic-impact.shtml.

9. Brint, S. (2018). *Two cheers for Higher Education: Why American Universities are stronger than ever—and how to meet the challenges they face.* Princeton, NJ: Princeton University Press.

10. Brint, S. (2019). Is this Higher Education's golden age? *The Chronicle of Higher Education: The Chronicle Review.* Retrieved from: https://www.chronicle.com/interactives/golden-age.

11. Lederman, D. (2019a, Jan. 16). Why MOOCs didn't work in 3 data points. *Inside Higher Education.* Retrieved from: https://www.insidehighered.com/digital-learning/article/2019/01/16/study-offers-data-show-moocs-didnt-achieve-their-goals.

12. Lederman, D. (2019b, Jan. 16). How many public universities can "go big" online? *Inside Higher Education.* Retrieved from: https://www.insidehighered.com/digital-learning/article/2019/03/20/states-and-university-systems-are-planning-major-online.

13. Brint, S. (2018). *Two cheers for Higher Education: Why American Universities are stronger than ever—and how to meet the challenges they face.* Princeton, NJ: Princeton University Press.

14. Smulowitz, S. (2014). Planned organizational change in Higher Education: Dashboard indicators and stakeholder sensemaking—A case study (Unpublished doctoral dissertation). Rutgers, The State University of New Jersey, New Brunswick, NJ.

15. Weick, K. E. (1976). Educational organizations as loosely coupled systems. *Administrative Science Quarterly, 21,* 1–19.

16. Ruben, B. D. (1983). A system-theoretic view. In W. B. Gudykunst (Ed.), *Intercultural communication theory* (pp. 131–145). Beverly Hills, CA: Sage.

Smulowitz, S. (2014). Planned organizational change in Higher Education: Dashboard indicators and stakeholder sensemaking—A case study (Unpublished doctoral dissertation). Rutgers, The State University of New Jersey, New Brunswick, NJ.

Thayer, L. (1968). *Communication and communication systems.* Homewood, IL: Irwin.

von Bertalanffy, L. (1950). An outline of general systems theory. *The British Journal for the Philosophy of Science, 1*(2), 134–165.

17. Ruben, B. D., & Stewart, L. P. (2006). *Communication and human behavior* (5th ed.). Boston, MA: Pearson Education.

18. Miller, J. G. (1965). Living systems: Basic concepts. *Behavioral Science, 10*(3), 193–237.

Ruben, B. D. (1983). A system-theoretic view. In W. B. Gudykunst (Ed.), *Intercultural communication theory* (pp. 131–145). Beverly Hills, CA: Sage.

Thayer, L. (1968). *Communication and communication systems.* Homewood, IL: Irwin.

von Bertalanffy, L. (1950). An outline of general systems theory. *The British Journal for the Philosophy of Science, 1*(2), 134–165.

19. Smulowitz, S. (2014). Planned organizational change in Higher Education: Dashboard indicators and stakeholder sensemaking—A case study (Unpublished doctoral dissertation). Rutgers, The State University of New Jersey, New Brunswick, NJ.

20. Mohrman, S. A., Mohrman, A. M., & Ledford, G. E. (1989). Interventions that change organizations. In A. M. Mohrman, S. A. Mohrman, G. E. Ledford, E. E. Lawler, & Associates (Eds.), *Large scale organizational change.* San Francisco, CA: Jossey-Bass Publishers, Inc.

Chapter 6

Leadership Requires Commitment

WHAT YOU CAN EXPECT TO
LEARN IN THIS CHAPTER

• What are the six high-priority practices for leading successful change efforts in higher education?

A consistent, high-priority practice for successful change efforts in higher education and in industry is a leader who is committed to the planned change effort[1] Without solid leadership, the change effort is doomed to fail.[2] Leaders show commitment to the planned change effort in a variety of ways. Research indicates the top ways leaders demonstrate that they are committed to the planned organizational change effort are by setting a vision; being clear and reducing uncertainty; providing timely feedback; maintaining momentum, priority, and urgency; and providing the appropriate and timely resources.[3]

VISION

One of the first ways a leader can demonstrate their commitment to the planned change effort is to set the vision and tone.[4] This is especially important as they work toward establishing and initiating the change effort with members of the organization.[5]

A vision establishes direction for the change effort, provides consistent and compelling justification for the change, focuses the organization, and encourages organizational members to stick with the change effort. It clearly tells organizational members where they are going and it connects to the existing mission. A vision of where the institution is today and where it is headed upon integration of the change effort must be consistently articulated by the leader.[6] This provides organizational members with an idea of the discrepancy between the two and a compelling need for the change.[7]

Most, if not all, leaders realize the value of a vision but fail when it comes to the creation and consistent communication of that vision.[8] In many instances, this is due to the amount of time or perceived time involved with this process. Other leaders discuss vision only at the beginning stages of a change effort. Reality is that, especially in the depths of change, organizational members need to be reminded about the ultimate vision of the change effort as often as possible. These reminders reinforce the need for the change effort and each organizational members' impact on the change effort.

It is in defining this image of the future, or the vision, leaders or change agents of an institution play a key role for they are setting the tone of the change effort and changing the identity, and culture, of the institution. Changing the identity of the institution also means that those within the institution must change how they identify with the institution. In many cases, their identity is associated closely with the existing identity of the institution.[9] Think about what it is that the organization stands for, or represents—the core values.

Leaders and change agents should clearly communicate the vision to inspire organizational members to recognize the need for change and to take a leap of faith that the change effort will transform their current perception of the institution into an institution that they can identify with and belong to.[10] In doing so, leaders need to take into account differences between the new vision and the ways in which existing values, beliefs, and identities of organizational members might be adapted or cause conflict.[11] These differences include normative concerns, context, salience, culture, and the worldview of individuals.

- Normative concerns are considered when an individual's values and beliefs are in agreement with the core institutional values and beliefs and even the values and beliefs of an industry, such as higher education, as a whole.[12] Successful change implementation programs take into account norms of the institution such as faculty governance, tradition, and continuity.[13]
- An individual's context is typically "taken for granted" and "based on a set of individual and personal life experiences—such as nationality, education, job function—it is likely to influence how we relate to and work together as a team."[14] Due to the loosely coupled nature of institutions of higher education, each subunit relies on different constituencies and social networks of support—some of them political. When faced with an overall institutional change these subunits tend to react in a way that will preserve their constituency groups.[15] Within each subunit exist independent worldviews, which enable its members to find a socially constructed "way of looking at the world," a certain way to do things and a certain way of interacting with other members to support their culture and normative concerns.[16]

- Saliency describes the relative impact or relevance of the message on the receiver. The same message might be understood differently by different organizational members. The leader should take into account all the different ways a message could be interpreted.
- Organizational members not only represent themselves as an individual but also represent other groups such as belonging to the faculty, administration, or a specific discipline. The values held in these groups come from a culture unique to those groups. Leaders should take into account the different cultural groups that exist on campus and consider the leap of faith those members will be required to take to join the change effort.

CLARITY AND REDUCING UNCERTAINTY

The leader needs to ensure that all organizational members have clarity about the goals, or vision, of the planned change effort. If leaders aren't clear about the vision and goals of the change effort, this will cause others in the organization to also have uncertainty. Uncertainty often happens when organizational members don't know what will happen in the future. This can cause anxiety and stress for some organizational members and frustration and shutdown for others. In addition, uncertainty can cause some organizational members to fixate on possible outcomes rather than focus on their job.

Organizational members of the Case Study Large University were concerned and unmotivated because they didn't understand the benefit of the change effort to their department and their role, specifically, within the University. A staff member neatly summarized what many others expressed, "I think people's attitude was really about disinterest to frustration. How do we do this? And maybe shutdown because what does this have to do with me? Why should I care?"[17]

Much research has been completed about the causes and effects of uncertainty on organizational members. Three types of uncertainty are as follows:

- Strategic uncertainty—what are the reasons, benefits, and planning of the change effort, and how does this impact the future of the organization?
- Structural uncertainty—how does the change effort impact reporting structures, reallocation of services, and physical relocation of staff?
- Job-related uncertainty—are there promotion opportunities, changes to the job or job security issues?[18]

In the Case Study Large University, members reported staff shortages, low morale, and no salary increases for three to four years. A staff member exclaimed, "People feared for the safety of their job because of budget cuts."[19] Another staff member said that because of job security concerns, they started to think about learning new skills and professional development options in case they either found another job or their existing job was eliminated. This speaks directly to the fear that organizational members had surrounding the uncertainty of the change effort.

The more clarity organizational members have about the benefits of the change effort, the more likely they are to support and see the change effort through to success. However, if organizational members don't have access to or don't understand this type of information, they will either incorporate the effort sporadically or not at all.[20]

In addition, if organizational members don't trust the process or that the change effort will make a difference, then the effort will be doomed to fail. This can come from an inherent mistrust in the leader or the introduction of too many change efforts in too short of time that aren't seen through to fruition.

For example, about every three to five years, Case Study Small University introduced a new learning management system. For the first two years, the faculty were attending sessions about using the new learning management system, but over time, the number of faculty who attended these sessions drastically dropped off. Instead, urgent faculty phone calls to the administrator increased because they waited until they needed to use a specific component of the learning management system. Or, faculty adopted a different online program that was not supported by the University because they found it easier to use.

The new system was doomed before it began because the faculty grew tired of learning and relearning systems that would just be replaced every so many years. To the faculty, it was a waste of time to attend the learning management system sessions. Instead, they chose to call the administrator if there was something they couldn't figure out for themselves. Even if it meant that they were in a crisis situation such as entering midterm or final grades. Or, even if they had to learn the new online program on their own.

In the Case Study Large University, mistrust was rampant about the goals of the change effort. Some organizational members thought that the change effort was a fad that would disappear quickly. For example, a director shared, "They don't want to uncover dirt . . . they want to paint a pretty picture."[21]

A senior leader explained, "To someone such as myself who's got a bigger view it's . . . a lesson learned about an important communication component in this process that we shouldn't ever miss the people in the trenches. They should really understand the benefits that are derived from their work."[22]

FEEDBACK

Another way that leaders show commitment to the change effort is by giving and gathering feedback from organizational members.[23] Providing feedback to organizational members is essential because it adds an opportunity to rework underutilized programs, reengage organizational members, and remind organizational members of the vision.[24]

Leaders who fail to keep organizational members tuned into the importance of the change effort will lose the benefit of the effort. As a result, leaders will often end up thinking the change effort wasn't as effective as it could have been and might begin looking for a new change effort. The problem wasn't the change effort. The problem was leader's follow through and communication.

Organizational members in Case Study Large University were overwhelmingly critical about the lack of information available to them about the change effort. Members addressed the importance of hearing more about the effort so that it would become a natural "part of the conversation," provide clarity, reduce uncertainty, and as a result, there would be less resistance.

Providing a formal way for organizational members to assess and give feedback to leaders and change agents about the change effort is just as valuable. Unfortunately, many change effort plans provide information from a top-down approach only. These top-down approaches lose the opportunity to gain valuable information from organizational member's evaluation of the effort.[25]

MOMENTUM, PRIORITY, AND URGENCY

When it comes to long-term change efforts in higher education, the focus is on patience and persistence.[26] A decade can easily pass by before the results of a change effort are fully integrated into the culture. Persistence combined with continuous processes that produce gradual change over time are more likely to produce success in institutions of higher education rather than quick fixes.[27]

Momentum plays a big part in a planned change effort and leaders need to be seen as keeping the effort a priority. Erratic activities by those in charge of the planned change effort can have a negative impact on the success of the effort.[28] Organizational members may feel the change effort has failed if due dates keep moving, the topic stops showing up on agendas, leaders don't expect or insist on participation, there is an absence of discussion about the effort, or because of perceived inactivity.[29]

If this happens, organizational members may shift priorities away from the change effort and assume that the change effort has either failed or fizzled.[30] As a result, organizational members may revert back to their comfortable, previous processes and simply abandon the change effort.

In Case Study Large University, organizational members reported that the change effort stopped showing up on the agenda prepared by the leader. Not only were organizational members confused, but after some time of no mention of the change effort, they were convinced the effort had stalled or stopped.

At the time the effort "stopped," many organizational members were beginning to see some results. Organizational members became frustrated because they perceived the entire effort to be a waste of time and an exercise in futility.

Some of the organizational members thought there were too many competing priorities. A senior leader said, "Everyone knows it's important but they could never prioritize it."[31] Others blamed a lack of support from leadership, "If you don't have someone driving the bus it's not going anywhere."[32] A lesson learned from this case study is that leaders need to show their commitment to the change effort by creating a sense of urgency about the change effort and its impact on the future of the organization.[33]

Another damaging effect of the loss of momentum and organizational members perceiving that the change effort has stopped is that the next change effort to be introduced is almost surely doomed. Organizational members will remember that time after time when they act on a request from leaders to change, the effort comes to a complete stop. A director from Case Study Large University stated, "We do nothing but produce reports to say that we have reports."[34]

RESOURCES

Leaders show commitment to the change effort by providing resources organizational members feel are necessary. Beyond the obvious, some members may be concerned that they don't have the capability to participate in the change effort.

In Case Study Large University, a senior leader describes their frustration, "There was no one in all the units that report to me who had the skills to measure their goals. We didn't have the money. We didn't have the time. We couldn't do surveys. We didn't have anybody to code the data if we did interviews and we didn't have anybody to produce a report. It was beyond our background and training."[35]

Members' attitudes coupled with these performance concerns will contribute to the extent the change effort will be used in their own work and could create a major pause to the change effort.[36] Robust planning can help ensure that resources are identified, coordinated, and used effectively between all levels of the organization.[37] Although sometimes unforeseen situations arise that could make securing resources so that the effort can be continued is a challenge.[38]

Examples of resources include, but are not limited to, the following:

- benchmarking,
- funding,
- survey software,
- access to data,
- access to statisticians,
- people to enter and code data,
- additional personnel (staff and change agents), and
- leader's promise to shield a department from cutbacks if their data showed poor performance.

SUMMARY

Leadership requires commitment. If organizational members sense the leader is not committed to the planned organizational change effort, they will perceive it to be a waste of time and may abandon the effort. Leaders need to ensure they develop and communicate a compelling vision of the change effort so that organizational members will embrace the need to change.

Organizational members require clarity about the goals of the change effort. Uncertainty about goals can interfere with the progress of the change effort. Leaders need to ensure they provide timely feedback to organizational members about the change effort. They also need to gather feedback from organizational members to gain valuable insights to help the change effort succeed.

Should organizational members perceive a lack of momentum, priority, or urgency about the change effort, they may perceive that the change effort has stalled or stopped and this may cause them to halt their activities. Organizational members may also halt their efforts because of a lack of or perceived lack of resources. Leaders should monitor all these potential issues of commitment and ensure they meet them for increased success with the change effort. The next two chapters provide additional information about increasing success.

NOTES

1. Lewis, L. K., Schmisseur, A., Stephens, K., & Weir, K. (2006). Advice on communicating during organizational change: The content of popular press books. *Journal of Business Communication, 43*(2), 1–25.

2. Aune, B. P. (1995). The human dimension of organizational change. *Review of Higher Education, 18*(2), 149–173.

Lueddeke, G. R. (1999). Toward a constructivist framework for guiding change and innovation in higher education. *The Journal of Higher Education, 70*(3), 235–260.

3. Smulowitz, S. (2014). Planned organizational change in Higher Education: Dashboard indicators and stakeholder sensemaking—A case study (Unpublished doctoral dissertation). Rutgers, The State University of New Jersey, New Brunswick, NJ.

4. Guskin, A. (1996). Facing the future: The change process in restructuring universities. *Change, The Magazine of Higher Learning, 28*(4), 27-37.

Smulowitz, S. (2014). Planned organizational change in Higher Education: Dashboard indicators and stakeholder sensemaking—A case study (Unpublished doctoral dissertation). Rutgers, The State University of New Jersey, New Brunswick, NJ.

5. Aune, B. P. (1995). The human dimension of organizational change. *Review of Higher Education, 18*(2), 149–173.

Newcombe, J. P., & Conrad, C. F. (1981). A theory of mandated academic change. *The Journal of Higher Education, 52*(6), 555–577.

6. Guskin, A. (1996). Facing the future The change process in restructuring universities. *Change, The Magazine of Higher Learning, 28*(4), 27-37.

7. Armenakis, A. A., & Harris, S. G. (2009). Reflections: Our journey of organizational change research and practice. *Journal of Change Management, 9*(2), 127–142.

8. Smulowitz, S. (2014). Planned organizational change in Higher Education: Dashboard indicators and stakeholder sensemaking—A case study (Unpublished doctoral dissertation). Rutgers, The State University of New Jersey, New Brunswick, NJ.

9. ASHE-ERIC Higher Education Report. (2001). Special issue: Understanding and facilitating organizational change in the 21st century: Recent research and conceptualizations. *ASHE-ERIC Higher Education Report, 28*(4), 1–162.

10. Gioia, D. A., & Thomas, J. B. (1996). Identity, image, and issue interpretation: Sensemaking during strategic change in academia. *Administrative Science Quarterly, 41*, 370–403.

11. Conrad, C. (1978). A grounded theory of academic change. *Sociology of Education, 51*(2), 101–112.

12. Lewis, L. K., & Seibold, D. R. (1996). Communication during intraorganizational innovation adoption: Predicting users' behavioral coping responses to innovations in organizations. *Communication Monographs, 63*, 131–157.

Simsek, H., & Louis, K. S. (1994). Organizational change as paradigm shift: Analysis of the change process in a large, public university. *The Journal of Higher Education, 65*(6), 670–695.

13. ASHE-ERIC Higher Education Report. (2001). Special issue: Understanding and facilitating organizational change in the 21st century: Recent research and conceptualizations. *ASHE-ERIC Higher Education Report, 28*(4), 1–162.

Johnstone, D. B., Dye, N. S., & Johnson, R. (1998). Collaborative leadership for institutional change. *Liberal Education, 84*(2), 12-20.

14. Gluesing, J. C., & Gibson, C. B. (2004). Designing and forming global teams. In H. W. Lane, M. L. Maznevski, M. E. Mendenhall, & J. McNett (Eds.), *Handbook of global management* (pp. 199–226). Malden, MA: Blackwell Publishing.

Smulowitz, S. M. (2007). When does culture matter, and to whom? *Journal of Intercultural Communication Studies 16*(1), 1–13.

15. Boyce, M. E. (2003). Organizational learning is essential to achieving and sustaining change in higher education. *Innovative Higher Education, 28*(2), 119–136.

16. Simsek, H., & Louis, K. S. (1994). Organizational change as paradigm shift: Analysis of the change process in a large, public university. *The Journal of Higher Education, 65*(6), 670–695.

17. Smulowitz, S. (2014). Planned organizational change in Higher Education: Dashboard indicators and stakeholder sensemaking—A case study (Unpublished doctoral dissertation). Rutgers, The State University of New Jersey, New Brunswick, NJ.

18. Bordia, P., Hobman, E., Jones, E., Gallois, C., & Callan, V. J. (2004). Uncertainty during organizational change: Types, consequences, and management strategies. *Journal of Business and Psychology, 18*(4), 507–532. Quote p. 509.

19. Smulowitz, S. (2014). Planned organizational change in Higher Education: Dashboard indicators and stakeholder sensemaking—A case study (Unpublished doctoral dissertation). Rutgers, The State University of New Jersey, New Brunswick, NJ.

20. Klein, K. J., & Sorra, J. S. (1996). The challenge of innovation implementation. *Academy of Management Review, 21*(4), 1055–1080.

21. Smulowitz, S. (2014). Planned organizational change in Higher Education: Dashboard indicators and stakeholder sensemaking—A case study (Unpublished doctoral dissertation). Rutgers, The State University of New Jersey, New Brunswick, NJ.

22. Smulowitz, S. (2014). Planned organizational change in Higher Education: Dashboard indicators and stakeholder sensemaking—A case study (Unpublished doctoral dissertation). Rutgers, The State University of New Jersey, New Brunswick, NJ.

23. Smulowitz, S. (2014). Planned organizational change in Higher Education: Dashboard indicators and stakeholder sensemaking—A case study (Unpublished doctoral dissertation). Rutgers, The State University of New Jersey, New Brunswick, NJ.

24. Lewis, L. K. (2000). Communicating change: Four cases of quality programs. *The Journal of Business Communication, 37*(2), 128–155.

25. Lewis, L. K. (2007). An organizational stakeholder model of change implementation communication. *Communication Theory, 17*, 176–204.

26. Guskin, A. (1996). Facing the future The change process in restructuring universities. *Change, The Magazine of Higher Learning, 28*(4), 27-37.

Simsek, H., & Louis, K. S. (1994). Organizational change as paradigm shift: Analysis of the change process in a large, public university. *The Journal of Higher Education, 65*(6), 670–695.

27. Interestingly enough, this same approach to personal change efforts is also true. For example, it is proven that making small, incremental changes increases the likelihood that an individual will stick to personal change plans like weight loss. Burchard, B. (2017). *High performance habits: How extraordinary people become that way.* USA: Hay House, Inc.

Kezar, A. (2005). Consequences of radical change in governance: A grounded theory approach. *The Journal of Higher Education, 76*(6), 634–668.

Miller, D., & Friesen, P. (1980). Archetypes of organizational transition. *Administrative Science Quarterly, 25*(2), 268–299.

Schuster, J. H., & Finkelstein, M. J. (2007). On the brink: Assessing the status of the American Faculty. Research & Occasional Paper Series: CSHE. 3.07. *Center for Studies in Higher Education.*

28. Colvin, T. J., & Kilmann, R. H. (1990). Participant perceptions of positive and negative influences on large-scale change. *Group and Organizational Studies, 15,* 233–248.

29. Gersick, C. J. G. (1991). Revolutionary change theories: A multilevel exploration of the punctuated equilibrium paradigm. *The Academy of Management Review, 16*(1), 10–36.

Levinson, D. J. (1978). *The seasons of a man's life.* New York, NY: Knopf.

Newcombe, J. P., & Conrad, C. F. (1981). A theory of mandated academic change. *The Journal of Higher Education, 52*(6), 555–577.

30. Smulowitz, S. (2014). Planned organizational change in Higher Education: Dashboard indicators and stakeholder sensemaking—A case study (Unpublished doctoral dissertation). Rutgers, The State University of New Jersey, New Brunswick, NJ.

31. Smulowitz, S. (2014). Planned organizational change in Higher Education: Dashboard indicators and stakeholder sensemaking—A case study (Unpublished doctoral dissertation). Rutgers, The State University of New Jersey, New Brunswick, NJ.

32. Smulowitz, S. (2014). Planned organizational change in Higher Education: Dashboard indicators and stakeholder sensemaking—A case study (Unpublished doctoral dissertation). Rutgers, The State University of New Jersey, New Brunswick, NJ.

33. Guskin, A. (1996). Facing the future The change process in restructuring universities. *Change, The Magazine of Higher Learning, 28*(4), 27-37.

Gersick, C. J. G. (1991). Revolutionary change theories: A multilevel exploration of the punctuated equilibrium paradigm. *The Academy of Management Review, 16*(1), 10–36.

Smulowitz, S. (2014). Planned organizational change in Higher Education: Dashboard indicators and stakeholder sensemaking—A case study (Unpublished doctoral dissertation). Rutgers, The State University of New Jersey, New Brunswick, NJ.

34. Smulowitz, S. (2014). Planned organizational change in Higher Education: Dashboard indicators and stakeholder sensemaking—A case study (Unpublished doctoral dissertation). Rutgers, The State University of New Jersey, New Brunswick, NJ.

35. Smulowitz, S. (2014). Planned organizational change in Higher Education: Dashboard indicators and stakeholder sensemaking—A case study (Unpublished doctoral dissertation). Rutgers, The State University of New Jersey, New Brunswick, NJ.

36. Lewis, L. K., & Seibold, D. R. (1993). Innovation modification during intraorganizational adoption. *Academy of Management Review, 18,* 322–354.

Smulowitz, S. (2014). Planned organizational change in Higher Education: Dashboard indicators and stakeholder sensemaking—A case study (Unpublished doctoral dissertation). Rutgers, The State University of New Jersey, New Brunswick, NJ.

37. Lueddeke, G. R. (1999). Toward a constructivist framework for guiding change and innovation in higher education. *The Journal of Higher Education, 70*(3), 235–260.

38. Lueddeke, G. R. (1999). Toward a constructivist framework for guiding change and innovation in higher education. *The Journal of Higher Education, 70*(3), 235–260.

Chapter 7

The Importance of Leading through a Change Agent

WHAT YOU CAN EXPECT TO LEARN IN THIS CHAPTER

- What is a change agent and how do they complement organizational leaders?
- What are the responsibilities of change agents and how do they help ensure a successful change effort?

Leadership commitment doesn't stop with the activities described in the previous chapter. Even though the leader should be seen as the main organizational member to facilitate the change effort, they need to appoint at least one organizational member who will take on the role of change agent. Often leaders need to move onto another task to keep the organization running at optimal performance. The change agent can focus solely on the planned change effort and is responsible for three key functions: organizational member participation, change effort priority and vision.

The change agent assumes most of the responsibility of the day-to-day operations of the planned change effort. First, getting organizational members to participate and feel empowered through communication and processes is at the heart of the successful change effort.[1]

Here, change agents use strategies such as meetings where members can talk and make sense of, rather than being talked to about the planned change effort.[2] The importance of this type of face-to-face meeting in institutions of higher education should be noted as a way to combat the "uncoordinated" characteristic associated with loosely coupled higher education systems.[3] It is a work-around to the silos that are characteristic of higher education.

OUTLETS FOR ORGANIZATIONAL
MEMBERS TO SHARE

More successful change efforts are a result of organizational members who had an outlet to talk with other members. As these members talk with one another, they learn new information about the change effort. This process promotes sensemaking, creates shared meaning, and enables them to cocreate a new shared reality about the change effort.[4]

Learning is the best way to replace the current shared reality with a new, shared reality, especially when that learning includes an understanding of other organizational member's cognitive maps, or worldview.[5] These members are more likely than leaders to influence other members of the organization because they have credibility and social influence with their peers.

Social influence can benefit the change effort because there is reliability with talking about the change effort with a friend who is also a fellow organizational member.[6] These fellow organizational members can use their social influence to share meaning, sway organizational members' (even leader's) opinions and emotional reactions of the change effort, and take action through discussions.[7]

As organizational members engage in these discussions, learn from each other and make sense of their situation, they are cocreating their new reality together. Organizational members look for cues to help them make sense of what's happening.[8] Cues include items such as the lack of rewards, symbols of achievement, "cheerleading," stories, message reinforcement, and importance placed on the effort by senior leaders.[9]

Organizational members attach meaning to these cues.[10] Discussions with fellow organizational members help increase their knowledge about the change effort through "disagreement and disconfirmation of expectations" and cues.[11] This is an important step to overcome the different interpretations of the same communication event as seen through other member's worldview.

Studies show that informal discussions between organizational members provide greater contribution to the change effort.[12] This is welcome news because organizational member attitudes and ongoing interactions toward the new change effort will partially affect the way the new effort is made a part of their work process.[13] Over time, the change effort takes on a new meaning brought about by organizational member interaction as they create a new shared reality together.[14] Overall, it's a good thing that word-of-mouth is one of the most used channels of communication in a change effort.[15]

Giving organizational members an opportunity to discuss the change effort shows a leader's good faith in them to work through the change effort challenges.[16] Additionally, when organizational members share their concerns and troubles with each other, stress caused by the change effort can be reduced or at least cushioned.[17] This happens because participants can discuss their fears about the planned change program and discover collectively that those fears will most likely never occur.[18] The leader, or change agent, should provide outlets for organizational members to participate in such sharing through the implementation plan.[19]

Also important to this process is that this open sharing provides an opportunity for organizational members to feel part of the process. This helps members cocreate legitimacy of the leader and also influences the outcomes of the change effort.[20]

PARTICIPATION, EMPOWERMENT, AND INVOLVEMENT

Involving organizational members helps reduce the damaging effects of uncertainty and demonstrates leaders' commitment to the change effort.[21] However, in reality, participation is underused in practice.[22]

Participation provides an abundance of positive outcomes for change efforts including increased organizational member commitment, an increase in organizational member clarity about the vision, and a decrease in resistance.[23] Including organizational members as participants in a planned change effort also provides them with a sense of ownership and commitment rather than feeling like a "target of change," which will make them less likely to resist the change effort.[24]

Participation allows organizational members to contribute their expertise to the planned change effort, something we know members like to do.[25] This type of participation can be complex and involve organizational members contributing at a high level on small work teams, at a more simple level during conversations at a town hall meeting, or a combination of the two. Some of the more simple conversations can include the leader asking organizational members questions such as, "if you were trying to solve XYZ issue, what are some ways you might do it?"

Leaders may be surprised at some of the rather informed and illuminating answers they will receive from organizational members, especially those who are in the trenches dealing with the details of the change effort on a daily basis. Once this question is asked, it opens a dialogue between the leader, change agent, and the organizational members.

This allows for open communication about the issue and provides an opportunity for organizational members to have input about the proposed planned change effort to solve the issue. If the leader or change agent uses the suggestion, organizational members are more likely to be fully invested in adapting and integrating the change into their daily routines. However, organizational members are likely to be invested because they had an opportunity to be involved in the discussion.

Participation in a planned change effort can lead to organizational members feeling empowered, which can provide them with a sense of ownership in and the impetus to complete the change effort.[26] Empowered organizational members are more likely to spread messages about the change effort into the organization through their informal networks. This, in turn, can show increased positive results.[27] These members are also more likely to stay with the organization.[28]

Participation of a diverse group of organizational members (e.g., different levels and departments in the organization) can increase appreciation for others' perspectives in the organization, increase support for the change effort, and increase the likelihood that organizational members will work together.[29] This is especially important for institutions of higher education and other loosely coupled organizations where members have different perceptions of reality, which stem from their membership in different organizational levels and divisions.[30]

Bringing together diverse groups of constituents, such as faculty and members of the administration or board of trustees, will enable a greater understanding of each other's perspectives as well as a quicker realization that they are each involved for the betterment of the overall institution and its students.[31] Research shows that using this process, "rapport came easier than expected and camaraderie was rampant," helping to bring successful change to organizations.[32]

Leaving organizational members out of the change effort, either by not including them in planning or not making them aware of the effort has several damaging effects. Some members feel left out or unimportant to the process, and others assume that the change effort is not important. Case Study Large University was a casualty of uninvolved members. Frustrations were high among those interviewed. A director commented, "Nothing's really shared," and a staff member replied, "I don't think any of my colleagues know anything about it."[33]

PROCESS

A second responsibility of the change agent is to ensure the change effort process is moving along as planned. This role frees up the leader from day-to-day project management tasks to be able to focus on the bigger picture of leading the organization.

However, it is imperative that the leader be visibly committed and keep the change effort at the top priority. Otherwise, organizational members will see the leaders' "absence" as a sign that the change effort is not important. This can lead members to abandon the change effort. That means that the change agent is responsible to loop the leader back in so that organizational members see the support.

The change agent(s) should be involved as early as possible in the process—from inception if possible. This person will be involved in all meetings, organization-wide to department and individual. The change agent will meet with groups of organizational members (department heads, staff, faculty, and so on) about the process as it pertains to their area of responsibility. They will do this as needed throughout the change effort to ensure clarity of vision and goals and sustained momentum.

The Case Study Large University change agent was able to overcome some perceptions that the change effort was busy work. Through education about the goals of the change effort, some organizational members stated that they were more inclined to buy into the process. A senior leader said, "When we had conversations about this . . . it was sort of infectious in that other groups were anticipating when they would become a part of this process."[34]

In essence, the change agent is a project manager who needs to have the ability to ensure all members at all levels of the organization are educated about their role in the process and are able to carry out their part to meet deadlines and goals. For the most part, the change agent will not have direct supervisory role with members of the organization. Therefore, it is important that they establish trust and credibility with organizational members from the very beginning.

The change agent will need to figure out which areas of the organization need what kinds of help and to be able to access resources for them. In addition, the change agent will need to be able to "nudge" organizational members to keep the effort moving forward.[35] Further, the change agent is responsible for keeping the leader updated on change effort progress and setbacks and ensure that the change effort is a priority for the leader. Often the leader has to move along to the next big picture effort to keep the organization moving forward. It is imperative that the change agent keep the leader visible and involved.

In Case Study Large University, the change agent needed to reeducate organizational members that the results of the change effort were "not about the piece of paper. It was about the conversations they had. How they came to the decisions on the paper. The examination of what they're doing and why it works. It's about the process."[36]

The third responsibility of a change agent is the creation of a vision if the leader has not already done this.[37] The vision will provide clarity for organizational members about the need for, process, and benefits of the change effort.[38] See the earlier discussion on vision in chapter 6.

Often, leaders will be able to identify organizational members who function as campus opinion leaders. These organizational members have positive social influence over their peers. If appropriate, the leaders should include these opinion leaders as change agents or in other visible ways for the effort because their involvement will signal integrity to the process. Change agents should be master project managers, detail-oriented, and good time managers.

Opinion leaders and change agents should have a grasp of the existing power structures within the overall institution and be able to tap into them. In addition, they should be able to determine ahead of time potential conflict, resistors, motivations, and distractions.[39] Change agents need to be aware of other individual and group social influencers on campus, ways in which to make best use of these informal networks, and reasoning for potential resistance to change.[40]

SUMMARY

The change agent assumes the day-to-day responsibilities for the success of the planned change effort. They need to keep the wheels moving and the leader visible. Often leaders become rightfully distracted with other timely and pressing situations that arise. Leaders need to have someone they can trust to manage the change effort.

Change agents ensure organizational members are participating in the change effort and feel empowered. This provides members with a sense of ownership in the program and helps lead it to success.

Moving the change effort along is a second role of the change agent. Often complex, the change agent will ensure that everyone is meeting deadlines. If this is not happening, the change agent needs to determine if there are barriers that need to be removed or resources and support that can facilitate meeting the deadline.

If the leader has not already created a vision, this is a third responsibility for the change agent. The next critical leadership action is monitoring the communication environment.

NOTES

1. Lewis, L. K., Schmisseur, A., Stephens, K., & Weir, K. (2006). Advice on communicating during organizational change: The content of popular press books. *Journal of Business Communication, 43*(2), 1–25.

2. Lewis, L. K., Schmisseur, A., Stephens, K., & Weir, K. (2006). Advice on communicating during organizational change: The content of popular press books. *Journal of Business Communication, 43*(2), 1–25.

3. ASHE-ERIC Higher Education Report. (2001). Special issue: Understanding and facilitating organizational change in the 21st century: Recent research and conceptualizations. *ASHE-ERIC Higher Education Report, 28*(4), 1–162. Quote p. 117.

4. Barge, J. K., & Fairhurst, G. T. (2008). Living leadership: A systemic constructionist approach. *Leadership Quarterly, 4*(3), 227–251.

Smulowitz, S. (2014). Planned organizational change in higher education: Dashboard indicators and stakeholder sensemaking—a case study (Unpublished doctoral dissertation). Rutgers, The State University of New Jersey, New Brunswick, NJ.

5. Crossan, M. M., Lane, H. W., & White, R. E. (1999). An organizational learning framework: From intuition to institution. *Academy of Management Review, 24*(3), 522–537.

6. Albrecht, T., & Hall, B. (1991). Facilitating talk about new ideas: The role of personal relationships in organizational innovation. *Communication Monographs, 58*, 273–288.

7. Barge, J. K., & Fairhurst, G. T. (2008). Living leadership: A systemic constructionist approach. *Leadership Quarterly, 4*(3), 227–251.

Fairhurst, G. T. (2008). Discursive leadership: A communication alternative to leadership psychology. *Management Communication Quarterly, 21*(4), 510–521.

Fairhurst, G. T. (1993). Echoes of the vision: When the rest of the organization talks Total Quality. *Management Communication Quarterly, 6*, 331–371.

Timmerman, C. E. (2003). Media selection during the implementation of planned organizational change: A predictive framework based on implementation approach and phase. *Management Communication Quarterly, 16*(3), 301–340.

Zorn, T. (2002). The emotionality of information and communication technology implementation. *Journal of Communication Management, 7*(2), 160–171.

8. Weick, (1995). *Sensemaking in organizations*. Thousand Oaks, CA: Sage.

9. Bolman, L. G., & Deal, T. E. (1991). *Reframing organizations: Artistry, choice and leadership*. San Fransisco, CA: Jossey-Bass.

Gersick, C. J. G. (1991). Revolutionary change theories: A multilevel exploration of the punctuated equilibrium paradigm. *The Academy of Management Review, 16*(1), 10–36.

Lewis, L. K. (2000). Communicating change: Four cases of quality programs. *The Journal of Business Communication, 37*(2), 128–155.

Simsek, H., & Louis, K. S. (1994). Organizational change as paradigm shift: Analysis of the change process in a large, public university. *The Journal of Higher Education, 65*(6), 670–695.

10. Schneider, B. (1990). The climate for service: An application for the climate construct. In B. Schneider (Ed.), *Organizational climate and culture* (pp. 383–412). San Francisco, CA: Jossey-Bass Publishers.

11. Piderit, S. K. (2000). Rethinking resistance and recognizing ambivalence: A multidimensional view of attitudes toward an organizational change. *Academy of Management Review, 25*(4), 783–794.

12. Lewis, L. K., & Seibold, D. R. (1993). Innovation modification during intraorganizational adoption. *Academy of Management Review, 18*, 322–354.

13. Lewis, L. K., & Seibold, D. R. (1993). Innovation modification during intraorganizational adoption. *Academy of Management Review, 18*, 322–354.

14. Rogers, E. M. (1995). *Diffusion of innovations* (4th ed.). New York: Free Press. pp. 371–404.

15. Lewis, L. K. (1999). Disseminating information and soliciting input during planned organizational change: Implementers' targets, sources, and channels for communicating. *Management Communication Quarterly, 13*(1), 43–75.

16. Aune, B. P. (1995). The human dimension of organizational change. *Review of Higher Education, 18*(2), 149–173.

17. Ashford, S. J. (1988). Individual strategies for coping with stress during organizational transitions. *The Journal of Applied Behavioral Science, 24*, 19–36.

18. Aune, B. P. (1995). The human dimension of organizational change. *Review of Higher Education, 18*(2), 149–173.

19. Ashford, S. J. (1988). Individual strategies for coping with stress during organizational transitions. *The Journal of Applied Behavioral Science, 24*, 19–36.

20. Barge, J. K., & Fairhurst, G. T. (2008). Living leadership: A systemic constructionist approach. *Leadership Quarterly, 4*(3), 227–251.

Fairhurst, G. T. (2008). Discursive leadership: A communication alternative to leadership psychology. *Management Communication Quarterly, 21*(4), 510–521.

21. Bordia, P., Hobman, E., Jones, E., Gallois, C., & Callan, V. J. (2004). Uncertainty during organizational change: Types, consequences, and management strategies. *Journal of Business and Psychology, 18*(4), 507–532.

Smulowitz, S. (2014). Planned organizational change in higher education: Dashboard indicators and stakeholder sensemaking—a case study (Unpublished doctoral dissertation). Rutgers, The State University of New Jersey, New Brunswick, NJ.

22. Lewis, L. K., & Russ, T. L. (2011). Soliciting and using input during organizational change initiatives: What are practitioners doing? *Management Communication Quarterly, 26*(2), 267–294.

23. Lewis, L. K., Hamel, S. A., & Richardson, B. K (2001). Communicating change to nonprofit stakeholders: Models and predictors of implementers' approaches. *Management Communication Quarterly, 15*, 5–41.

24. Aune, B. P. (1995). The human dimension of organizational change. *Review of Higher Education, 18*(2), 149–173.

25. Lewis, L. K., & Russ, T. L. (2011). Soliciting and using input during organizational change initiatives: What are practitioners doing? *Management Communication Quarterly, 26*(2), 267–294.

26. Johnstone, D. B., Dye, N. S., & Johnson, R. (1998). Collaborative leadership for institutional change. *Liberal Education, 84*(2), 12-20.

Lewis, L. K., Schmisseur, A., Stephens, K., & Weir, K. (2006). Advice on communicating during organizational change: The content of popular press books. *Journal of Business Communication, 43*(2), 1–25.

27. Aune, B. P. (1995). The human dimension of organizational change. *Review of Higher Education, 18*(2), 149–173.

Lewis, L. K., Schmisseur, A., Stephens, K., & Weir, K. (2006). Advice on communicating during organizational change: The content of popular press books. *Journal of Business Communication, 43*(2), 1–25.

28. Lewis, L. K., Schmisseur, A., Stephens, K., & Weir, K. (2006). Advice on communicating during organizational change: The content of popular press books. *Journal of Business Communication, 43*(2), 1–25.

29. Johnstone, D. B., Dye, N. S., & Johnson, R. (1998). Collaborative leadership for institutional change. *Liberal Education, 84*(2), 12-20.

30. Gallivan, M. J. (2001). Meaning to change: How diverse stakeholders interpret organizational communication about change initiatives. *IEEE Transactions on Professional Communication, 44*, 243–266.

31. Johnstone, D. B., Dye, N. S., & Johnson, R. (1998). Collaborative leadership for institutional change. *Liberal Education, 84*(2), 12-20.

32. Aune, B. P. (1995). The human dimension of organizational change. *Review of Higher Education, 18*(2), 149–173. Quote p. 166.

33. Smulowitz, S. (2014). Planned organizational change in higher education: Dashboard indicators and stakeholder sensemaking—a case study (Unpublished doctoral dissertation). Rutgers, The State University of New Jersey, New Brunswick, NJ.

34. Smulowitz, S. (2014). Planned organizational change in higher education: Dashboard indicators and stakeholder sensemaking—a case study (Unpublished doctoral dissertation). Rutgers, The State University of New Jersey, New Brunswick, NJ.

35. Smulowitz, S. (2014). Planned organizational change in higher education: Dashboard indicators and stakeholder sensemaking—a case study (Unpublished doctoral dissertation). Rutgers, The State University of New Jersey, New Brunswick, NJ. Quote p. 191.

36. Smulowitz, S. (2014). Planned organizational change in higher education: Dashboard indicators and stakeholder sensemaking—a case study (Unpublished doctoral dissertation). Rutgers, The State University of New Jersey, New Brunswick, NJ.

37. Lewis, L. K., Schmisseur, A., Stephens, K., & Weir, K. (2006). Advice on communicating during organizational change: The content of popular press books. *Journal of Business Communication, 43*(2), 1–25.

38. Smulowitz, S. (2014). Planned organizational change in higher education: Dashboard indicators and stakeholder sensemaking—a case study (Unpublished doctoral dissertation). Rutgers, The State University of New Jersey, New Brunswick, NJ.

39. ASHE-ERIC Higher Education Report. (2001). Special issue: Understanding and facilitating organizational change in the 21st century: Recent research and conceptualizations. *ASHE-ERIC Higher Education Report, 28*(4), 1–162. Quote p. 155.

40. ASHE-ERIC Higher Education Report. (2001). Special issue: Understanding and facilitating organizational change in the 21st century: Recent research and conceptualizations. *ASHE-ERIC Higher Education Report, 28*(4), 1–162.

Chapter 8

Leaders and the Communication Environment

The Critical Connection

WHAT YOU CAN EXPECT TO LEARN IN THIS CHAPTER

- How does communication and information influence planned organizational change?
- What is cocreation of reality and how does it impact planned organizational change?
- How can a leader's mindset influence the success or failure of planned organizational change?

COMMUNICATION AND INFORMATION

The key element of success for leading planned organizational change efforts is communication.[1] Most leaders who implement change efforts say communication is a top obstacle.[2]

To begin, it's important to distinguish communication processes and outcomes from information flow and strategy used in planned change efforts. Wait a minute. Isn't it all the same, you might ask? Nope, and here's why.

Information exchange, or how information flows from person to person, and information strategies are typically used during change efforts to introduce, promote, and coordinate the change effort to organizational members. Communication is the process by which we impose our meanings upon messages that we receive and send. These meanings are based on previous experiences, values, and beliefs, and are typically taken for granted by us.

These meanings also vary and change based on context and further experiences. They also help form our individual realities and sense of self. This

95

includes the way we act and the decisions we make during an organizational change. Will we accept or resist the change? Will we use our social actions and influence to encourage others to accept or resist the change?

Communication and information processing enable the leader to monitor the communication environment. A failure to do so can decrease the chance of success of the overall change effort. Concrete items that must be paid attention to include the messages created, how those messages get to and from members of the organization, lack of information exchange, and lack of monitoring the sensemaking going on in the organization.[3]

Looking at the organizational change as a disruption to members' normal daily routines will help to understand the process. People, in general, really don't like change. Remember when you doctor asks you if you've been eating better and exercising? How did that change work out for you? Again, for some of us, change is no problem. Some of us thrive on change. But for the vast majority of people, change is difficult and very uncomfortable. It can set even the most mild-mannered of us into a tizzy.

We naturally want to revert back to what we did before the change was implemented because it's comfortable, safe, and easy. Our mind fights the change because learning something new, like a procedure or practice, takes work. Much of the time we are not convinced that it is worth our time. Yes, you heard that right. How many times have you been asked to do something different that resulted in busy work that was quickly forgotten or replaced by something else, and then something else? What did you think? Waste of time. Right? We prefer the way things are now, even if that's crazy and unproductive. At least it's our crazy.

As the leader or change agent, you use information exchange and strategies for introducing, promoting, and coordinating change implementation.[4] Leaders or change agents use formal communication to announce the change to organizational members.[5] This is typically a deliberate, thought out and planned one-way form, or exchange, of information. Most of us call this strategy "decide and announce." Most of us hate it. Our hate for this strategy goes all the way back to when Mom and Dad influenced our worldview by saying, "Because I said so."

Organizational members take that information and determine their reality for it through sensemaking and negotiation of meaning with each other. As we make sense of our environment and especially the information from the leader about the change, we rely on our experiences. We also engage in social interactions with other organizational members. For example, we might ask other members' opinions about the reasons for the change or how the change will affect our work. These social interactions occur through communication.[6]

As organizational members engage in social interactions, they are creating and cocreating their social reality about how they understand the change effort, what it means to them and how they will respond to it.[7] This is of great importance to leaders and change agents because organizational members interpret information about the change effort based on their perceptions of reality and the meaning it holds for them.[8] The meanings derived come about based on the individual's perception of what's going on and the context within which it takes place.[9]

As organizational members use communication and information processing to make sense of the change for themselves and with others, they monitor the environment for any changes or new information. As they continually interact with the environment, gaining new information, organizational members will continue to cocreate their organizational reality over and over. Simultaneously, they communicate and make sense of the new information with other members.

Organizational "change is created, sustained, and managed in and by communication."[10] Organizational members make sense of and cocreate their social reality and understanding of change efforts as they and the leader or change agent socially interact with each other.[11] These social actions, or interactions, between organizational members determine the success or failure of change efforts.[12]

While organizational members are trying to make sense of the change, they have the opportunity to use their social influence with others in the organization. Some organizational members have more influence than others. As the leader or change agent, you will want to identify these members early on and ensure they are clear about the goals. You want these organizational members to advocate for others to support the change.

Throughout the change effort, leaders and change agents should monitor the communication environment, the reality that's being cocreated among organizational members. Upon learning that there is a lack of clarity, leaders and change agents must produce corrective messages to ensure the organizational members are on the same page to allow for successful change.[13]

COCREATION OF REALITY

Think about the last time something was going on in your life and you weren't really sure why or what to do about it. First, you most likely relied on your experiences. Then, you probably sought others' thoughts about the situation. As you did so, you and the others probably made connections about events, happenings, and so on. Each person you spoke with about the situation provided yet another piece of information—sort of like piecing together a puzzle—to figure out the situation. This "figuring out" as a dyad or group is when you cocreate your reality. It also restores the system. That is, it gets the group into a new status quo.

As a dyad or group, you discussed all the connections and ideas about the situation to try to make sense of it. Then, at some point, there was a moment when everything became clear. Each member of the group left with an understanding of the situation as created in, or made sense to, the group. And, guess what? This group understanding could be totally wrong or right! But as far as the group is concerned, it's right.

With that in mind, realize that there are other groups in the same organization going through the same process and perhaps coming up with different understandings of the same situation. Most likely these groups in the same organization are operating with a different set of understanding, and thus reality, of the situation. Now imagine that these are your employees and they have been discussing your change program.

As the leader, it is your responsibility to monitor the communication environment, or what organizational members are talking about and how they are cocreating reality. What worries them? What questions do they have?

How can you and your team make corrective messaging to them to help them make sense of, fill in the puzzle pieces, and better understand the change program objectives, timeline, investment, and most importantly what's in it for them? How can you direct the way organizational members talk about, think, and understand the reality of the planned change effort and its impact on the organization and each organizational member?

WORLDVIEW

One of the most important precursors to any change is to assess the leader and organizational member's worldviews. Every interpretation of the information and communication about the change effort depends on each person's worldview. First, as leaders, we need to discern our own worldviews. Having a deep awareness of the way we understand "how things are" is important. This view shapes the way we look at and evaluate everything from how families "ought to" spend dinner time to how coworkers "should" clean the coffee pot.

Our worldview provides a structured, unconscious belief that there is one way things "should" or "ought to" be done. However, you don't own the only way to think about or get things done. You have either generated your own rules for how things "should be," or adopted them from others.

As we seek to truly understand others, we must be sure that we are not imposing our worldview on them. That is, we must be sure to really hear and understand everything. Many times, we hear and pay attention only to what's said or done that is familiar to us. We need to be sure that we also attend to "other people's experiences and concerns" and that we are able to understand that the world is not black and white.[14] Each person interprets their experiences in their own way, given their worldview.

From time-to-time, our worldview benefits from a thorough assessment and awareness of our own vulnerabilities and hopes as this will make us more open to discovering what we have in common and difference with others' worldviews. In doing so, we will learn that it's beneficial to question our worldview and doing so may help us to become a bit more empathetic of others worldviews.[15] This is important as leaders of change efforts, and leaders in general, because we need to be able to remove our filters so that we can truly understand and respect each other's ideas and each other as human beings.[16]

Coming into a position of leadership with this mindset shift will open your eyes to opportunities and ideas that may have never occurred to you otherwise. Your openness will also show your empathy for others and as a result increase your credibility and trustworthiness. This, in turn, will increase the level of commitment your organizational members will have for you.

Further, this mindset shift will help you understand and recognize quickly that organizational members, especially those members at different levels within the organization, will have different views about the change effort. And, that those different views are sometimes at the root of discrepancies and conflict.[17]

For example, Case Study Large University shows that senior leaders were concerned about the best way to use the change effort to show the strengths of their division to external constituents. Directors and staff members were concerned with how the change effort could help improve department operations and effectiveness.[18] Obviously, this discrepancy caused much frustration with all members of the organization because they were working toward different goals.

Leaders need to clearly communicate the goal and continuously monitor the communication environment to be sure that all organizational members understand the goal in the same way. If, like in this example, leaders find that some organizational members have a discrepancy in their understanding of the goal, then leaders should communicate a corrective message.

Connect this to the concept of a lint filter. Just as the filter keeps out lint (and sometimes rocks, candy wrappers and golf tees) it also provides us with a way to pay attention to some (but not all) messages. However, even if we pay attention to a message, we may not react to it. Further, our filter is more in-tune with messages that are similar to our own worldview—or the rules we use in life about how things "are" or "should be."

A large disparity in worldview about the change effort in Case Study Large University came from the lack of involvement and awareness about the change effort. Senior directors seemed oblivious that anyone in the organization would be unaware or uninvolved in the change effort. Senior leaders expected directors to keep their staff involved and aware of organizational happenings. However, many staff were unaware of the change effort, showing a failure of information flow and exchange from leaders and change agents to directors.

NONVERBAL COMMUNICATION

We also take into account nonverbal communication, things like crossing our arms, rolling our eyes, leaning forward, looking at your mobile device, where people position themselves around the conference table, and so on. As people communicate, these types of nonverbal cues help us to determine what's really being said. You might hear someone say to you that they aren't upset with you. However, their nonverbal communication might say something different.

For example, they may have an upset facial expression, crossed arms, and even a tear in their eye. You better believe they are upset. Walking away or just reacting on their verbal statement that they are not upset with you would also send a nonverbal message. If you care about the person, walking away would send the wrong message. A step in the right direction might be if, instead, you were to apologize. Or, at the very least, find out why they are upset. You might find out that there is a simple explanation and resolution that might otherwise create a much larger damaging effect if it goes unresolved.

INTENTIONAL AND PLANNED
VERSUS UNINTENTIONAL AND
UNPLANNED COMMUNICATION

Often leaders and other organizational members will spend much time preparing for formal, more planned, and intentional communication to others in the organization. However, they give less thought to unplanned and unintentional communication. The difference might be thought about as informal conversations versus a speech that addresses the organization as a whole. One could argue that most of us engage in this informal, unplanned communication frequently throughout the day. Even with well-thought-out and planned communication, leaders and other organizational members can communicate unintentionally to others.[19]

The difference is in the details. Here's where the filter metaphor discussed earlier comes into play in what could be a game-changing way. Senior leaders create a message to promote the planned change effort and organizational members interpret this message. It could be that the organizational member's interpretation of the message was far from what the senior leader intended. Or it could be right on.

Either way the filter may cause organizational members to "worry," become skeptical, and perhaps start looking for another job. Other organizational member filters may produce feelings of excitement and a desire to engage in efforts to make the change happen because they trust leadership and are committed to the leader and/or the organization. This is the ideal situation.

Looking at Case Study Large University, many staff members were either unaware or uninformed about the goals of the change effort. Among staff concerns were anxiety over whether the change effort meant that they would ultimately lose their job. Some of the staff stated they were actively job searching and others stated that they were engaging in professional development opportunities in case they needed to suddenly find another job.

Most of the participants in Case Study Large University perceived that the effort had failed. This was directly contributable to unintentional cues from leaders such as a perceived lack of priority, urgency, resources, feedback, momentum, awareness, and involvement of members of the organization. Organizational members engaged in sensemaking to interpret these environmental cues.

Their cocreated reality of the situation was that the change effort stalled or came to an early finish. As a result, they stopped working on the change effort. This was reinforced by the leaders who stopped asking for information from the directors and staff. And the vicious cycle kept going. The leader's inaction and lack of corrective messages further reinforced the perception that the change effort had failed.

Let me tell you another story about Rick who was the admissions director at the university Susan worked for. Susan was a specialist in the marketing department and responsible to help Rick achieve his admissions goals. Susan did not report directly to Rick. However, Rick held a leadership position in the university. One day Rick came into her office full of enthusiasm and explained the success they would have if they rolled out this new program to their admissions team. He preplanned his pitch to Susan and she was extremely motivated and excited. She focused all her efforts toward meeting this goal over the next two weeks.

After two weeks of preparation, Susan was set to present her plan, including mock-ups of new advertisements and admissions materials to Rick. An hour before her meeting with Rick, he burst into her office full of enthusiasm just as he did two weeks ago; only with an unplanned pitch to Susan. This time Rick had another idea. Again, Susan was excited, but a little hesitant as she had just spent weeks working through Rick's first idea.

When she asked Rick about the first idea he said, "Forget about what I said last week. THIS is how we need to proceed." As Rick continued to explain his newest idea, Susan glanced around the room at all the materials she had prepared to present to Rick during their meeting. As Rick went on and on telling Susan all about his new idea, all she could think about was the time and effort involved in creating a program that Rick would never hear about and that would never come to fruition.

What do you think happened next? You got it! Susan began to resist Rick's ideas by not doing anything. Over the next few weeks, Rick repeated his behavior with new ideas and Susan got into the habit of getting "tied up with other projects" and not accomplishing anything for Rick. Rick and Susan developed some "personality conflicts" and thus began the start to a difficult working relationship. It's a vicious cycle.

When Susan asked Rick about his first idea and he said to forget about it, he lost her. If, instead Rick had taken a few minutes to listen to Susan, things could have gone much better for their continued working relationship. To Susan, Rick's unplanned comment "forget what I said yesterday" over and over unintentionally communicated to her that he was indecisive, and it was a waste of her time to work on any of his projects.

Susan's work process was disrupted by a change in the way Rick wanted to approach admissions recruiting. At first, Susan was on board even though it took effort. Perhaps she had trust in Rick or was committed to the organization. However, through communication and information processing, Susan's filter, the previous experiences with Rick, led her to believe that Rick would just keep wasting her time. This was Susan's way of making sense of the situation to create boundaries and return to the status quo—the way things were—before Rick had his great ideas.[20]

If Rick had listened to Susan's new program and taken the time to negotiate the program with her, they would have had a chance to cocreate a restored version of their entire admissions system. This would allow Susan to move past the urge to return to the status quo, enable harmony, and increase performance within their system.[21]

An unintended consequence is the effect of this interaction on the rest of the organization. While Susan and Rick were certainly attending to their jobs in a meaningful way, they were not working together to benefit the organization as a whole. What was Rick's goal and how is that being fulfilled? What impact does Susan's inaction have on admissions recruiting and growth for the organization? If the result is a dip in attendance, will there be layoffs?

This is "systems thinking" where one action in one part of a system affects many other parts of a system. As was evidenced here, organizational members, Rick and Susan, used communication and information processing to make sense of what's going on.[22] In this instance, Susan determined that Rick's requests were a waste of time and Rick determined that Susan could not be counted on to help with admissions support.

When organizational members work together, they can accomplish much more than going it alone.[23] Similarly, when organizational members make a change at one level, all other levels of the organization are affected either positively or negatively.[24] A systems level of thinking must be used to avoid negative unintended consequences when leaders are planning a change effort.

Institutions of higher education differ from traditional organizations in that the institution of higher education is characterized by loosely coupled components—or silos. Changes in each of these silo areas may have a great impact on the rest of the institution. This means that academic leaders should pay particular attention to the communication environment: the way organizational members interact, think about their current reality, make sense of, and cocreate their reality (as opposed to merely exchanging information) at each level of the organization to be better prepared for large-scale, planned organizational change efforts.[25]

SUMMARY

Communication is the process by which we impose our meanings upon messages that we receive and send. These meanings are based on previous experiences, values, and beliefs, and are typically taken for granted by us. These meanings vary and change based on context and further experiences and help form our individual realities and sense of self.

Factors such as nonverbal communication, unintentional communication, unplanned communication, culture, and social influence can affect the way we interpret and understand what we say and the experiences we have.[26] These factors can also affect the actions of organizational members and the consequences of that behavior. Most importantly, these factors affect the perception of the success or failure of the planned organizational change effort.

NOTES

1. Smulowitz, S. (2014). Planned organizational change in Higher Education: Dashboard indicators and stakeholder sensemaking—A case study (Unpublished doctoral dissertation). Rutgers, The State University of New Jersey, New Brunswick, NJ.

2. Lewis, L. K. (2000). "Blindsided by that one" and "I saw that one coming": The relative anticipation and occurrence of communication problems and other problems in implementers' hindsight. *Journal of Applied Communication Research, 28*(1), 44–67.

3. Smulowitz, S. (2014). Planned organizational change in Higher Education: Dashboard indicators and stakeholder sensemaking—A case study (Unpublished doctoral dissertation). Rutgers, The State University of New Jersey, New Brunswick, NJ.

4. Lewis, L. K. (2007). An organizational stakeholder model of change implementation communication. *Communication Theory, 17*, 176–204.

Smulowitz, S. (2014). Planned organizational change in Higher Education: Dashboard indicators and stakeholder sensemaking—A case study (Unpublished doctoral dissertation). Rutgers, The State University of New Jersey, New Brunswick, NJ.

5. Lewis, L. K. (2011). Organizational change: Creating change through strategic communication. Malden, MA: Wiley-Blackwell.

6. Berger, P. L., & Luckmann, T. (1967). *The social construction of reality: A treatise in the sociology of knowledge.* Garden City, NY: Doubleday.

7. Berger, P. L., & Luckmann, T. (1967). *The social construction of reality: A treatise in the sociology of knowledge.* Garden City, NY: Doubleday.

Ford, J., & Ford, L. W. (2010). Stop blaming resistance to change and start using it. *Organizational Dynamics, 39*(1), 24–36.

Poole, M. S. (2009). Adaptive structuration theory. In E. Griffin (Ed.), *A first look at communication theory* (7th ed., pp. 235–246). New York: McGraw Hill.

8. Blumer, H. (1979). Symbolic interaction. In R. W. Budd & B. D. Ruben (Eds.), *Interdisciplinary approaches to human communication* (pp. 135–153). Rochelle Park, New Jersey: Hayden Book Company, Inc.

Luckmann, T. (2008). On social interaction and the communicative construction of personal identity, knowledge and reality. *Organization Studies, 29*(2), 277–290.

Ruben, B. D. (1979). General system theory. In R. W. Budd & B. D. Ruben (Eds.), *Interdisciplinary approaches to human communication* (pp. 95–118). Rochelle Park, New Jersey: Hayden Book Company, Inc.

Thayer, L. (1979). Communication: Sine qua non of the behavioral sciences. In R. W. Budd & B. D. Ruben (Eds.), *Interdisciplinary approaches to human communication* (pp. 7–31). Rochelle Park, New Jersey: Hayden Book Company, Inc.

Weick, K. E. (2001). *Making sense of the organization.* Malden, MA: Blackwell Publishing.

9. Halloran, J. D. (1985). Information and communication: Information is the answer, but what is the question? In B. D. Ruben (Ed.), *Information & behavior: Vol. 1* (pp. 27–39). New Brunswick: Transaction Books.

Thayer, L. (1979). Communication: Sine qua non of the behavioral sciences. In R. W. Budd & B. D. Ruben (Eds.), *Interdisciplinary approaches to human communication* (pp. 7–31). Rochelle Park, New Jersey: Hayden Book Company, Inc.

Smith, A. G. (1979). Anthropology. In R. W. Budd & B. D. Ruben (Eds.), *Interdisciplinary approaches to human communication* (pp. 57–70). Rochelle Park, New Jersey: Hayden Book Company, Inc.

10. Ford, J. D., & Ford. L. W. (1995). The role of conversations in producing intentional change in organizations. *The Academy of Management Review, 20*(3), 541–570. Quote p. 560.

11. Berger, P. L., & Luckmann, T. (1967). *The social construction of reality: A treatise in the sociology of knowledge.* Garden City, NY: Doubleday.

Ford, J. D., & Ford, L. W. (1995). The role of conversations in producing intentional change in organizations. *The Academy of Management Review, 20*(3), 541–570.

Lewis, L. K. (2007). An organizational stakeholder model of change implementation communication. *Communication Theory, 17*, 176–204.

Poole, M. S. (2009). Adaptive structuration theory. In E. Griffin (Ed.), *A first look at communication theory* (7th ed., pp. 235–246). New York: McGraw Hill.

Weick, K. E. (1995). *Sensemaking in organizations.* Thousand Oaks, CA: Sage.

12. Lewis, L. K. (2007). An organizational stakeholder model of change implementation communication. *Communication Theory, 17*, 176–204.

13. Lewis, L. K. (2007). An organizational stakeholder model of change implementation communication. *Communication Theory, 17*, 176–204.

Smulowitz, S. (2014). Planned organizational change in Higher Education: Dashboard indicators and stakeholder sensemaking—A case study (Unpublished doctoral dissertation). Rutgers, The State University of New Jersey, New Brunswick, NJ.

14. Shane, P. (1990). Why are so many people so unhappy? Habits of thought and resistance to diversity in legal education. *Iowa Law Review, 75*, 1033–1056. Quote p. 1036.

15. Shane, P. (1990). Why are so many people so unhappy? Habits of thought and resistance to diversity in legal education. *Iowa Law Review, 75*, 1033–1056.

16. Shane, P. (1990). Why are so many people so unhappy? Habits of thought and resistance to diversity in legal education. *Iowa Law Review, 75*, 1033–1056.

17. Conrad, C. (1978). A grounded theory of academic change. *Sociology of Education, 51*(2), 101–112.

Johnstone, D. B., Dye, N. S., & Johnson, R. (1998). Collaborative leadership for institutional change. *Liberal Education, 84*(2).

18. Smulowitz, S. (2014). Planned organizational change in Higher Education: Dashboard indicators and stakeholder sensemaking—A case study (Unpublished doctoral dissertation). Rutgers, The State University of New Jersey, New Brunswick, NJ.

19. Ruben, B. D., & Gigliotti, R. A. (2019). *Leadership, communication, and social influence: A theory of resonance, activation, and cultivation.* Bingley/West Yorkshire, UK: Emerald Publishing.

20. Berger, P. L., & Luckmann, T. (1967). *The social construction of reality: A treatise in the sociology of knowledge.* Garden City, NY: Doubleday.

Weick, K. E. (1979). *The social psychology of organizing* (2nd ed.). Reading, MA: Addison Wesley.

21. Berger, P. L., & Luckmann, T. (1967). *The social construction of reality: A treatise in the sociology of knowledge.* Garden City, NY: Doubleday.

Burr, V. (2003). *Social constructionism* (2nd ed.). New York, NY: Routledge.

Ruben, B. D. (1983). A system-theoretic view. In W. B. Gudykunst (Ed.), *Intercultural communication theory* (pp. 131–145). Beverly Hills, CA: Sage.

Smulowitz, S. (2014). Planned organizational change in Higher Education: Dashboard indicators and stakeholder sensemaking—A case study (Unpublished doctoral dissertation). Rutgers, The State University of New Jersey, New Brunswick, NJ.

Thayer, L. (1979). Communication: Sine qua non of the behavioral sciences. In R. W. Budd & B. D. Ruben (Eds.), *Interdisciplinary approaches to human communication* (pp. 7–31). Rochelle Park, New Jersey: Hayden Book Company, Inc.

von Bertalanffy, L. (1975). General system theory. In R. W. Budd & B. D. Ruben (Eds.), *Interdisciplinary approaches to human communication* (pp. 95–118). Rochelle Park, NJ: Hayden Book Company, Inc.

22. Ruben, B. D. (1979). General system theory. In R. W. Budd & B. D. Ruben (Eds.), *Interdisciplinary approaches to human communication* (pp. 95–118). Rochelle Park, New Jersey: Hayden Book Company, Inc.

Ruben, B. D., & Kim, J. Y. (Eds.). (1975). *General systems and human communication theory.* Rochelle Park, NJ: Hayden Book Company, Inc.

Ruben, B. D., & Stewart, L. P. (2006). *Communication and human behavior* (5th ed.). Boston, MA: Pearson Education.

Smulowitz, S. (2014). Planned organizational change in Higher Education: Dashboard indicators and stakeholder sensemaking—A case study (Unpublished doctoral dissertation). Rutgers, The State University of New Jersey, New Brunswick, NJ.

Thayer, L. (1979). Communication: Sine qua non of the behavioral sciences. In R. W. Budd & B. D. Ruben (Eds.), *Interdisciplinary approaches to human communication* (pp. 7–31). Rochelle Park, New Jersey: Hayden Book Company, Inc.

23. Smulowitz, S. (2014). Planned organizational change in Higher Education: Dashboard indicators and stakeholder sensemaking—A case study (Unpublished doctoral dissertation). Rutgers, The State University of New Jersey, New Brunswick, NJ.

24. Mohrman, S. A., Mohrman, A. M., & Ledford, G. E. (1989). Interventions that change organizations. In A. M. Mohrman, S. A. Mohrman, G. E. Ledford, E. E. Lawler & Associates (Eds.), *Large scale organizational change.* San Francisco, CA: Jossey-Bass Publishers, Inc.

Ruben, B. D. (1979). General system theory. In R. W. Budd & B. D. Ruben (Eds.), *Interdisciplinary approaches to human communication* (pp. 95–118). Rochelle Park, New Jersey: Hayden Book Company, Inc.

von Bertalanffy, L. (1950). An outline of general systems theory. *The British Journal for the Philosophy of Science, 1*(2), 134–165.

von Bertalanffy, L. (1975). General system theory. In R. W. Budd & B. D. Ruben (Eds.), *Interdisciplinary approaches to human communication* (pp. 95–118). Rochelle Park, NJ: Hayden Book Company, Inc.

25. Smulowitz, S. (2014). Planned organizational change in Higher Education: Dashboard indicators and stakeholder sensemaking—A case study (Unpublished doctoral dissertation). Rutgers, The State University of New Jersey, New Brunswick, NJ.

26. Barge, J. K., & Fairhurst, G. (2008). Living leadership: A systemic constructionist approach. *Leadership Quarterly, 4*(3), 227–251.

Ruben, B. D., DeLisi, R., & Gigliotti, R. A. (2017). *A guide for leaders in higher education: Core concepts, competencies and tools.* Sterling, VA: Stylus Publishing.

Chapter 9

Organizational Change Buy-In Commitment Loop

WHAT YOU CAN EXPECT TO LEARN IN THIS CHAPTER

- What are some elements that enable organizational members to buy into the planned organizational change effort?
- How can a leader impact organizational member buy-in to future planned organizational change efforts?

All organizational change efforts begin with a spark, or something that causes the leader to determine that a change is necessary. Perhaps this spark is the need to grow enrollment, reduce binge drinking, increase diversity, or address changing student needs. This spark might lead to a change that could be smaller in scope like replacing a paper form with an online form, or larger in scope like the introduction of a new student information system.

This spark can come from internal or external prompts. For example, the *Spellings Commission Report* was an external spark that set institutions of higher education across the United States to understand their choices for improving assessment of student learning outcomes.[1] Similarly, the spark can be internal such as the need for an academic department to reallocate funds to be able to launch a new student engagement initiative or for a new dean to keep the candy bowl full throughout the year.

What follows is a model for fast-tracking organizational member buy-in to your planned, organizational change effort. This new model shows a pathway to move organizational members from awareness of the change effort (see figure 9.1, #1) to buy-in (#4).

Once the spark occurs, the planning stage of the change program begins. The leader may choose to start this stage alone or immediately involve others

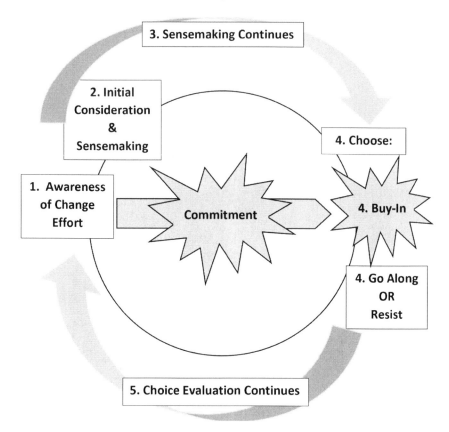

Figure 9.1   Organizational Change Buy-In / Commitment Loop.

to identify a list of alternative options (figure 9.1, #2) to solve the need. This list is often initially generated based on the worldview of those involved. At this point, it is up to the leader to determine (a) whether to look for other alternative options; (b) to evaluate and choose from the alternative options on their own; (c) to include others in search of additional alternative options and a solution to the spark; or (d) do nothing.

Many issues come into play at this stage of the process. First is the leader's power to decide whether to include others in the decision-making about the planned change. Depending on the size and scope of the need and the range of those organizational members who will be affected by the need, the leader will determine if participation from others is necessary.

If the decision is small enough in scope, the leader may not need to involve organizational members. For example, a new dean decided to purchase enough candy for the office to last the entire semester. The dean didn't involve anyone in the decision. Not many decisions will be this simple and low pressure. Unless your decision is this simple, it is always best to include organizational members from the beginning.

The chairperson of an academic department in Case Study Small University, sent an email to department members to ask who would like to be involved in the search committee for a new faculty hire. No one responded. A few weeks later, one of the faculty members stopped to ask the department chairperson if they could chair the search committee. The chairperson agreed, but didn't tell any of the other faculty members in the department about the agreement. The chairperson sensed a lack of interest from the faculty and thought they wouldn't care about such a small decision.

A few weeks later, as the hiring process was getting started, faculty began to receive emails from the chair of the search committee. Confused, the faculty began the sensemaking process to figure out what was happening. Did they miss a meeting and subsequent vote to elect the chair of the search committee? Was this a planned action? Why weren't they included? Eventually the faculty met as a group and aired their displeasure with the process. The faculty officially voted and ended up electing the same person chair for the search committee.

In the end, the search process went well. However, trust in and commitment to the chairperson plummeted. Faculty became skeptical about future actions of the chairperson. Even a small decision about who's going to facilitate the hiring process can have long-lasting implications for leaders and future planned organizational change efforts.

INVOLVING ORGANIZATIONAL MEMBERS IN DECISION-MAKING ABOUT THE CHANGE

While leaders have a big picture view of where the organization is today and where it needs to be in the future, they need to rely on organizational members who are working day-to-day to keep things running. These organizational members will often have greater knowledge about the spark that led to the need for change because of their closeness to the situation. Often organizational members have access to information that the leader may not. Therefore, it is in the best interest of the organization for the leader to involve organizational members in the decision-making process.

As organizational members learn about the change effort they determine whether they share their information about the situation with the leader or stay silent. Sometimes, just the action of involving organizational members in decision-making will be enough to entice them to share their knowledge. Other times, issues of trust, commitment, and self-interest play a role in the organizational member's silence.[2]

If those issues are overcome, and especially if organizational members are committed to the organization or the leader, then their participation in the decision-making will have a greater likelihood of happening. Typically, the leader will assemble a select group of organizational members to discuss the spark and perhaps the leader's predisposed alternative option list (figure 9.1, #2). Some discussion will occur and the organizational members will develop or add to the predisposed alternative option list, and perhaps even remove some of the initial options on the list.

Depending on the intensity of the options on the list, there may be a need for organizational members to work outside this meeting to collect more information and report back to the group, evaluating the alternative options (figure 9.1, #2). In doing so, some of the options on the list will become irrelevant and others may become more desirable. In addition, other, new options might surface. Either way, the group will evaluate the alternative options on the list and choose the option that best solves their need.

Early in this process, the leader will make a formal announcement to make all organizational members aware of the change effort. As organizational members learn about the change effort, they will initially decide whether to buy into, go along with or resist the change (figure 9.1, #4). Between the time they learn about the change effort and have to take action or become impacted by the change effort, organizational members will continue to use sensemaking.

The decision to buy into, go along with, or resist the change is dependent upon a multitude of issues such as organizational member commitment to the organization and the leader, trust in the leader, participation and voice, emotions, worldview, and more.[3] The process of sensemaking will help organizational members to determine whether they buy-into, go along with, or resist the change effort (figure 9.1, #3).

Those organizational members who are committed and have a voice are more likely to buy-in. At the same time, those organizational members who buy-in and participate in the process are more likely to increase their commitment. If the change effort results in a positive outcome for them, then they are more likely to become an advocate and use their social influence with others in the organization the next time a planned change effort occurs.

VOICE

The considerations of voice include power of leaders, commitment of organizational member, inclusion of a third party such as a union in the organization, interest, and benefit to nonorganizational members. Issues of voice immediately bring to the forefront the concept of power. Leaders have the power to consider the voice of the organizational member as irrelevant, a threat to authority, or a valuable asset.[4] At the same time, organizational members also espouse power of voice in several ways.

One way organizational members can espouse power of voice is through their stage of employment. This can lead to power, or a lack of power, of voice for organizational members. Think about this on a continuum from low voice to high voice with adjunct faculty and untenured assistant professors having low voice, associate professors in the middle and full professors having high voice.

Depending on the institution, the administrative side can act similarly with staff secretaries and assistant directors having low voice, directors in the middle, and vice presidents and the president having high voice. The addition of a union for faculty or staff can change this dynamic a bit because the union can act as a collective voice to speak out without fear of retribution—even when the group cannot do so on their own.

Another dynamic for voice is the concept of social influencers. These influencers can come from inside or outside of the organization and can help organizational members bring forth compelling evidence and support for their voices. In some instances, organizational members may be able to bring in speakers or testimony from industry experts about a specific topic. For example, many assessment experts have been instrumental to help organizational members convince administration to add a budget line for travel to workshops and conferences.

Another example is the growing need for additional student psychological, academic, and other support on campuses. Faculty are often the first group within the organization to recognize this growing need and use their network across their discipline to find resources and ideas from other organizations across the country. As faculty talk with each other on campus, they share this information and in some instances have begun committees to focus specifically on student needs.

Sometimes, people outside the organization exercise social influence because it is of interest and benefit to them and to the organization. For example, the "Me Too" movement has led indirectly to changes in the policies of many colleges and universities across the United States. Leaders must consider the internal and external social influencers and organizational member commitment to these groups.

When considering voice, one should also look to the commitment of organizational members. The more commitment that organizational members possess, the more they are likely to use their voice. Conversely, the less commitment that organizational members possess, the less likely they are to use their voice. Even if more committed organizational members use their voice to express disdain (or even resistance) about a change effort, this should be viewed as a positive expression. Leaders should take this opportunity to find out why these members are providing a signal that the direction of the change effort may miss the mark.

Leaders have an obligation to listen to concerns, which may raise awareness of an unintended consequence that may have gone unnoticed otherwise. If leaders choose to ignore these warnings, the change effort could lead to unforeseen negative results. Worse, choosing to ignore warnings from your committed organizational members might send a message that their voice is meaningless. The next time these organizational members see red flags, they may choose to join less committed members and withhold information to let the change effort fail.

WHY GIVE ORGANIZATIONAL MEMBERS VOICE?

Most organizational members want to succeed. They want to do well and excel in their job. The environment in most colleges and universities is one that fosters support and help for students. Typically, leaders evaluate the impact of their staff to determine outcomes on performance and goals. What if, instead, leaders provided a mechanism for staff to evaluate their own impact on performance and goals?

Faculty have a peer-review system in place consisting first with their department, and then a board on rank and tenure. The process consists of faculty presenting their successes in research, teaching, and service to their peers. It is up to the individual faculty member to make a case for why their peers should promote them. Often the requirements for these promotions are vague, leaving the candidate in a constant state of anxiety. What are some options that you, as a leader, could provide to faculty, the departments, and the board?

Staff promotions and salary increases, on the other hand, operate in a more traditional manner. Typically the leader conducts a performance review and meets with the staff member to share their thoughts about the staff member's performance throughout the year. What happens when the staff member has the ability to create goals and assess themselves? The instances of this process has proven to (a) be much more strenuous than what the leader will develop; and (b) provide more engaging for the staff member who will almost always do everything in their power to meet and exceed these goals because they are more invested in goals that they had a chance to express.

This relates back to the concept of buy-in. Combining buy-in with participation increases organizational member commitment. Commitment combined with voice increases organizational member buy-in and makes it less likely that these members will leave the organization (even if they experience low job satisfaction). Increased commitment and positive outcomes increase positive sharing and turning your organizational members into ambassadors who will exert their social influence on others in the organization. This is key to your planned change efforts in the future as well as employee retention.

NEGLECT

Organizational members who are not committed to the organization have a reason. In some instances, they were never committed to the organization, and in others, their commitment waned over years for a number of reasons. Perhaps throughout their employment, their voice was ignored, their involvement was not permitted, or they suffered retribution.

If the organizational member used their voice and it was ignored, these members may feel that they have little to no ability to be able to affect the organization, especially organizational changes.[5] Perhaps these organizational members came to distrust the actions and promises of leaders.[6] This distrust might stem from leaders who broke commitments to organizational members. Often this type of distrust can lead to feelings of hurt, disappointment and mistrust.

Some, but not all, organizational members who are not fully committed to the organization will cause disruption. At times, this disruption can be considered neglect. Neglect is when organizational members purposefully do their job wrong or without care.[7]

Often this carelessness becomes a burden on other organizational members who need to pick up the slack for these members. Such acts can be as small as complaining about work processes or fellow organizational members. Or they can be as disruptive as protesting or undermining work processes or fellow organizational members. Generally, the most visible disruption from these organizational members comes with large-scale planned change efforts.

For example, they might be the person in the room to stand up and express hostility toward the change effort while others are trying to figure out how to make it work. That's the best-case scenario as the leader can see which members they need to reach out to. The real problem is when an organizational member silently decides to create a disruption that you will find out about only when the damaging effects have been done. For example, the leader of a department may decide to not inform department members about the change effort, reducing its overall success.

BUY-IN/COMMITMENT LOOP

Getting buy-in from organizational members is a crucial part of the leader's work. Once the organizational member buys-into the process, they will move forward with their support for the change effort. However, realize that throughout the change effort, the organizational member will continue to evaluate and make sense of (#5) their choice to buy-into the change effort over and over again.

It's critical throughout the change process that the leader monitors the communication environment to ensure that all organizational members have a clear understanding of the goals and progress of the change effort. Should the leader find out that there are organizational members that are uncertain about the goal and/or progress, the leader will need to produce corrective messages. This process will help organizational members reaffirm that their decision to buy-into the change effort was the right choice.

Organizational members evaluate their overall change effort experience (figure 9.1, #5). These evaluations frame their perspectives and potential to buy-into future change efforts. These evaluations also frame their degree of commitment to the leader. As organizational members participate in and feel they have a voice, are well-informed, continually evaluate and reaffirm their choice to buy-into the change effort, they are increasing their commitment to the leader.

When organizational member's commitment to the leader increases, the potential for them to quickly buy-into the next change effort increases. The payoff is that the more organizational members who are committed to the leader, the more likely the organizational change effort is to succeed.

These committed organizational members are likely to instantly buy-into the next change effort. In doing so, they will bypass the time it takes to engage in deep sensemaking (see figure 9.1). These organizational members will become advocates for the leader and the change effort and use their social influence to encourage other members to buy-into the change.

Once organizational members use the buy-in/commitment loop, they will continually engage in evaluation of their choice to buy-in. The leader is never immune from evaluation by organizational members. As a result, the leader must always ensure organizational members have clarity about goals, receive timely and accurate information about the change effort and can trust the leader's choices. Ideally, organizational members will continue to use the buy-in/commitment loop and use their social influence to bring other members through that loop as well for future change efforts.

SUMMARY

All planned organizational change efforts begin with a spark that the leader identifies as a gap. As the leader implements the change effort participation, voice and monitoring the communication environment become paramount to increase the likelihood of successful change. If the planned change is successful and organizational members perceive they can trust the leader, their commitment to the leader may increase.

Over time and with consistency, organizational members may not need as much time for sensemaking prior to buying into the change effort. Ideally, organizational members will move directly into buy-in and act as social influencers to other organizational members.

NOTES

1. U.S. Department of Education. (2006). *The Spellings Commission report.* Washington, DC: Department of Education.

2. Allen, N. J., & Meyer, J. P. (1990). The measurement and antecedents of affective, continuance and normative commitment to the organization. *Journal of Occupational Psychology, 63*, 1–18.

Fulmer, C. A., & Ostroff, C. (2017). Trust in direct leaders and top leaders: A trickle-up model. *Journal of Applied Psychology, 102*(4), 648.

Thomas, G. F., Zolin, R., & Hartman, J. L. (2009). The central role of communication in developing trust and its effect on employee involvement. *The Journal of Business Communication, 46*(3), 287–310.

3. It is beyond the scope of this chapter to discuss each reason organizational members may resist or buy into the planned organizational change effort.

4. Hamilton, G. G., & Feenstra, R. C. (1997). Varieties of hierarchies and markets: An introduction. In M. Orru, N. W. Biggart & G. G. Hamilton (Eds.), *The economic organization of East Asian capitalism* (pp. 55–96). Thousand Oaks, CA: Sage.

Whitley, R. (2003). From the search for universal correlations to the institutional structuring of economic organization and change: The development and future of organization studies. *Organization, 10*(3), 481–501.

5. Edwards, P., Collinson, D., & Rocca, G. D. (1995). Workplace resistance in Western Europe: A preliminary overview and a research agenda. *European Journal of Industrial Relations, 1*(3), 283–316.

6. Naus, F., van Iterson, A., & Roe, R. (2007). Organizational cynicism: Extending the exit, voice, loyalty, and neglect model of employees' responses to adverse conditions in the workplace. *Human Relations, 60*(5), 683–718.

7. Allen, M. M. C. (2014), Hirschman and voice. In A. Wilkinson, J. Donaghey, T. Dundon & R. Freeman (Eds.), *The handbook of research on employee voice* (pp. 36–51). Cheltenham and New York: Edward Elgar Press.

Part III

Leadership Toolkit

This is a hands-on leadership toolkit to help you get organized and take step-by-step action for your planned, organizational change. As you work through this toolkit, it will be helpful to refer back to earlier chapters to integrate best practices and determine your current and desired actions.

Chapter 10

Phase 1

Self-Discovery

WHAT YOU CAN EXPECT TO LEARN IN THIS CHAPTER

- What are the major elements of self-discovery?
- How do your worldview and assumptions cloud your ability to lead?

One of the most overlooked ways to experience success is to first look inward. Knowing what's in your filter enables you to understand how you view the world as you do. The way you think, act, and behave impacts the change effort you lead in a bigger way than you are aware. There are three ways that lead to self-discovery: (1) Self-awareness of your worldviews; (2) leadership assumptions, style, and competencies; and (3) the recognition and plan for how you want to lead. In chapter 8, we discussed the filter that you and everyone else has—the filter that enables you to understand how you view the world as you do—your worldview.

IT ALL BEGINS WITH YOU: BECOMING SELF-AWARE

Your thoughts, behaviors, and actions depend on your worldview. Now, keep in mind that every person you encounter has their own unique worldview that, in turn, shapes the way they think, behave and act. No two people are the same. No two people think the same. Research shows that even twins brought up in the same environment have different worldviews.[1] The same goes for organizations whether they are traditional organizations or institutions of higher education.

Why is it that you have your specific worldview? Well, there's the way you were raised and socialized, where you went to school, your friends and family, and even other places you worked. All these experiences from birth through now lead you to your current worldview—your mental reality—and rules for the way things are. You learned some of these rules along the way from others and created other rules from your life experiences.

Think about the last time you saw a baby or toddler. They don't care if they burp (or worse) in public. They don't care how messy they get when they eat or what they say to anyone at any time. They have not yet learned that it's inappropriate to put your food into someone else's hair or that yelling out in the middle of church that they need more cereal is better kept to a whisper. As far as they know, they need more cereal and everyone should help them get it. After repeated learning the "no yelling in church" rule from our parents week after week, we incorporate that rule into our worldview. We become socialized into church culture, for example.

We create other rules on our own, share them with others and sustain them through communication. For example, in chapter 8, Susan created a rule that she should be "busy" whenever Rick asked for help. Susan's prior experience taught her that Rick's projects were a waste of her time. This experience helped Susan create a new rule, or worldview, for her behavior.

Over time and with other experiences, Susan's "Rick rule" may change or stay the same if she experiences repeated behaviors and especially if others share similar "Rick" experiences with Susan. Social sharing and influence help cocreate and sustain Susan's "Rick rule." Managing and adapting these worldviews occurs through communication as we cocreate our reality with others socially.[2]

Your worldview impacts the way you think, act, behave, and "predicts your ability to create positive change."[3] What if you could change the way you think, act, and behave, and become happier, more productive, and able to create positive change? Think about how you interact with others. Is it in a positive or negative way? Do people enjoy when you stop to talk with them or do they bury their nose in their desk and appear busy so they don't have to get into too much discussion with you? Do you wonder why people act defensively around you? Or are you greeted with enthusiasm?

One of the most overlooked ways to experience success is to first look inward. Changing your worldview changes your thoughts, behaviors, and actions. These new, more positive thoughts, behaviors and actions help to increase your happiness. Being happy helps you become more productive and successful.[4]

We live in the age of information overload. That is, we are exposed to more information than we can possibly pay attention to. Think about all the information you receive in a given day, then think about the information you receive just about the change program you plan to implement or are implementing. Now think about the top pieces of information from each that stick out in your mind. Is that information positive or negative? What information will you talk about tonight when you get home? Let's take a bet that it's the negative information that will be weighing in on your thoughts.

Recently, a friend spent three weeks in Europe, visiting London and Paris. When the friend returned home, the first story about the trip was about the trouble getting through the airport. Similarly, a family member had an amazing New York City weekend. Again, the first story was about a rude waiter. Why is it that we seem to be destined to think about negative experiences rather than positives ones? The reason is simple. We allow ourselves to focus on those negative experiences at the expense of positive experiences.[5]

What if, instead of focusing on the negative experiences or the five employees who complain about the change program, that we instead focus on the positive experiences or the other 500 employees who are moving through the change program with a positive outlook? Or, perhaps it's us who bring the negativity. Think about your self-talk.[6] You know, those moments during the day or week where we doubt ourselves. We might hear a voice in our head that says "people are going to resist this change effort, so why even bother," or "is this change effort something in my range of expertise or should I just throw in the towel?"

No matter what those negative voices are in your head, let them pass. Instead, use positive self-talk. You might say, "People might resist, but once they understand the value of the change program they'll be on board." Or "there may be some resources to help implement this change effort, just like that time with the other project."

As your worldview becomes more positive, you'll see a 23 percent increase in the amount of energy during stressful periods, 31 percent higher productivity, and a 40 percent increase in the opportunity to advance in your career.[7] All this is a direct result of changing your worldview, which, in turn, changes your thoughts, beliefs, and actions.

Yes, some people are just happier than others—that's genetics and that controls 50 percent of our happiness.[8] But your job is stressful, you say? Yes, that's your circumstance and that controls another 10 percent of your happiness.[9] That leaves 40 percent of your happiness up for grabs. By changing your worldview, you can change the way you think about, act, and behave. By doing this, you can increase your happiness by up to 40 percent and your productivity by up to 31 percent. So why not try? Aren't we all looking to find a way to be more productive and happy?

But there's more good news. Are you ready? When we shift our worldview to a more positive outlook, our bodies give off chemicals that increase our ability to generate energy, success, and to see more opportunities.[10]

And the best news of all is that happy is catchy! That's right. The happy you have will rub off onto others around you—think about a happier workplace and home. To make the shift, there are a number of intentional activities you can do daily. These activities have a stronger effect on your happiness than your genetics and circumstances.[11] Try incorporating some of these habits for twenty-one days and see the difference in yourself and those around you.[12]

A few strategies to get started on shifting your worldview to feel happier and become successful:

1. Have a vision so that you will have something to strive for moving forward.
2. Live in the present so that you won't miss the happy moments that could go unnoticed.
3. Begin a gratitude habit. Use a journal just for this and record three things you are grateful for each day.
4. Smile.
5. Meditate.
6. Exercise.
7. Practice random acts of kindness.
8. Buy something for someone else.
9. Make relationships and social connections important.
10. Donate old blankets to an animal shelter.

DISCOVERING ASSUMPTIONS AND MANAGING PERCEPTIONS

The second part of self-discovery is to assess your leadership assumptions, style, and competencies. You are reading this book because either you are an academic leader or you aspire to become one in the near future. If you are an academic leader, think about how this happened. Perhaps you were a department chairperson and decided that administration was more suiting to your lifestyle and skills. Perhaps the administration asked you to lead an initiative. Maybe you came from industry.[13]

Assumptions

Whatever the reason and from wherever you came, you first need to make an inventory of the assumptions you've brought along with you (see table 10.1). These assumptions should be about what it's like working in academia, as a faculty member, as an administrator and how faculty and administrators work together. These assumptions should also include your ideas about how

Table 10.1   Assumptions Checklist #1

Topic	Assumption
Working in higher education:	
Working as a faculty member:	
Working as an administrator:	
How faculty and administrators work together:	

work gets done, who should be responsible for what and how people hold themselves accountable.

In a recent conversation with an administrator who went back to school for her doctorate and is now a faculty member, the administrator shared that while the work as an administrator was demanding and stressful, she never realized the intense workload of faculty during the semester until she became one. In fact, she shared feelings of guilt about thinking poorly of faculty either who refused to take on committee work or who fell behind with their committee work.

Conversely, a new administrator shared their remorse about leaving the faculty. He said that while he was excited about the possibility to affect many more students, he missed the opportunity to develop relationships through teaching that would have a greater effect on a smaller amount of students. He also missed the "freedom" from big, seemingly impossible issues such as declining enrollment, increased expenses, and the multitude of other pressures administrators face. He said he now feels as if it's his job to shelter the faculty from some of these issues because he never had to face them in his role as a faculty member.

If you aspire to become an academic leader, do the same soul-searching about your assumptions and experiences and include them on Checklist #2 (see table 10.2). Why is it that you want to become an academic leader? What leadership roles have you had in the past? Reflect on those positions, your accomplishments, your subordinates, and times you failed. What did you learn? How did your subordinates feel about you? Would they work for you again? Why is that? Were you able to make effective change or did you find that your subordinates were always resisting and putting up roadblocks to your ideas? Why do you think you had failures? What made a difference between times of failure and accomplishment?

Think about your perspective as well as other person's perspectives. Faculty members and administrators need to focus on very different issues facing their institution of higher education. The key to making a good institution of higher education great is to be able to set aside differences, acknowledge the difference in perspectives, and figure out how to use those differences to work together.

Table 10.2   Assumptions and Experiences Checklist #2

Topic	*Assumptions and Experiences*
Why do you want to become a leader in higher education?	
What leadership roles have you had in the past?	
What did you learn from these roles?	
What did you learn from accomplishments from your previous roles?	
What did you learn from failures from your previous roles?	
What was the key difference in your failures and successes? What does this tell you?	
What did you learn from subordinates from your previous roles?	
How did your subordinates feel about you? Why?	
Would they work for you again? Why?	
Were you able to make effective change? Why?	
Did subordinates resist and create roadblocks? Why?	

Your Expertise Can Be Limiting

For those faculty who are arm-twisted or even go willingly into the administrative side, be aware of your expertise. Yes, you are an expert in an area of great importance. However, this expertise does not always translate well into leadership roles, especially during times of organizational change.

Think about it. You are accustomed to being the most knowledgeable person in the room about your area of expertise. That has afforded you many privileges. For example, you might make a mistake about an admissions statistic or procedure. As a faculty member, who is an expert in one area, you might not be expected to know about these topics as you come to the table with built-in credibility.

As an administrator, others will expect you to be knowledgeable about these topics. You will be the "newbie" who has quite a learning curve. This is going to be a new feeling for you. One that may make you very uncomfortable. One that you will need to learn to accept and move forward.

Monitor your self-talk about this experience. Keep in mind that you have amazing experience that no one else has. Allow yourself time to learn all the new processes and information. Be authentic. Surround yourself with other awesome leaders just like you. Support and learn from one another. Only by accepting and embracing this new learning opportunity can you become an effective leader—especially in times of planned organizational change.

LEADERSHIP STYLES

With your newly discovered leadership assumptions, now is the time to determine your leadership style. Chapter 4 provides a good review of a majority of the different leadership styles, including those that are based on competencies and skills. The good news is that leadership is an ability that can be learned over time. You do not have to be born a leader. There are people who are everyday leaders, making impact in big and small ways. There are people who lead informally and others who are formal leaders. You don't need a fancy title to be a leader. And, you certainly don't need a fancy title to be a good leader.

Then there are followers. If there are leaders, there must be followers. Leadership is defined by the way the leader and followers create their reality together. They do so by the way they interact and communicate with each other. At times, then, one could argue that the leadership role is actually fulfilled by the followers and at other times, by the leader. Think about the times where your leadership influenced situations where your role was not the official leader. For example, a colleague recently began a new internship process with her students. Soon, all faculty in the department were using the same process. This is leadership at work. No fancy title needed.

A quick review of some of the leadership styles provides us with an idea of some of the criteria that are used to assess ones leadership abilities. Note that these criteria differ depending on the style of leadership. For example, table 4.1 shows that the focus and point of view change based on the type of leadership style. That is, some leadership styles focus on the leader and others on the followers. At the same time, some leadership styles focus on the leader behavior, trait, skill, and even interaction with followers.

An examination of leadership competencies is a nice complement to the leadership styles inventory listed in chapter 4. The categories of analytical, personal, communication, positional and organizational competencies transcend beyond leadership behaviors and traits as discussed in chapter 4 (see table 4.2) to examine leader's knowledge and skills.[14] This is an excellent resource for readers who have reviewed the leadership styles in chapter 4 and determined that your leadership falls into multiple styles.

Once you have recognized your existing worldview and assumptions, determined your desired worldview, and leadership style or competencies the next step is to determine how to enact those. This is where you put your positive energy to work.

1. Use the checklists to benchmark your assumptions and worldview.
2. Make shifting your worldview and checking those assumptions a priority. Integrate at least one of the methods described before into your life for twenty-one days.
3. Add more of these methods, one at a time, every twenty-one days.
4. Conduct a gap analysis[15] of the leadership style or competencies you desire. Which are the areas where you excel and which are the areas

where you can improve? Ask others opinions of your areas of strengths and improvement. Often other people are better able to tell you where you excel and need improvement. You will find areas of strength you didn't really think about. This will surprise you.

5. Make a list of the areas where you excel. Think about why that is. How can these areas help you with your change effort?

6. Make a list of the areas where you need improvement. Think about why that is. What situations can you reflect upon where improvement in these areas would have made a difference? How so?

7. Find a resource to help you with your areas of improvement. Or, find someone you can put in charge of those areas—delegate.

8. Make a plan to move forward with your change effort using these analyses and assessments.

SUMMARY

The first step for leaders is self-discovery because understanding oneself is a precursor to being able to understand and lead others. The way you think, behave, and act depends on your worldview. Your worldview is your mental reality, or a set of rules, you have developed for the way the world operates. Everyone, even twins, has a different worldview. Understanding your own worldview will help you to recognize differences you may have with others' thoughts, behaviors, and actions.

The second step of self-discovery is to assess your leadership assumptions, styles, and competencies. Use the checklist provided to list your assumptions and review the leadership styles and competencies provided in chapter 4 to determine your unique style. Finally, recognize your leadership strengths and weaknesses. Learn how you can improve on your weaknesses or delegate those responsibilities. Maximize your strengths. Once you have yourself figured out, it's time to focus on the other members of your organization.

NOTES

1. Delgado, J. M. R. (1979). Neurophysiology. In R. W. Budd & B. D. Ruben (Eds.), *Interdisciplinary approaches to human communication* (pp. 119–134). Rochelle Park, NJ: Hayden Book Company, Inc.

Dervin, B. (1977). Useful theory for librarianship: Communication, not information. *Drexel Library Quarterly, 13*(3), 16–32.

2. Barge, J. K., & Fairhurst, G. T. (2008). Living leadership: A systemic constructionist approach. *Leadership Quarterly, 4*(3), 227–251.

Fairhurst, G. T. (2008). Discursive leadership: A communication alternative to leadership psychology. *Management Communication Quarterly, 21*(4), 510–521.

3. Achor, S. (2013). *Before happiness: The five hidden keys to achieving success, spreading happiness, and sustaining positive change.* New York, NY: Random House.

4. Achor, S. (2013). *Before happiness: The five hidden keys to achieving success, spreading happiness, and sustaining positive change.* New York, NY: Random House.

5. Achor, S. (2013). *Before happiness: The five hidden keys to achieving success, spreading happiness, and sustaining positive change.* New York, NY: Random House.

6. Achor, S. (2013). *Before happiness: The five hidden keys to achieving success, spreading happiness, and sustaining positive change.* New York, NY: Random House.

7. Achor, S. (2013). *Before happiness: The five hidden keys to achieving success, spreading happiness, and sustaining positive change.* New York, NY: Random House.

8. Achor, S. (2013). *Before happiness: The five hidden keys to achieving success, spreading happiness, and sustaining positive change.* New York, NY: Random House.

9. Achor, S. (2013). *Before happiness: The five hidden keys to achieving success, spreading happiness, and sustaining positive change.* New York, NY: Random House.

10. Achor, S. (2013). *Before happiness: The five hidden keys to achieving success, spreading happiness, and sustaining positive change.* New York, NY: Random House.

11. Lyubormirsky, S. (2008). *The how of happiness: A new approach to getting the life you want.* New York, NY: The Penguin Press.

12. Achor, S. (2013). *Before happiness: The five hidden keys to achieving success, spreading happiness, and sustaining positive change.* New York, NY: Random House.

Coelho, P. (2014). *The alchemist.* New York, NY: HarperOne, Publishers.

Strobel, K. (n.d.). Kim Strobel Happiness Coach: Women rising. Retrieved from https://kimstrobel.com/.

13. Perlmutter, D. D. (2017, Jan. 1). Administration 101: Deciding to lead. *The Chronicle of Higher Education.* https://www.chronicle.com/article/Administration-1 01-Deciding/238757.

14. Gigliotti, R. A. (2019). An introduction to competencies and competency-based leadership. In R. A. Gigliotti (Ed.), *Competencies for effective leadership: A framework for assessment, education and research.* Bingley, UK: Emerald Publishing Limited.

15. In addition, or alternatively, you can use a preexisting assessment. Many of the leadership styles in chapter 4 already have these. See a list at Northouse, P. (2016). *Leadership: Theory and practice* (7th ed.). Los Angeles: Sage Publications.

Chapter 11

Phase 2

Organizational Member Discovery

WHAT YOU CAN EXPECT TO
LEARN IN THIS CHAPTER

- What are the three phases of organizational member discovery?
- How do emotion, cognition, and sensemaking connect to planned, organizational change efforts?

Now that you have made self-discovery a priority, you should have an idea of your existing and more positive desired worldviews; your existing and desired leadership style and competencies; and a plan to use these newfound abilities to move forward with your change effort. This is an excellent start to the next part of your path to success. Next you will gain a better understanding of organizational member skills, competencies, beliefs, values, biases, habits, and vision.

Just as you discovered when you learned about your own worldviews, you will need to figure out the worldviews of those around you. This will help you to understand why they probably have a different way of looking at and thinking about the change effort and even your organization.

What do people think about the change effort? To find this out, you will need to monitor the communication environment. What are organizational members saying—or better yet—not saying? What worries organizational members? What do they discuss at the water cooler, out for lunch, and when they see each other in the halls? What rumors are there? What truths are there? What do they know that you don't that could make your job a heck of a lot easier?

Step 1: Understand Organizational Member's Worldview

Step one of discovering your organizational members is to really understand them. What keeps them up at night and causes them so much frustration that they talk about it over and over again to coworkers, family, and friends? What gets them angry? What stresses do they have? Where are their sources of anxiety? What do they fear? Are these issues work or personal related or both?

For example, you may have an organizational member who has been asked to complete a task for which they don't have the skills. While this is an immediate work issue, it is also a personal issue of development and could cause them to worry about job security if they execute poorly. Would you prefer organizational members spend work time worrying or working?

Next, you'll need to figure out their hopes for the future—both personal and work related. Again you will find areas of overlap. Your organizational members may hope that in the near future, they receive a raise or get a promotion. Maybe they are invested in an increase in enrollment so that they continue to have a job.

Once you have an idea of the areas that keep your organizational members up at night and the areas of their hope, then you need to figure out what they really want or need. As in the last example, an organizational member may tell you that they want to increase enrollment, but what they might not tell you is that their real motivation is to have a job. To uncover this, keep asking, "why." Behind every want and need there is a why, some benefit that the organizational member receives. It's the "what's in it for me" that we all look out every day.

Ideally, you and your team will be able to develop a persona for each area in your organization that represents the wants, needs, and worries of your organizational members. For example, you might develop a persona, called Frank, another called Mary, and so on. Frank is your representative faculty member and Mary is your representative administrative director. Depending on your organization, you may need more or less of these personas.

As you and the team determine messaging and other change effort elements, you will refer back to the worries, wants, needs, and desires of these personas. You'll find that using the persona name during meetings will help you to think directly about each to better focus messages.

Step 2: Create your Main Message to be used Throughout the Change Effort

Step two happens as you develop your message to the organization about the change effort. Use the information you've gathered about your organizational members (Frank, Mary, and so on) as you develop this message. When you create your message, you want to think about it in two separate parts, cognitive and emotion. Then you want to figure out how the desired end point you've determined for the change effort meets the wants, needs, desires and hopes of your organizational members. Frequently, professionals in the advertising industry use this technique.

First, let's take a look at cognition, emotion, and sensemaking as they are critical connectors to the success of the change effort. The cognitive part is our rational side. It tells us, logically, why we did or should do something. However, our emotions are quick to take over and can often precede our cognitive, more rational side.[1] Further, our emotions are so strong at times that they have the ability to affect the way we experience and interpret situations and information.[2] This goes way back to the caveman days where our emotions instinctively taught us either to flee a situation or to fight.[3]

So, yes, it was your emotional side that appeared when you freaked out because the last person to use the coffee pot didn't clean it. Later on, your rational cognitive side tried to justify the freak out.[4] If you can get so worked up over a coffee pot, imagine how worked up organizational members will get over a change effort.

Any change effort will bring about a disruption to the normal flow of events in the organization. Emotions associated with change effort include fear, anger, anxiety, and hope.[5] Luckily, we can manage messages associated with a planned change effort.

Positive emotions are associated with an increased positive outlook on change efforts.[6] Helping organizational members to have positive emotions about the change effort can lead to greater success.[7]

Sometimes, we aren't quite sure how we feel about a situation. Should we be worried? Will it all work out? Will my job still be there? How will this change affect me? At these moments, we use sensemaking to figure it all out.[8] First, we try to make sense of the situation ourselves using our worldview. Then, we take our worldview to others in the organization and share it with them. They share their worldview with us and from there we're off solving all the reasons the coffee pot never gets cleaned by our lazy coworker or all the possible reasons for and consequences of the change effort that was just announced. As organizational members share their experiences and thoughts, they are cocreating their shared reality of what's happening.[9]

While we are busy cocreating our reality a few things are happening. First, we have in mind our own worldview. Second, we are ingesting others' worldviews. Some of these others may be exercising their social influence to get us to see things the way they do.[10] As they do this, their goal is to move our shared reality to their preferred reality or worldview.[11] The fancy term for this is "sensegiving."

While all this is happening, we also have a stir of emotions. Perhaps something we just remembered or something someone else told us stirred up the memory of a previous situation and the corresponding emotion you had to that situation. Well, guess what? We tend to respond to similar situations with similar emotions so you are likely to experience that same emotion again.[12] At the same time, we may unconsciously mimic others' emotions and feelings.[13] Groups tend to develop shared emotions and cognitive beliefs about change efforts.[14] Emotions are catchy. Let's hope there's some positivity and happiness there!

Next, you'll need to figure out the connection between the desired change effort outcomes and the wants, needs, desires, and hopes of your organizational members. There are many ways to do this. A favorite is the Venn diagram. In one circle, write out all the issues the change effort will solve, and in other, write out all the hopes, fears, wants, needs, and so on of the organizational members. Which information overlaps? "A la, peanut butter sandwiches," there you have it![15]

Take the information that overlaps and make it your main message. You might have to pretty it up, ensuring that you are connecting on an emotional and logical level. Determine where the overlap relates to Maslow's Hierarchy of Needs. There might be several levels that could apply. Use the level that best fits your organizational member's emotions and cognition. Is the concern a lower level, "safety" for employment, or is it a higher level self-actualization?

Try to reduce the overlap message to one word. Every time there's a message about the change effort that overlap needs to be included. Hammer it home. This process is used in the advertising industry. It's why we "prefer" Coke over Pepsi—we identify with Coke's "happiness" more so than what Pepsi is selling.

Step 3: Conduct Assessments and Create a Resource List

Step three of the organizational member discovery is an assessment of their readiness to change.[16] The Organizational Change Recipients' Beliefs Scale assesses organizational members level of buy-in to the change effort; perception of areas of weakness that could impact the change effort negatively; and provide leaders and change agents with areas where they could increase buy-in of organizational members.[17] Questions such as, "I believe the change from [*this*] to [*that*] will have a favorable effect on our operations" as well as perceptions about leadership and resources are included.[18]

In addition to this assessment, the happiness mindset information from chapter 10 and an assessment of organizational subject matter experts should also be considered. The emphasis placed on the happiness of organizational members is a growing trend.

We know that (a) change efforts are stressful and can trigger negative emotions; (b) emotions often take over before our cognitive responses; (c) positive emotions can positively influence a successful change outcome; and (d) emotions are catchy. There are a multitude of happiness coaches and consultants who can truly transform the workplace into a more positive and happy environment. Some provide key-note speaking, free classes, and group and one-on-one coaching.

Another valuable assessment is of subject matter experts in your organization. Certainly start with what you know. Who in your organization is good at what types of processes, tasks, and knowledge? Sometimes administrators forget that they have tremendous resources in-house, both within the administration and on the faculty.

Nothing frustrates faculty more than paying another consulting organization hundreds of thousands of dollars to do the same work that they can do with students or in a faculty group. Well, maybe more frustrating to faculty is that they are not even involved when the consultants are hired. Hello- someone's already written the book about that. Maybe they are on your campus. Maybe their friend at another college wrote the book. In any event, get them involved. Remember that buy-in/commitment loop? This allows voice and participation, which we know increases commitment.

After you figure out what internal talents you know you have, the next step is to ask what talents are out there. A brilliant woman worked in Case Study Small University for years as a department secretary. She applied for an assistant dean job and finally everyone discovered that she was more qualified for the job than the PhD they flew in to interview. You certainly have hidden gems on your campus as well.

As you assess the desired goals for the change effort, you'll also need to determine what resources you'll need to achieve those goals. In addition, keep in mind that things just pop up. So having a list of who's good at what will be really handy when that unexpected situation pops up. You'll know who to go to first. And, you'll have a better idea of the areas where you need to spend money to get outside expertise.

QUICK GUIDE TO STEPS IN THE DISCOVERY OF ORGANIZATIONAL MEMBERS' WORLDVIEW

1. Understand organizational member's worldview:
   a. Anger
   b. Hope
   c. Wants/Needs
   d. Persona
2. Create your main message that will be used throughout the change effort:
   a. Cognition

   b. Emotion
   c. Sensemaking/sensegiving
3. Conduct assessments and create a resource list:
   a. Readiness
   b. Happiness
   c. Create subject matter expert resources list

SUMMARY

The three steps to organizational member discovery are understanding their worldviews, creating a main message, and conducting assessments and a resource list. Leaders can learn much about organizational member's worldviews by assessing their points of anger, hope, wants, and needs.

Leaders can use this information to create a main message for the change effort that taps into organizational member emotions and cognition and facilitates their sensemaking. Finally, leaders and their team can conduct and analyze readiness and happiness assessments and create a master resources list to help with the change effort.

These phases cannot guarantee success. However, taken together, the leader is strengthening organizational member commitment to them. In turn, a stronger committed organizational member over time should buy into future planned organizational change efforts more easily. Further, these more committed organizational members should also become key social influencers for the leader and future change efforts.

NOTES

1. Steigenberger, N. (2015). Emotions in sensemaking: A change management perspective. *Journal of Organizational Change Management, 28*(3), 432–451.

2. Lerner, J. S., & Keltner, D. (2000). Beyond valence: Toward a model of emotion-specific influences on judgement and choice. *Cognition & Emotion, 14*(4), 473–493.

3. Steigenberger, N. (2015). Emotions in sensemaking: A change management perspective. *Journal of Organizational Change Management, 28*(3), 432–451.

4. Weick, K. E. (1979). *The social psychology of organizing* (2nd ed.). Reading, MA: Addison Wesley.

5. Antonacopoulou, E. P., & Gabriel, Y. (2001). Emotion, learning and organizational change. *Journal of Organizational Change Management, 14*(5), 435–451.

Bartunek, J. M., Balogun, J., & Do, B. (2011). Considering planned change anew: Stretching large group interventions strategically, emotionally and meaningfully. *The Academy of Management Annals, 5*(1), 1–52.

Huy, Q. N. (1999). Emotional capability, emotional intelligence, and radical change. *Academy of Management Review, 24*(2), 325–345.

Saunders, M. N., Altinay, L., & Riordan, K. (2009). The management of post-merger cultural integration: Implications from the hotel industry. *The Service Industries Journal, 29*(10), 1359–1375.

Steigenberger, N. (2015). Emotions in sensemaking: A change management perspective. *Journal of Organizational Change Management, 28*(3), 432–451.

Vaara, E. (2000). Constructions of cultural differences in post-merger change processes: A sensemaking perspective on Finnish-Swedish cases. *Management Communication Quarterly, 3*(3), 81–110.

6. Shin, J., Taylor, M. S., & Seo, M. G. (2012). Resources for change: The relationships of organizational inducements and psychological resilience to employees' attitudes and behaviors toward organizational change. *Academy of Management Journal, 55*(3), 727–748.

7. Steigenberger, N. (2015). Emotions in sensemaking: A change management perspective. *Journal of Organizational Change Management, 28*(3), 432–451.

8. Weick, K. E. (1995). *Sensemaking in organizations.* Thousand Oaks, CA: Sage.

9. Berger, P. L., & Luckmann, T. (1967). *The social construction of reality: A treatise in the sociology of knowledge.* Garden City, NY: Doubleday.

Burr, V. (2003). *Social constructionism* (2nd ed.). New York, NY: Routledge.

Ruben, B. D. (1983). A system-theoretic view. In W. B. Gudykunst (Ed.), *Intercultural communication theory* (pp. 131–145). Beverly Hills, CA: Sage.

Smulowitz, S. (2014). Planned organizational change in Higher Education: Dashboard indicators and stakeholder sensemaking—A case study (Unpublished doctoral dissertation). Rutgers, The State University of New Jersey, New Brunswick, NJ.

Thayer, L. (1968). *Communication and communication systems.* Homewood, IL: Irwin.

von Bertalanffy, L. (1975). General systems theory. In R. W. Budd & B. D. Ruben (Eds.), *Interdisciplinary approaches to human communication* (pp. 95–118). Rochelle Park, NJ: Hayden Book Company, Inc.

10. Ruben, B. D., DeLisi, R., & Gigliotti, R. A. (2017). *A guide for leaders in higher education: Core concepts, competencies and tools.* Sterling, VA: Stylus Publishing.

11. Gioia, D. A., & Chittipeddi, K. (1991). Sensemaking and sensegiving in strategic change initiation. *Strategic Management Journal, 12*(6), 433–448.

12. Rafferty, A. E., Jimmieson, N. L., & Armenakis, A. A. (2013). Change readiness: A multilevel review. *Journal of Management, 39*(1), 110–135.

Steigenberger, N. (2015). Emotions in sensemaking: A change management perspective. *Journal of Organizational Change Management, 28*(3), 432–451.

13. Bartel, C. A., & Saavedra, R. (2009). The collective construction of work group moods. *Administrative Science Quarterly, 45*(2), 197–231.

14. Armenakis, A. A., & Harris, S. G. (2009). Reflections: Our journey of organizational change research and practice. *Journal of Change Management, 9*(2), 127–142.

Smith, K. K., & Crandell, S. D. (1984). Exploring collective emotion. *American Behavioral Scientist, 27*(6), 813–828.

15. Sesame Street. (2012). A la peanut butter sandwiches. The Amazing Mumford.

16. Armenakis, A. A., Bernerth, J. B., Pitts, J. P., & Walker, H. J. (2007). Organizational change recipients' beliefs scale: Development of an assessment instrument. *The Journal of Applied Behavioral Science, 43*, 481–505.

Armenakis, A. A., & Harris, S. G. (2009). Reflections: Our journey of organizational change research and practice. *Journal of Change Management, 9*(2), 127–142.

17. Armenakis, A. A., Bernerth, J. B., Pitts, J. P., & Walker, H. J. (2007). Organizational change recipients' beliefs scale: Development of an assessment instrument. *The Journal of Applied Behavioral Science, 43*, 481–505.

18. Armenakis, A. A., Bernerth, J. B., Pitts, J. P., & Walker, H. J. (2007). Organizational change recipients' beliefs scale: Development of an assessment instrument. *The Journal of Applied Behavioral Science, 43*, 481–505. Quote p. 494.

Chapter 12

Phase 3

Implementation

WHAT YOU CAN EXPECT TO
LEARN IN THIS CHAPTER

- What are the eight steps to a successful planned organizational change effort?
- What are the six steps of the awareness program?

Finding the right balance to lead a successful planned organizational change effort can be a daunting task even for a leader who has done so before. Let's look at the steps and key factors for a successful planned change implementation program.[1]

STEPS TO SUCCESSFUL PLANNED
CHANGE PROGRAMS

Step 1: Planning
Step 2: Awareness
Step 3: Agreement
Step 4: Involvement
Step 5: Commitment
Step 6: Action
Step 7: Integration
Step 8: Assessment

Step 1: Planning

The first step to a successful planned change program is proper planning and assessing the organization's capacity to successfully tackle the change effort.[2] Before involving others in the organization, the leader should have already conducted the self-discovery process in chapter 10. This includes an analysis of leader worldviews; a possible shift of those worldviews integrating happiness; a gap analysis of leadership styles and competencies; resources to improve in leadership areas and/or delegation strategy; and a plan to use these self-discovery strategies to move forward with the rest of planning for the change effort.

The organizational capacity to tackle the change effort includes an assessment of the leader's commitment and resources required to implement the change effort.[3] The reasons, business, and otherwise, goals and vision for change must be determined along with an identification of the areas where change is required. In addition, organizational members must participate in the process to prepare and finalize plans for action.[4] Keep in mind that these steps don't always flow from one to the other in order. Sometimes they occur in tandem.

Because the change effort requires buy-in from all organizational members, and because there will be a multitude of worldviews, it's imperative to begin the planning step by involving organizational members from all areas and in all levels of the organization to form a change team. From defining goals to choosing a change strategy, the more organizational members involved, the more chance of success the change effort has. The team is led by the leader, who is visible to all organizational members as the person in charge and committed to the effort. A change agent is appointed.

The change team determines the need for the change effort first by conducting a SWOT analysis or similar analysis that considers issues both internal and external to the organization. The internal assessments should include analyses of the leader and organizational members as discussed in chapters 10 and 11, as well as a variety of key performance indicators that relate to the change effort. These could be financial, student satisfaction, admission rates, and so on. The environmental scan will analyze any external force that could impact the organization such as government regulations, economy, population statistics, and more.

Next, team members will discuss which subsystems and members of the organization will be affected; identify skeptics and opinion leaders; and assess organizational member's potential commitment to and capability to make the change. Then the goal(s) and vision must be defined, made clear, and agreed upon. The rollout plan, including strategies and tactics, will be developed next. This should include crafting of the key message to be used throughout the effort.

This key message is the same one that was discussed in chapter 11 that provides an overlap between the desired outcome of the change effort and the wants, needs, desires, and hopes of the organizational members. This key message will be specific and consistent in topics such as the vision, need to change, urgency, plan, goals, benefits, and expectations for the change program for individuals, teams, and the organization as a whole. This message should be, "clear, brief, focused, memorable, energizing, future-oriented, and responsive to constituent issues."[5] Keep in mind that this messaging will be key to helping organizational members commit to the planned change effort. The planning team will agree on, document, and assign responsibilities and deadlines to the plan.[6] Finally, team members must begin their campaign to prepare organizational members for step two.

Step 2: Awareness

Think of this step as a continuum from unaware to fully aware.[7] An awareness program to make all organizational members fully aware of the need to change as developed in the SWOT analysis is implemented by the change team.[8] Again, keep in mind that the steps for successful change are not linear. In fact, they overlap quite a bit. There are six stages of the awareness program:

1. Kickoff
2. Formulation of smaller working teams
3. Weekly team activity reports
4. Formal opportunities for organizational members to get together to talk about the change effort
5. Formal progress updates
6. A celebration when the effort has achieved its goal and become a part of the normal way of doing things.

1. Kickoff

The change effort begins with a formal kickoff event where the leader will clearly and briefly explain the need for the change, outlining the decisions that led to this choice. What is the problem? What are the alternatives, choices, and consequences of each? Present the information clearly and guide organizational members to understand what you learned and how that informed the decisions you made about the change effort. Provide them with sensegiving to help them see a clear vision of the future and why this change effort is needed, is urgent, and is a priority.

Review the resources, capabilities, and contingency plans in place to support the change effort. Publicly commit your dedication to the change effort and outline strategies, processes, and a timeline for events, deadlines, progress, and plans for feedback. Be clear that you believe that you have the right people in place, including your organizational members, for a successful change effort.

Pointedly share the idea that to accomplish the change effort successfully, everyone will be responsible to keep the effort an urgent priority. Further explain that if something gets in the way of keeping the effort a priority that they need to "raise a flag" and let someone know who can remove their obstacle. Develop an easy way for these issues to be submitted directly to the leader or change agent. Then have a process in place to reply to the organizational member immediately and to solve the issue quickly. If you make a promise and fail to follow through, the change effort and your credibility will likely be questioned. This will delay or derail the change effort.

Throughout the kickoff, it is critical that organizational members are infused with your joy over the future vision of what's to come from it. Smile. Tell them why you are grateful about the opportunity to make this change. Share your happiness and positivity. Remember it's catchy! Make a splash. Get organizational members excited. Give them a t-shirt, maybe some other goodies they can have in front of them to keep the effort in the front of their mind. Have balloons, cake, singers—whatever means celebration to your organizational members.

2. Formulation of Smaller Working Teams

As more organizational members become aware of the change effort, there is a need to involve them in smaller, working teams. The role of these teams will depend on the goals of the change effort. In some instances, there might be a team with a focus on admissions, in others assessment, and so on. Be sure to tap into that in-house subject matter expert list you compiled in chapter 11 for team membership. However, don't stop there. You should be able to gather a sample of many different organizational members. Think about involving not only administrative and faculty but also facilities and food service members. These members are especially aware of issues with students, faculty, and staff as their daily work involves interaction with most, if not all, organizational members.

3. Weekly Team Activity Reports

The next step of the awareness program is the production of a weekly team activity report indicating key happenings with the change program. Depending on the organization, there may be several channels to distribute the report. For example, postings in the cafeteria, paycheck stuffers, information slides on televisions monitors in hallways and break areas, email, hard copy delivered to offices and departments, bulletin boards, the university portal, and any other channels appropriate for your organizational members. The administrative marketing department may have information about what channels are best for each organizational member group. If not, this might be a good time for a communication audit.

4. Formal Opportunities for Organizational Members to Get Together to Talk about the Change Effort

As discussed throughout this book, it is imperative to monitor the communication environment, provide a method to promote sensemaking, and decrease levels of uncertainty and skepticism. One way to do this is through formal town meetings held periodically, which include time for organizational members from all levels to get together to catch up with each other, discuss the change effort, and ask questions. As organizational members talk with each other about the change effort, they will be sharing their worldviews, hearing others' worldviews, and continuing to cocreate a shared reality of the change effort.

Leaders can take this opportunity to monitor the communication, learn about any incorrect rumors or messages, and to make corrective messages so that all organizational members share the same understanding of the vision and goals for the change effort. At the same time, organizational members have an opportunity to socially influence the direction and thinking of the leader and other organizational members.

Communication, in this sense, involves the way organizational members use information to make sense of their situation and cocreate their social reality. This is accomplished through the back-and-forth negotiation of meaning and the social influence of organizational members. As such, the leader should always be prepared to see things from others worldview.

5. Formal Progress Updates

Formal progress updates should occur in person, if possible. Any public presentations should also be recorded and uploaded to the University portal so that organizational members not in attendance can watch them at a later time. The town meeting is an ideal way to hold these.

Provide information to the organizational members about the progress made on each initiative of the change effort, any obstacles, and measures to remove the obstacles. It's also important to review the vision, goals, timeline, restate the leader's commitment to the effort and providing resources, and remind organizational members of their part of the plan.

One of the most important things to do is to acknowledge the efforts of those within the organization who have made a distinctive effort or achievement to further the change effort. Acknowledge as many people as you can because this is a moment to celebrate.

Who doesn't like to be acknowledged for their work? It doesn't take much. Bring in an ice cream truck, serve lunch, have cake or coffee or both. Give them a reason to get out of their office and come to the meeting. And, smile. Be positive. Remember, your emotions can spread to others!

6. Celebration

It may seem odd to include the final celebration in an awareness campaign, but think about it as the last attempt to catch anyone who is still not aware of the change effort. There may be recently hired organizational members or the occasional member who really had no clue.

Go big. Your organizational members have conquered their fears and anxieties and have completed a major turnaround for your organization. Yes, they now work for a better organization and their job is safe. However, remember that they accomplished some version of the change that you wanted. It was hard work, at times. They put their faith in your direction. Tell them how proud they made you. Celebrate with them. Pop some bubbly (if that's allowed), bring in the band. Be sure to clearly spell out what their accomplishments mean to the organization, to their department, and especially to them as individuals.

If you've been taking photos along the way, have your marketing department (or maybe a student group) assemble a slide show of all the major steps along the way to show at this event. It will remind organizational members of just how far they have come. Send everyone home with some sort of memento. Again, it doesn't have to be anything expensive or big. It could be something to put into their office, something to use at home or something for their car. You'd be amazed how far a t-shirt or other university swag goes.

Step 3: Understanding of and Agreement about the Need to Change

As leaders or change agents create, provide, and exchange information and messages to organizational members about the change effort, it is with the intention that those messages and information will enable organizational members to become aware of the need, priority, and urgency for change.[9] However, this awareness does not come without much hard work.

At this stage, the change team needs to assess organizational member's perceptions about the organization's and their own readiness and capability to change. The organization's readiness and capability to change was assessed by a SWOT in step 1. Hopefully, it's ready. Now you need to find out if your organizational members share that belief. There are five beliefs your organizational members need and you can assess them using the Organizational Change Recipient's Beliefs Scale.[10]

The readiness model assesses organizational member's perception of whether or not the organization is ready and capable of tackling the change effort. In doing so, leaders must provide organizational members with a legitimate and clear vision for the change that provides clear evidence of a gap, or *discrepancy*, between the current and desired organizational state or performance.[11]

This establishes a sense of urgency and helps organizational members to understand reasons for and goals of the change effort. Most importantly, this will help organizational members to come to the conclusion that there is a need for the change, and come to agreement that the chosen change effort to remove the discrepancy is *appropriate* to solve the problem faced by the organization.[12]

Efficacy, or the belief by organizational members that they are capable of completing the change effort, is the next part of the model.[13] This is reinforced by *principal support*, where leaders, change agents, and peers (perhaps informal leaders and social influencers) are viewed by organizational members as supportive, committed, and willing to provide enough resources to see the change effort through.[14]

Elements of trust and values in the organization, leaders and change agents play a role here. Especially where change efforts are frequent, organizational members may not trust that "this is the time they really mean it!" If organizational member values match those of the organization, it is more likely that organizational members will find support valid.

Finally with *valence*, there must be an expected benefit of the change effort for everyone involved.[15] Leaders can provide extrinsic, such as increased department resources and pay increases, or intrinsic rewards, such as "more autonomy for decision making" to organizational members.[16] Many organizational members find a benefit of change efforts is that their department and individual work processes improve in some meaningful way.[17]

Step 4: Involvement

As the awareness campaign rolls out, the change team will recruit organizational members from all levels of the organization to take a bigger role in the effort. This stage of involvement may happen in several different steps. The first step may occur prior to the formation of the change team. Another may occur during the awareness campaign, prior to the rollout plan, or any other opportunities that arise during the change effort.

It's never too late to get someone involved. Involve everyone in the organization. Even if some people are involved only in meetings about the change effort or they decide that they just want to show up for ice cream and cake. The opportunity to get involved must be genuine and available to everyone.

Organizational members who are involved in actions from defining goals, choosing a change strategy, collecting data and more are more likely to support the program and see it through.[18] In addition, the more involved organizational members are, the more they believe that

- they can carry out and complete the change,
- the change strategy that was chosen was the right one,
- there really is a need for change, and
- there are benefits to the change.[19]

Step 5: Commitment

Leaders need to commit publicly to support the change and the change strategy.[20] To do so, leaders and change agents need to spend some time to determine what type and how much commitment is needed on their part and for organizational members at all levels of the organization. In smaller organizations, holding focus groups or interviewing organizational members helps to accomplish this goal. However, if the organization is large, spans several states or countries, and consists of people working in dispersed locations (e.g., telecommuting), then a quantitative survey similar to the five beliefs scale detailed earlier is ideal.[21]

The survey should focus on the five beliefs—(a) discrepancy: organizational members see a reason to change; (b) appropriateness: members agree that the change strategy chosen is the right one; (c) efficacy: we are capable of making the change; (d) visible leadership commitment: leaders and change agents are visibly supportive of the change effort; and (e) valence: there is a benefit that is appealing to me—and the awareness program:—the information provided by the weekly team activity report and other discussion opportunities keep me informed about the change effort.

In addition to the survey, the leader will complete a Visible Leadership Commitment Checklist (see box 12.1) and the results from both will be compiled into a Dashboard of key planned change indicators, which will be administered and analyzed by the change agent. Results of the survey, checklist, and Dashboard will be presented quarterly to the change team, leaders, and organizational members.

BOX 12.1 VISIBLE LEADERSHIP COMMITMENT CHECKLIST

Indicate what you are doing as a leader of this change effort for the following key factors:

1. How (will you) are you monitoring organizational member sensemaking process?
2. How (will you) are you monitoring organizational member uncertainty?
3. How (will you) are you monitoring organizational member skepticism?
4. How (will you) are you providing feedback to organizational members?
5. How (will you) are you gathering feedback from organizational members?
6. How (will you) are you keeping the organizational change effort a top priority?
7. What types of rewards (will you) do you provide, and how, to organizational members?
8. How (will you) do you share success stories with organizational members?
9. How (will you) do you share stories about the vision with organizational members?
10. How (will you) do you monitor and reassess resource allocation?
11. How (will you) do you know you have enough change agents?
12. How (will your) are your change agents making sure that organizational members from all levels are aware, involved, and engaged?
13. How (will your) are your change agents working with organizational members to fulfill the change effort?
14. How (will you) are you keeping momentum strong?
15. How (will you) are you showing your confidence in change agents, strategies, change team, and organizational members' abilities to complete the change effort?
16. How (will you) are you telling stories about the values and meaning of the change effort?
17. How (will you) do you ensure that the perspectives from all levels of the organization are heard?
18. What (will your) does your Success Dashboard tell you about the health of your change effort?
19. What (will) do the results of the employee survey tell you about the health of your change effort?

Source: Smulowitz, S. (2014). Planned organizational change in Higher Education: Dashboard indicators and stakeholder sensemaking—A case study. (Unpublished doctoral dissertation). Rutgers, The State University of New Jersey, New Brunswick, NJ.

Note: Slightly adapted from original source.

The importance of measuring these items periodically throughout the change program is to ensure that organizational members have confidence that the change program is important to the health of the organization and that it is fully supported by everyone in the organization. If the change agent finds that organizational members show a decrease in any of the indicators, then the change agent, along with the change team and any other organizational members who want to be involved, can determine the appropriate strategy to improve that indicator.

For example, should the survey reveal that the people do not perceive that they are fully aware of the progress of the change program, then the change agent can increase or add elements to the awareness program. If the survey shows that all or most of the indicators are declining, then the change agent can modify the program so that it does not fail. It is important to include organizational members in this step so that they feel part of and buy into the process.

Step 6: Action

This is considered the implementation phase, where organizational members are working toward the change.[22] Begin the kickoff with some fanfare where the leaders, change agents, and change team gather all organizational members to celebrate the start of the new vision. This is a key opportunity for leaders to show they are committed to the change effort by telling the story of the vision and showing confidence in the rollout.

Periodically throughout the change program process, the survey and leadership checklist should be administered again and the key performance indicators should be updated regularly on the Dashboard. Ensuring the awareness program is taking place is essential as is monitoring the communication environment and employee sensemaking of the change effort. Throughout the effort, the leader should continue to tell success stories and engage in conversation with organizational members about the change program.

Step 7: Integration

To get to the integration stage is the cause for great celebration because this is when the change has become routine in the organization—part of the culture. It becomes the new way of "how things are done around here." This is the time to have the big celebration and recognize organizational member's hard work. This is also the time for the leader to further reinforce and show continuing support for any new "processes, structures and mechanisms" that have been created to sustain the change effort.[23]

Step 8: Assessment

Not everyone is a fan of assessment so expect to see eye rolls. Remind organizational members that assessment provides a way to ensure time, resources, and money are being spent in the right places.[24] In addition, assessment provides an opportunity to demonstrate the success of your change effort.[25]

While this is listed as the last step, there should be assessment happening at least quarterly to determine if the key performance indicators are being met. These will differ depending on the goals of the change effort. One key performance indicator might be the number of incoming freshmen, another may display retention numbers, and another may display fundraising goals and so on (see table 12.1).

Certainly, another look at this data at the expected end point of the change effort is expected. Was the initial or modified goal of the change effort met? What was learned throughout the process? How can those lessons become a part of a continuous plan to improve going forward?

SUMMARY

There are eight steps to a successful planned organizational change effort. Careful planning of each step of the change effort is recommended for increased success. The second step, awareness, is important for every member of the organization at every level of the organization. This is often the step that impedes success. When organizational members have agreement for the need to change, they often find themselves becoming more involved, which increases the chance that they will see the change through to fruition.

It is vital that leaders are seen as and remain fully committed to the change effort. Once organizational members perceive that leaders are no longer committed to the effort, then they will abandon it as well. Action or implementation of the change effort is when organizational members are moving forward with the change. The goal of the effort is to make it a permanent part of the organization so that it is integrated and becomes part of the culture.

Finally, there must be an assessment of the change effort. Was the goal met? What lessons were learned throughout the process? How can those lessons be used to strengthen the organization moving forward? Although these steps are discussed here in a linear fashion, some of the steps occur simultaneously or overlap. Leaders, change agents and the change team need to be aware of the importance of each step and be prepared for challenges that can arise at each step.

Table 12.1   Sample Dashboard with Key Performance Indicators

	2016	2017	2018	2019
Admissions Applications				
My Institution	20,000	21,000	22,000	23,000
Peer Institution	21,000	22,000	23,000	24,000
Aspirant Institution	24,000	25,000	27,000	30,000
Admissions Deposits				
My Institution	10,000	12,000	13,000	15,000
Peer Institution	11,000	12,000	14,000	14,500
Aspirant Institution	12,000	13,000	15,000	16,000
Admissions Enrollment				
My Institution	8,000	10,000	11,000	13,000
Peer Institution	9,000	10,000	12,000	12,250
Aspirant Institution	10,000	11,000	13,500	15,000
Total Fundraising				
My Institution	$10,000,000	$12,000,000	$14,000,000	$16,000,000
Peer Institution	$10,500,000	$12,000,000	$14,500,000	$16,500,000
Aspirant Institution	$15,000,000	$18,500,000	$20,000,000	$23,500,000
Student Satisfaction: Career Services				
My Institution	78% ex/good	80% ex/good	82% ex/good	86% ex/good
Peer Institution	78% ex/good	79% ex/good	79% ex/good	80% ex/good
Aspirant Institution	86% ex/good	89% ex/good	90% ex/good	93% ex/good
Student Satisfaction: Academics				
My Institution	92% ex/good	93% ex/good	94% ex/good	95% ex/good
Peer Institution	90% ex/good	90% ex/good	90% ex/good	90% ex/good
Aspirant Institution	97% ex/good	97% ex/good	98% ex/good	98% ex/good

Note: Dashboard key indicators will vary by institution and change program. These key indicators are for example only.

NOTES

1. The Steps to Successful Planned Change Programs was adapted from several sources including the following: Armenakis & Harris, 2002; Lewin, 1945; Lippitt, Watson & Westley, 1958; Neely, 1999; Ruben, 2009a; Weisbord, 1987.

2. Smulowitz, S. (2014). Planned organizational change in Higher Education: Dashboard indicators and stakeholder sensemaking—A case study (Unpublished doctoral dissertation). Rutgers, The State University of New Jersey, New Brunswick, NJ.

Weisbord, M. R. (1987). Toward third-wave managing and consulting. *Organizational Dynamics, 15*(3), 5–24.

3. Smulowitz, S. (2014). Planned organizational change in Higher Education: Dashboard indicators and stakeholder sensemaking—A case study (Unpublished doctoral dissertation). Rutgers, The State University of New Jersey, New Brunswick, NJ.

4. Tromp, S. A., & Ruben, B. D. (2004). *Strategic planning in higher education: A leader's guide. Planning and Improvement in Colleges and Universities* (2nd ed.). Washington, DC: NACUBO.

5. Ruben, B. D. (2009). *Understanding, planning and leading organizational change: Core concepts and strategies.* Washington, DC: National Association of College and University Business Officers. Quote p. 19.

6. Tromp, S. A., & Ruben, B. D. (2004). *Strategic planning in higher education: A leader's guide. Planning and Improvement in Colleges and Universities* (2nd ed.). Washington, DC: NACUBO.

7. Smulowitz, S. (2014). Planned organizational change in Higher Education: Dashboard indicators and stakeholder sensemaking—A case study (Unpublished doctoral dissertation). Rutgers, The State University of New Jersey, New Brunswick, NJ.

8. Smulowitz, S. (2014). Planned organizational change in Higher Education: Dashboard indicators and stakeholder sensemaking—A case study (Unpublished doctoral dissertation). Rutgers, The State University of New Jersey, New Brunswick, NJ.

9. Armenakis, A. A., Harris, S. G., & Mossholder, K. W. (1993). Creating readiness for organizational change. *Human Relations, 46*(June), 681–703.

Lewin, K. (1946). Action research and minority problems. *Journal of Social Issues, 2*(4), 34–46.

Lippitt, R., Watson, J., & Westley, B. (1958). *Dynamics of planned change.* New York, NY: Harcourt Brace.

Ruben, B. D. (2009). *Understanding, planning, and leading organizational change: Core concepts and strategies.* Washington, DC: National Association of College and University Business Officers.

Smulowitz, S. (2014). Planned organizational change in Higher Education: Dashboard indicators and stakeholder sensemaking—A case study (Unpublished doctoral dissertation). Rutgers, The State University of New Jersey, New Brunswick, NJ.

10. Armenakis, A. A., Bernerth, J. B., Pitts, J. P., & Walker, H. J. (2007). Organizational change recipients' beliefs scale: Development of an assessment instrument. *The Journal of Applied Behavioral Science, 43*, 481–505.

11. Armenakis, A. A., Bernerth, J. B., Pitts, J. P., & Walker, H. J. (2007). Organizational change recipients' beliefs scale: Development of an assessment instrument. *The Journal of Applied Behavioral Science, 43*, 481–505.

Armenakis, A. A., & Harris, S. G. (2002). Crafting a change message to create transformational readiness. *Journal of Organizational Change Management, 15*(2), 169–183.

Holt, D. T., Armenakis, A., Field, H. S., & Harris, S. G. (2007). Readiness for organizational change: The systematic development of a scale. *The Journal of Applied Behavioral Science, 43*(2), 232–255.

Holt, D. T., Armenakis, A., Harris, S. G., & Field, H. S. (2007). Toward a comprehensive definition of readiness for change: A review of research and instrumentation. *Research in Organizational Change and Development, 16*, 289–336.

12. Armenakis, A. A., Bernerth, J. B., Pitts, J. P., & Walker, H. J. (2007). Organizational change recipients' beliefs scale: Development of an assessment instrument. *The Journal of Applied Behavioral Science, 43*, 481–505.

Armenakis, A. A., & Harris, S. G. (2002). Crafting a change message to create transformational readiness. *Journal of Organizational Change Management, 15*(2), 169–183.

13. Armenakis, A. A., Bernerth, J. B., Pitts, J. P., & Walker, H. J. (2007). Organizational change recipients' beliefs scale: Development of an assessment instrument. *The Journal of Applied Behavioral Science, 43*, 481–505.

Armenakis, A. A., & Harris, S. G. (2002). Crafting a change message to create transformational readiness. *Journal of Organizational Change Management, 15*(2), 169–183.

Holt, D. T., Armenakis, A., Field, H. S., & Harris, S. G. (2007). Readiness for organizational change: The systematic development of a scale. *The Journal of Applied Behavioral Science, 43*(2), 232–255.

Holt, D. T., Armenakis, A., Harris, S. G., & Field, H. S. (2007). Toward a comprehensive definition of readiness for change: A review of research and instrumentation. *Research in Organizational Change and Development, 16*, 289–336.

14. Armenakis, A. A., Harris, S. G., & Mossholder, K. W. (1993). Creating readiness for organizational change. *Human Relations, 46*(June), 681–703.

Armenakis, A. A., Bernerth, J. B., Pitts, J. P., & Walker, H. J. (2007). Organizational change recipients' beliefs scale: Development of an assessment instrument. *The Journal of Applied Behavioral Science, 43*, 481–505.

15. Armenakis, A. A., Bernerth, J. B., Pitts, J. P., & Walker, H. J. (2007). Organizational change recipients' beliefs scale: Development of an assessment instrument. *The Journal of Applied Behavioral Science, 43*, 481–505.

Armenakis, A. A., & Harris, S. G. (2002). Crafting a change message to create transformational readiness. *Journal of Organizational Change Management, 15*(2), 169–183.

Holt, D. T., Armenakis, A., Field, H. S., & Harris, S. G. (2007). Readiness for organizational change: The systematic development of a scale. *The Journal of Applied Behavioral Science, 43*(2), 232–255.

Holt, D. T., Armenakis, A., Harris, S. G., & Field, H. S. (2007). Toward a comprehensive definition of readiness for change: A review of research and instrumentation. *Research in Organizational Change and Development, 16*, 289–336.

16. Armenakis, A. A., Bernerth, J. B., Pitts, J. P., & Walker, H. J. (2007). Organizational change recipients' beliefs scale: Development of an assessment instrument. *The Journal of Applied Behavioral Science, 43*, 481–505. Quote p. 488.

17. Smulowitz, S. (2014). Planned organizational change in Higher Education: Dashboard indicators and stakeholder sensemaking—A case study (Unpublished doctoral dissertation). Rutgers, The State University of New Jersey, New Brunswick, NJ.

18. Smulowitz, S. (2014). Planned organizational change in Higher Education: Dashboard indicators and stakeholder sensemaking—A case study (Unpublished doctoral dissertation). Rutgers, The State University of New Jersey, New Brunswick, NJ.

19. Armenakis, A. A., Harris, S. G., & Mossholder, K. W. (1993). Creating readiness for organizational change. *Human Relations, 46*(June), 681–703.

20. Armenakis, A. A., Harris, S. G., & Mossholder, K. W. (1993). Creating readiness for organizational change. *Human Relations, 46*(June), 681–703.

Ruben, B. D. (2009). *Understanding, planning, and leading organizational change: Core concepts and strategies.* Washington, DC: National Association of College and University Business Officers.

21. Armenakis, A. A., & Harris, S. G. (2002). Crafting a change message to create transformational readiness. *Journal of Organizational Change Management, 15*(2), 169–183.

22. Lewin, K. (1946). Action research and minority problems. *Journal of Social Issues, 2*(4), 34–46.

Lippitt, R., Watson, J., & Westley, B. (1958). *Dynamics of planned change.* New York, NY: Harcourt Brace.

Ruben, B. D. (2009). *Understanding, planning, and leading organizational change: Core concepts and strategies.* Washington, DC: National Association of College and University Business Officers.

23. Ruben, B. D. (2009). *Understanding, planning, and leading organizational change: Core concepts and strategies.* Washington, DC: National Association of College and University Business Officers.

24. Ruben, B. D. (2009). *Understanding, planning, and leading organizational change: Core concepts and strategies.* Washington, DC: National Association of College and University Business Officers.

25. Ruben, B. D. (2009). *Understanding, planning, and leading organizational change: Core concepts and strategies.* Washington, DC: National Association of College and University Business Officers.

Conclusion

The need for ongoing, planned organizational change in organizations is growing. This is true especially in institutions of higher education where the impetus for change has been particularly dramatic in the assessment of performance and outcomes, and in the use of the resulting information to document, report upon, and improve institutional effectiveness.

Leaders and those who desire to lead institutions of higher education can learn many important facts, concepts, and strategies to plan for, implement, and celebrate planned organizational change efforts. Attention to the role the leader plays and the associated perceived level of commitment by organizational members is not to be overlooked. If organizational members do not perceive the leader to be committed to the change effort, then they will find good reason to move onto other activities and even regress to structures or procedures they had in place prior to the introduction of the change effort. In particular, attention must be given to the following:

- Creation, clarity and communication of vision
- Communication and information exchange
- Sustained momentum
- Sustained priority
- Feedback to and from organizational members
- Resources
- Uncertainty reduction
- Participation and awareness of all organizational members

Considering planned change efforts as purposeful efforts to change, or disrupt, the dynamics and harmony of the system provide a good basis for understanding the complications of change effort in general. The disruption and subsequent attempts to restore harmony occur through communication and information processing. It is through these processes that members of a system cocreate the restored version of the system to enable organization and functionality.[1]

Communication can be both an impediment and a facilitator and, as such, is vital to any change effort. The lack of information exchange previous to and throughout the planned organizational change effort can lead to member uncertainty and skepticism about the

- purpose,
- commitment,
- benefit,
- importance,
- priority, and
- sustainability of the effort.

The culmination of these issues leads participants of the planned organizational change effort to experience frustration, disgust, and even shutdown, which can contribute to the perception that the effort failed. When, in fact, it wasn't the effort that failed, but a failure in the information exchange from the leader.

The decisions about communication strategy and frequency of information exchange made by leaders "affect the perceptions, concerns, assessments and interactions" of other members of the organization.[2] Without a continual give-and-take of information, negotiated meaning of messages and social influence organizational members will have a tough time making sense of the planned change effort and as a result will find it difficult to find harmony to restore the system.[3] It is the interaction and social influence between the different levels of employees that "in part" affect the outcomes of a planned, organizational change effort.[4] Thus, it is communication in the sense of a shared understanding of the purpose and goal of the effort as a key facilitator for a perception of leadership commitment throughout the organization about the change effort.[5]

This perception of the leader's commitment determines the way the organizational member views the planned change effort. As organizational members make sense of the change effort and the leaders' commitment they socially create their shared reality of the effort. This is a key moment where organizational members decide whether to buy-in, resist, or go along with the planned change effort.

This book gives you, the leader, the knowledge and tools to enact successful change. While every change is unique, you are certain to find strategies and tools here to aid your journey.

Persist and stay happy.

NOTES

1. Berger, P. L., & Luckmann, T. (1967). *The social construction of reality: A treatise in the sociology of knowledge.* Garden City, NY: Doubleday.

Burr, V. (2003). *Social constructionism* (2nd ed.). New York, NY: Routledge.

2. Lewis, L. K. (2007). An organizational stakeholder model of change implementation communication. *Communication Theory, 17,* 176–204. Quote p. 181.

3. Barge, J. K., & Fairhurst, G. T. (2008). Living leadership: A systemic constructionist approach. *Leadership Quarterly, 4*(3), 227–251.

Berger, P. L., & Luckmann, T. (1967). *The social construction of reality: A treatise in the sociology of knowledge.* Garden City, NY: Doubleday.

Fairhurst, G. T. (2008). Discursive leadership: A communication alternative to leadership psychology. *Management Communication Quarterly, 21*(4), 510–521.

Miller, J. G. (1965). Living systems: Basic concepts. *Behavioral Science, 10*(3), 193–237.

Ruben, B. D. (1983). A system-theoretic view. In W. B. Gudykunst (Ed.), *Intercultural communication theory* (pp. 131–145). Beverly Hills, CA: Sage.

Ruben, B. D., DeLisi, R., & Gigliotti, R. A. (2017). *A guide for leaders in higher education: Core concepts, competencies and tools.* Sterling, VA: Stylus Publishing.

Thayer, L. (1968). *Communication and communication systems.* Homewood, IL: Irwin.

von Bertalanffy, L. (1975). General systems theory. In R. W. Budd & B. D. Ruben (Eds.), *Interdisciplinary approaches to human communication* (pp. 95–118). Rochelle Park, NJ: Hayden Book Company, Inc.

Weick, K. E. (1979). *The social psychology of organizing* (2nd ed.). Reading, MA: Addison Wesley.

Weick, K. E. (1995). *Sensemaking in organizations.* Thousand Oaks, CA: Sage.

Weick, K. E. (2001). *Making sense of the organization.* Malden, MA: Blackwell Publishing.

Westley, B. H., & MacLean, M. S. (1970). A conceptual model for communications research. In K. K. Sereno & C. D. Mortensen (Eds.), *Foundations of communication theory* (pp. 103–107). New York, NY: Harper and Row Publishers.

4. Lewis, L. K. (2007). An organizational stakeholder model of change implementation communication. *Communication Theory, 17,* 176–204.

5. See also p. 151 Lewis, L. K. (2000). Communicating change: Four cases of quality programs. *The Journal of Business Communication, 37*(2), 128–155.

References

REFERENCES CH. 1

Argyris, C., & Schon, D. A. (1974). *Theory in practice: Increasing professional effectiveness.* San Francisco, CA: Jossey Bass.

Argyris, C., & Schon, D. A. (1978). *Organizational learning.* Reading, MA: Addison-Wesley.

Armenakis, A. A., Harris, S. G., & Mossholder, K. W. (1993). Creating readiness for organizational change. *Human Relations, 46*(June), 681–703.

Ashforth, B. E., & Mael, F. (1989). Social identity theory and the organization. *Academy of Management Review, 12*(1), 20–39.

Bordia, P., Hobman, E., Jones, E., Gallois, C., & Callan, V. J. (2004). Uncertainty during organizational change: Types, consequences, and management strategies. *Journal of Business and Psychology, 18*(4), 507–532.

Brower, R. S., & Abolafia, M. Y. (1995). The structural embeddedness of resistance among public managers. *Group and Organization Management, 20*(2), 149–166.

Burke, W. W. (2008). *Organization change: Theory and practice* (2nd ed.). Thousand Oaks, CA: Sage Publishing.

Cameron, K. S., & Quinn, R. E. (2006). *Diagnosing and changing organizational culture.* San Francisco, CA: Jossey-Bass.

Coch, L., & French, J. L. P. Jr. (1948). Overcoming resistance to change. *Human Relations, 1*(4), 512–532.

Dent, E. B., & Goldberg, S. G. (1999). Challenging "resistance to change." *Journal of Applied Behavioral Science, 35*(1), 45–47.

Fairhurst, G. T. (1993). Echoes of the vision: When the rest of the organizational talks Total Quality. *Management Communication Quarterly, 6*, 331–371.

Ford, J., & Ford, L. W. (2010). Stop blaming resistance to change and start using it. *Organizational Dynamics, 39*(1), 24–36.

Ford, J. D., Ford, L. W., & D'Amelio, A. (2008). Resistance to change: The rest of the story. *The Academy of Management Review (AMR), 33*(2), 362–377.

Gersick, C. J. G. (1991). Revolutionary change theories: A multilevel exploration of the punctuated equilibrium paradigm. *The Academy of Management Review, 16*(1), 10–36.

Kee, J. E., & Newcomer, K. E. (2008). Why do change efforts fail?: What can leaders do about it? *The Public Manager, 37*(3), 5–12.

Klein, K. J., & Sorra, J. S. (1996). The challenge of innovation implementation. *Academy of Management Review, 21*(4), 1055–1080.

Kotter, J. P., & Heskett, J. L. (1992). *Corporate culture and performance.* New York, NY: The Free Press.

Lewis, L. K. (1999). Disseminating information and soliciting input during planned organizational change: Implementers' targets, sources, and channels for communicating. *Management Communication Quarterly, 13*(1), 43–75.

Lewis, L. K. (2000). "Blindsided by that on" and "I saw that one coming": The relative anticipation and occurrence of communication problems and other problems in implementer' hindsight. *Journal of Applied Communication Research, 28*(1), 44–67.

Lewis, L. K. (2006). Employee perspectives on implementation communication as predictors of perceptions of success and resistance. *Western Journal of Communication, 70*(1), 23–46.

Lewis, L. K. (2011). *Organizational change: Creating change through strategic communication.* Malden, MA: Wiley-Blackwell.

Lewis, L. K., Schmisseur, A., Stephens, K., & Weir, K. (2006). Advice on communicating during organizational change: The content of popular press books. *Journal of Business Communication, 43*(2), 1–25.

Moullin, M. (2002). *Delivering excellence in health and social care.* Buckingham, UK: Open University Press.

Orlikowski, W. J. (1993). The duality of technology: Rethinking the concept of technology in organizations. *Organization Science, 3*(3), 398–427.

Piderit, S. K. (2000). Rethinking resistance and recognizing ambivalence: A multidimensional view of attitudes toward an organizational change. *Academy of Management Review, 25*(4), 783–794.

Poole, M. S., & Van de Ven, A. H. (2004). *Handbook of organizational change and innovation.* New York: Oxford University Press.

Ruben, B. D. (2009). *Understanding, planning, and leading organizational change: Core concepts and strategies.* Washington, DC: National Association of College and University Business Officers.

Schein, E. H. (1985). *Organizational culture and leadership.* San Francisco, CA: Jossey-Bass.

Shapiro, D. L., Lewicki, R. J., & Devine, P. (1995). When do employees choose deceptive tactics to stop unwanted organizational change? *Research on Negotiation in Organizations, 5*, 155–184.

Smulowitz, S. (2014). Planned organizational change in Higher Education: Dashboard indicators and stakeholder sensemaking—A case study (Unpublished doctoral dissertation). Rutgers, The State University of New Jersey, New Brunswick, NJ.

Standish Group. (2000). Extreme CHAOS. Retrieved from www.standishgroup.com /sample_research/index.php.

Steigenberger, N. (2015). Emotions in sensemaking: A change management perspective. *Journal of Organizational Change Management, 28*(3), 432–451.

Watson, T. J. (1982). Group ideologies and organizational change. *Journal of Management Studies, 19*(3), 259–275.

Weick, K. E., & Quinn, R. E. (1999). Organizational change and development. *Annual Review of Psychology, 50*, 361–386.

Wheatley, M. J., & Keller-Rogers, M. (1998). Bringing life to organizational change. *Journal of Strategic Performance Measurement April/May*, 6–13.

Zorn, T., Christensen, L. T., & Cheney, G. (1999). *Do we really want constant change? Beyond the bottom line series.* San Francisco, CA: Berrett-Koehler Communications Inc.

REFERENCES CH. 2

Adams, C., & Neely, A. (2000). The Performance Prism to boost M&A success. *Measuring Business Excellence, 4*(3), 19–23.

Armenakis, A. A., & Harris, S. G. (2009). Reflections: Our journey of organizational change research and practice. *Journal of Change Management, 9*(2), 127–142.

Bennis, W. G. (1993). *Beyond bureaucracy: Essays on the development and evolution of human organization.* San Fransisco, CA: Jossey-Bass Publishers.

Bennis, W. G. (1996). *Changing organizations.* New York, NY: McGraw-Hill Book Company.

Blake, R. R., & Mouton, J. S. (1964). *The managerial grid: Key orientations for achieving production through people.* Houston, TX: Gulf Publishing Co.

CHEA (2019). *2019-202 director of CHEA-recognized organizations.* Washington, DC: Council for Higher Education Accreditation.

Chin, R., & Benne, K. D. (1985). General strategies for effecting change in human systems. In W. G. Bennis, K. D. Benne, & R. Chin (Eds.), *The planning of change* (4th ed.). New York, NY: Holt, Rinehart & Winston.

Eckerson, W. (2011). *Performance dashboards: Measuring, monitoring and managing your business* (2nd ed.). Hoboken, NJ: John Wiley & Sons.

French, W. L., & Bell, Jr., C. H. (1990). *Organization development: Behavioral science interventions for organization improvement* (4th ed.). Englewood Cliffs, NJ: Prentice-Hall.

Friedlander, F., & Brown, L. D. (1974). Organization development. *Annual Review of Psychology, 33*, 313–341.

Kaplan, R. S., & Norton, D. P. (1996). *The balanced scorecard: Translating strategy into action.* Boston, MA: Harvard Business School Press.

Lewin, K. (1951). *Field theory in social science.* New York: Harper & Brothers Publishers.

Lewis, L. K., Schmisseur, A., Stephens, K., & Weir, K. (2006). Advice on communicating during organizational change: The content of popular press books. *Journal of Business Communication, 43*(2), 1–25.

Lippitt, R., Watson, J., & Westley, B. (1958). *Dynamics of planned change.* New York, NY: Harcourt, Brace.

Lunger, K. (2006). Why you need more than a dashboard to manage your strategy. *Business Intelligence Journal, 11*(4), 8–17.

Moullin, M. (2002). *Delivering excellence in health and social care.* Buckingham, UK: Open University Press.

Neely, A. (1999). The performance measurement revolution: Why now and what next? *International Journal of Operations and Production Management, 19*(2), 205–228.

Neely, A., Adams, C., & Crowe, P. (2001). The Performance Prism in practice. *The Academy of Management Review, 5*(2), 6–12.

Ruben, B. D. (2009a). *Understanding, planning, and leading organizational change: Core concepts and strategies.* Washington, DC: National Association of College and University Business Officers.

Ruben, B. D. (2009b). *Excellence in higher education guide 2009: An integrated approach to assessment, planning and improvement in colleges and universities.* Washington, DC: National Association of College and University Business Officers.

Ruben, B. D. (2009c). *Excellence in higher education workbook 2009: An integrated approach to assessment, planning and improvement in colleges and universities.* Washington, DC: National Association of College and University Business Officers.

Sashkin, M., & Burke, W. W. (1987). Organization development in the 1980's. *Journal of Management, 13*(2), 393–417.

Smulowitz, S. (2014). Planned organizational change in Higher Education: Dashboard indicators and stakeholder sensemaking—A case study (Unpublished doctoral dissertation). Rutgers, The State University of New Jersey, New Brunswick, NJ.

U.S. Department of Education. (2006). *The spellings commission report.* Washington, DC: Department of Education.

Weick, K. E., & Quinn, R. E. (1999). Organizational change and development. *Annual Review of Psychology, 50*, 361–386.

Weisbord, M. R. (1987). Toward third-wave managing and consulting. *Organizational Dynamics, 15*(3), 5–24.

REFERENCES CH. 3

Bateson, G. (1996). Communication. In H. B. Mokros (Ed.), *Interaction and identity: Information and behaviour: Vol. 5* (pp. 45–70). New Brunswick, NJ: Transaction Publishers.

Belkin, N. J., & Robertson, S. E. (1976). Information science and the phenomenon of information. *Journal of the American Society for Information Science, 27*(4), 197–204.

Berger, P. L., & Luckmann, T. (1967). *The social construction of reality: A treatise in the sociology of knowledge.* Garden City, NY: Doubleday.

Blumer, H. (1979). Symbolic interaction. In R. W. Budd & B. D. Ruben (Eds.), *Interdisciplinary approaches to human communication* (pp. 135–153). Rochelle Park, New Jersey: Hayden Book Company, Inc.

Burr, V. (2003). *Social constructionism* (2nd ed.). New York, NY: Routledge.

Craig, R. T. (1999). Communication theory as a field. *Communication Theory, 9*(2), 119–161.

Dance, F. (1967). *Human communication theory.* New York: Holt, Rinehart & Winston.

Delgado, J. M. R. (1979). Neurophysiology. In R. W. Budd & B. D. Ruben (Eds.), *Interdisciplinary approaches to human communication* (pp. 119–134). Rochelle Park, NJ: Hayden Book Company, Inc.

Dervin, B. (1977). Useful theory for librarianship: Communication, not information. *Drexel Library Quarterly, 13*(3), 16–32.

Frings, H. (1979). Zoology. In R. W. Budd & B. D. Ruben (Eds.), *Interdisciplinary approaches to human communication* (pp. 33–55). Rochelle Park, New Jersey: Hayden Book Company, Inc.

Halloran, J. D. (1985). Information and communication: Information is the answer, but what is the question? In B. D. Ruben (Ed.), *Information & behavior: Vol. 1* (pp. 27–39). New Brunswick: Transaction Books.

Katz, E., & Lazarsfeld, P. F. (1955). *Personal influence.* New York, NY: The Free Press.

Lasswell, H. D. (1948). The structure and function of communication in society. In L. Bryson (Ed.), *The communication of ideas: A series of addresses* (pp. 37–51). New York, NY: Institute for Religious and Social Studies.

Miller, J. G. (1965). Living systems: Basic concepts. *Behavioral Science, 10*(3), 193–237.

Mokros, H. B., & Ruben, B. D. (1991). Understanding the communication-information relationship: Levels of information and contexts of availabilities. *Knowledge: Creation, Diffusion, Utilization, 12*(4), 373–388. Quote p. 378.

Peters, J. D. (1999). Introduction: The problem of communication. In J. D. Peters (Ed.), *Speaking into the air: A history of the idea of communication* (pp. 1–31). Chicago: University of Chicago.

Rafaeli, S. (1988). From new media to communication. *Sage Annual Review of Communication Research: Advancing Communication Science, 16*, 110–134.

Ruben, B. D. (1972). General system theory: An approach to human communication. In R. W. Budd & B. D. Ruben (Eds.), *Approaches to human communication* (pp. 120–144). New York, NY: Spartan.

Ruben, B. D. (1979). General system theory. In R. W. Budd & B. D. Ruben (Eds.), *Interdisciplinary approaches to human communication* (pp. 95–118). Rochelle Park, NJ: Hayden Book Company, Inc.

Ruben, B. D. (1992). The communication-information relationship in system-theoretic perspective. *Journal of the American Society for Information Science, 43*(1), 15–27.

Ruben, B. D., & Stewart, L. P. (2006). *Communication and human behavior* (5th ed.). Boston, MA: Pearson Education.

Shannon, C. E., & Weaver, W. (1949). *The mathematical theory of communication.* Urbana, IL: University of Illinois Press.

Smith, A. G. (1979). Anthropology. In R. W. Budd & B. D. Ruben (Eds.), *Interdisciplinary approaches to human communication* (pp. 57–70). Rochelle Park, NJ: Hayden Book Company, Inc.

Thayer, L. (1968). *Communication and communication systems.* Homewood, IL: Irwin.

Thayer, L. (1979). Communication: Sine qua non of the behavioral sciences. In R. W. Budd & B. D. Ruben (Eds.), *Interdisciplinary approaches to human communication* (pp. 7–31). Rochelle Park, NJ: Hayden Book Company, Inc.

von Bertalanffy, L. (1950). An outline of general systems theory. *The British Journal for the Philosophy of Science, 1*(2), 134–165.

von Bertalanffy, L. (1968). General system theory: Foundations. In *Development Applications* (p. 3). New York, NY: George Braziller, Inc.

Watzlawick, B., Beavin, J., & Jackson, D. (1967). *Pragmatics of human communication.* London: Faber & Faber.

Weick, K. E. (1995). *Sensemaking in organizations.* Thousand Oaks, CA: Sage.

Weick, K. E. (1979). *The social psychology of organizing* (2nd ed.). Malden, MA: Blackwell Publishing.

Weick, K. E. (2001). *Making sense of the organization.* Malden, MA: Blackwell Publishing.

Westley, B. H., & MacLean, M. S. (1957). A conceptual model for communications research. *Journalism Quarterly, 34*(1), 31–38.

Wiener, N. (1966). Cybernetics. In A. G. Smith (Ed.), *Communication and culture: Readings in the codes of human interaction* (pp. 25–35). New York: Holt, Rinehart and Winston.

REFERENCES CH. 4

Achor, S. (2010). *The happiness advantage: How a positive brain fuels success in work and life.* New York, NY: CURRENCY.

Argyris, C. (1955). Organizational leadership and participative management. *The Journal of Business, 28*(1), 1–7.

Argyris, C., & Schon, D. A. (1978). *Organizational learning.* Reading, MA: Addison-Wesley.

Barge, J. K., & Fairhurst, G. (2008). Living leadership: A systemic constructionist approach. *Leadership Quarterly, 4*(3), 227–251.

Bass, B. M. (1985). *Leadership and performance beyond expectations.* New York: Free Press.

Bennis, W. G. (1959). Leadership theory and administrative behavior: The problem of authority. *Administrative Science Quarterly, 4,* 259–301.

Bion, W. R. (1961). *Experiences in groups.* London: Tavistock.

Blake, R. R., & McCanse, A. A. (1991). *Leadership dilemmas: Grid solutions.* Houston, TX: Gulf Publishing Company.

Blake, R. R., & Mouton, J. S. (1964). *The managerial grid.* Houston, TX: Gulf Publishing Company.

Blake, R. R., & Mouton, J. S. (1978). *The new managerial grid.* Houston, TX: Gulf Publishing Company.

Blake, R. R., & Mouton, J. S. (1985). *The managerial grid III.* Houston, TX: Gulf Publishing Company.

Blanchard, K., Zigarmi, D., & Nelson, R. (1993). Situational Leadership® after 25 years: A retrospective. *Journal of Leadership Studies, 1*(1), 22–36.

Blanchard, K., Zigarmi, D., & Zigarmi, D. (2013). *Leadership and the one minute manager: Increasing effectiveness through Situational Leadership® II.* New York: William Morrow.

Brubaker, D. L. (2006). *The charismatic leader: The presentation of self and the creation of educational settings.* Thousand Oaks, CA: Corwin Press.

Cobb, A. T., & Margulies, N. (1981). Organization development: A political perspective. *The Academy of Management Review, 6*(1), 49–59.

Conger, J., & Kanungo, R. (1987). Toward a behavioral theory of charismatic leadership in organizational settings. *The Academy of Management Review, 12*(4), 637–647.

George, B. (2003). *Authentic leadership: Rediscovering the secrets to creating lasting value.* San Francisco: Jossey-Bass.

Georgopoulous, B. S., Mahoney, G. M., & Jones, Jr., N. W. (1957). "A path-goal approach to productiv- ity." *Journal of Applied Psychology, 41,* 345–353.

Graen, G. B., & Uhi-Bien, M. (1995). Relationship-based approach to leadership: Development of leader-member exchange (LMX) theory of leadership over 25 years: Applying a multi-level, multi-domain perspective. *Leadership Quarterly, 6*(2), 219–247.

Heifetz, R. A. (1994). *Leadership without easy answers.* Cambridge, MA: Belknap Press.

Heifetz, R. A., & Laurie, D. L. (1997). The work of leadership. *Harvard Business Review, 7*(1), 124–134.

Hersey, P., & Blanchard, K. H. (1969). Life-cycle theory of leadership. *Training and Development Journal, 23,* 26–34.

Holmberg, I., & Tyrstrup, M. (2010). Well then – What now? An everyday approach to managerial leadership. *Leadership, 6*(4), 353–372.

House, R. (1971). A path goal theory of leader effectiveness. *Administrative Science Quarterly, 16*(3), 321–339.

House, R. J. (1977). A 1976 theory of charismatic leadership. In J. G. Hunt & L. L. Larson (Eds.), *Leadership: The cutting edge* (pp. 199–272). Carbondale: Southern Illinois University Press.

Jung, D., & Sosik, J. J. (2006). Who are the spellbinders? Identifying personal attributes of charismatic leaders. *Journal of Leadership & Organizational Studies, 12*, 12–27.

Katz, R. L. (1955). Skills of an effective administrator. *Harvard Business Review, 33*(1), 33–42.

Kets de Vries, M. F. R. (1979, July/August). Managers can drive their subordinates mad. *Harvard Business Review*, 125–134.

Kets de Vries, M. F. R. (1989). Leaders who self-destruct: The causes and cures. *Organizational Dynamics, 17*(4), 4–17.

Kets de Vries, M. F. R. (2009). *Reflections on leadership and character*. London: Wiley.

Kets de Vries, M. F. R. (2011). *Reflections on groups and organizations: On the couch with Manfred Kets de Vries*. London: Wiley.

Kirkpatrick, S. A., & Locke, E. A. (1991). Leadership: Do traits matter? *Academy of Management Executive, 5*(2), 48–60.

Labianca, G., Gray, B., & Brass, D. J. (2000). A grounded model of organizational schema change during empowerment. *Organization Science, 11*(2), 235–257.

Liden, R. C., Wayne, S. J., Zhao, H., & Henderson, D. (2008). Servant leadership: Development of a multidimensional measure and multi-level assessment. *Leadership Quarterly, 19*, 161–177.

Lieberson, S., & O'Connor, J. F. (1972). Leadership and organizational performance: A study of large corporations. *American Sociological Review, 37*(2), 117–130.

Martin, A. (2007). *Everyday leadership*. Center for Creative Leadership https://www.ccl.org/articles/white-papers/everyday-leadership/.

McDougall, J. (1985). *Theater of the mind*. New York: Basic Books.

Mumford, M. D., Zacaro, S. J., Harding, F. D., Jacobs, T. O., & Fleishman, E. A. (2000). Leadership skills for a changing world: Solving complex social problems. *Leadership Quarterly, 11*(1), 11–35.

Nadler, D. A., & Tushman, M. L. (1990). Beyond the charismatic leader: Leadership and organizational change. *California Management Review, 32*(2), 77–97.

Northouse, P. G. (2016). *Leadership: Theory and practice* (7th ed.). Los Angeles: Sage Publications, Inc.

Paulhus, D. L., & John, O. P. (1998). Egoistic and moralistic biases in self-perception: The interplay of self-deceptive styles with basic traits and motives. *Journal of Personality, 66*(6), 1025–1060.

Porras, J. I., & Berg, P. O. (1978). The impact of organization development. *Academy of Management Review, 3*, 249–266.

Porras, J. I., & Silvers, R. C. (1991). Organization development and transformation. *Annual Review of Psychology, 42*, 51–78.

Ruben, B. D. (2006). *What leaders need to know and do: A leadership competencies scorecard*. Washington, DC: NACUBO.

Ruben, B. D., DeLisi, R., & Gigliotti, R. A. (2017). *A guide for leaders in higher education: Core concepts, competencies and tools*. Sterling, VA: Stylus Publishing.

Sashkin, M., & Burke, W. W. (1987). Organization development in the 1980's. *Journal of Management, 13*(2), 393–417.

Smulowitz, S. (2014). Planned organizational change in Higher Education: Dashboard indicators and stakeholder sensemaking—A case study (Unpublished doctoral dissertation). Rutgers, The State University of New Jersey, New Brunswick, NJ.

Stogdill, R. M. (1948). Personal factors associated with leadership: A survey of the literature. *Journal of Psychology, 25*, 35–71.

Vroom, V. H. (1964). *Work and motivation.* New York: McGraw Hill.

Weick, K. E. (1995). *Sensemaking in organizations.* Thousand Oaks, CA: Sage.

REFERENCES CH. 5

Andrews, M. (2015, June 30). What do employers want? *Inside Higher Education.* Retrieved from: https://www.insidehighered.com/blogs/stratedgy/what-do-emplo yers-want.

Bienen, H. (2017, January 24). The role of major Universities in their local communities. *The Evolution.* Retrieved from: https://evolllution.com/revenue-streams/ market_opportunities/the-role-of-major-universities-in-their-local-communities/.

Brint, S. (2018). *Two cheers for Higher Education: Why American Universities are stronger than ever – and how to meet the challenges they face.* Princeton, NJ: Princeton University Press.

Brint, S. (2019). Is this Higher Education's golden age? The Chronicle of Higher Education: The Chronicle Review. Retrieved from: https://www.chronicle.com/ interactives/golden-age.

Community Relations. (2018). *Economic and community impact.* Scranton, PA: The University of Scranton. Retrieved from: https://www.scranton.edu/about/comm unity-relations/economic-impact.shtml.

Jaschik, S. (2019, January 23). For Provosts, more pressure on tough issues. *Inside Higher Education.* Retrieved from: https://www.insidehighered.com/news/survey /2019-inside-higher-ed-survey-chief-academic-officers.

Lederman, D. (2019a, January 16). Why MOOCs didn't work in 3 data points. *Inside Higher Education.* Retrieved from: https://www.insidehighered.com/digital-learni ng/article/2019/01/16/study-offers-data-show-moocs-didnt-achieve-their-goals.

Lederman, D. (2019b, January 16). How many public universities can "go big"online? *Inside Higher Education.* Retrieved from: https://www.insidehighered.com/digital-l earning/article/2019/03/20/states-and-university-systems-are-planning-major-online.

Miller, J. G. (1965). Living systems: Basic concepts. *Behavioral Science, 10*(3), 193–237.

Mohrman, S. A., Mohrman, A. M., & Ledford, G. E. (1989). Interventions that change organizations. In A. M. Mohrman, S. A. Mohrman, G. E. Ledford, E. E. Lawler & Associates (Eds.), *Large scale organizational change.* San Francisco, CA: Jossey-Bass Publishers, Inc.

Robinson, J. A. (2017, Oct. 16). Should all university property be tax exempt? *The James G. Martin Center for Academic Renewal.* Retrieved from: https://www.jam esgmartin.center/2017/10/university-property-tax-exempt/.

Ruben, B. D. (1983). A system-theoretic view. In W. B. Gudykunst (Ed.), *Intercultural communication theory* (pp. 131–145). Beverly Hills, CA: Sage.

Ruben, B. D., & Stewart, L. P. (2006). *Communication and human behavior* (5th ed.). Boston, MA: Pearson Education.

Schneider, M., & Klor de Alva, J. (2016, July 8). Why should rich universities get huge property tax exemptions? *The Washington Post.* Retrieved from: https://ww w.washingtonpost.com/news/grade-point/wp/2016/07/08/why-should-rich-univers ities-get-huge-property-tax-exemptions/?noredirect=on&utm_term=.280ff6ca324e.

Smulowitz, S. (2014). Planned organizational change in Higher Education: Dashboard indicators and stakeholder sensemaking—A case study (Unpublished doctoral dissertation). Rutgers, The State University of New Jersey, New Brunswick, NJ.

Thayer, L. (1968). *Communication and communication systems.* Homewood, IL: Irwin.

U.S. Department of Education. (2006). *The Spellings Commission report.* Washington, DC: Department of Education.

von Bertalanffy, L. (1950). An outline of general systems theory. *The British Journal for the Philosophy of Science, 1*(2), 134–165.

Weick, K. E. (1976). Educational organizations as loosely coupled systems. *Administrative Science Quarterly, 21*, 1–19.

REFERENCES CH. 6

Armenakis, A. A., & Harris, S. G. (2009). Reflections: Our journey of organizational change research and practice. *Journal of Change Management, 9*(2), 127–142.

ASHE-ERIC Higher Education Report. (2001). Special issue: Understanding and facilitating organizational change in the 21st century: Recent research and conceptualizations. *ASHE-ERIC Higher Education Report, 28*(4), 1–162.

Aune, B. P. (1995). The human dimension of organizational change. *Review of Higher Education, 18*(2), 149–173.

Bordia, P., Hobman, E., Jones, E., Gallois, C., & Callan, V. J. (2004). Uncertainty during organizational change: Types, consequences, and management strategies. *Journal of Business and Psychology, 18*(4), 507–532.

Boyce, M. E. (2003). Organizational learning is essential to achieving and sustaining change in higher education. *Innovative Higher Education, 28*(2), 119–136.

Burchard, B. (2017). *High performance habits: How extraordinary people become that way.* USA: Hay House, Inc.

Colvin, T. J., & Kilmann, R. H. (1990). Participant perceptions of positive and negative influences on large-scale change. *Group and Organizational Studies, 15*, 233–248.

Conrad, C. (1978). A grounded theory of academic change. *Sociology of Education, 51*(2), 101–112.

Gersick, C. J. G. (1991). Revolutionary change theories: A multilevel exploration of the punctuated equilibrium paradigm. *The Academy of Management Review, 16*(1), 10–36.

Gioia, D. A., & Thomas, J. B. (1996). Identity, image, and issue interpretation: Sensemaking during strategic change in academia. *Administrative Science Quarterly, 41*, 370–403.

Gluesing, J. C., & Gibson, C. B. (2004). Designing and forming global teams. In H. W. Lane, M. L. Maznevski, M. E. Mendenhall, & J. McNett (Eds.), *Handbook of global management* (pp. 199–226). Malden, MA: Blackwell Publishing.

Guskin, A. (1996). Facing the future: The change process in restructuring universities. *Change, The Magazine of Higher Learning, 28*(4), 27-37.

Johnstone, D. B., Dye, N. S., & Johnson, R. (1998). Collaborative leadership for institutional change. *Liberal Education, 84*(2), 12-20.

Kezar, A. (2005). Consequences of radical change in governance: A grounded theory approach. *The Journal of Higher Education, 76*(6), 634–668.

Klein, K. J., & Sorra, J. S. (1996). The challenge of innovation implementation. *Academy of Management Review, 21*(4), 1055–1080.

Levinson, D. J. (1978). *The seasons of a man's life.* New York, NY: Knopf.

Lewis, L. K. (2000). Communicating change: Four cases of quality programs. *The Journal of Business Communication, 37*(2), 128–155.

Lewis, L. K. (2007). An organizational stakeholder model of change implementation communication. *Communication Theory, 17*, 176–204.

Lewis, L. K., Schmisseur, A., Stephens, K., & Weir, K. (2006). Advice on communicating during organizational change: The content of popular press books. *Journal of Business Communication, 43*(2), 1–25.

Lewis, L. K., & Seibold, D. R. (1993). Innovation modification during intraorganizational adoption. *Academy of Management Review, 18*, 322–354.

Lewis, L. K., & Seibold, D. R. (1996). Communication during intraorganizational innovation adoption: Predicting users' behavioral coping responses to innovations in organizations. *Communication Monographs, 63*, 131–157.

Lueddeke, G. R. (1999). Toward a constructivist framework for guiding change and innovation in higher education. *The Journal of Higher Education, 70*(3), 235–260.

Miller, D., & Friesen, P. (1980). Archetypes of organizational transition. *Administrative Science Quarterly, 25*(2), 268–299.

Newcombe, J. P., & Conrad, C. F. (1981). A theory of mandated academic change. *The Journal of Higher Education, 52*(6), 555–577.

Schuster, J. H., & Finkelstein, M. J. (2007). On the brink: Assessing the status of the American Faculty. Research & Occasional Paper Series: CSHE. 3.07. *Center for Studies in Higher Education.*

Simsek, H., & Louis, K. S. (1994). Organizational change as paradigm shift: Analysis of the change process in a large, public university. *The Journal of Higher Education, 65*(6), 670–695.

Smulowitz, S. M. (2007). When does culture matter, and to whom? *Journal of Intercultural Communication Studies, 16*(1), 1–13.

Smulowitz, S. (2014). Planned organizational change in Higher Education: Dashboard indicators and stakeholder sensemaking—A case study (Unpublished doctoral dissertation). Rutgers, The State University of New Jersey, New Brunswick, NJ.

REFERENCES CH. 7

Albrecht, T., & Hall, B. (1991). Facilitating talk about new ideas: The role of personal relationships in organizational innovation. *Communication Monographs, 58*, 273–288.

ASHE-ERIC Higher Education Report. (2001). Special issue: Understanding and facilitating organizational change in the 21st Century: Recent research and conceptualizations. *ASHE-ERIC Higher Education Report, 28*(4), 1–162. Quote p. 117.

Ashford, S. J. (1988). Individual strategies for coping with stress during organizational transitions. *The Journal of Applied Behavioral Science, 24*, 19–36.

Aune, B. P. (1995). The human dimension of organizational change. *Review of Higher Education, 18*(2), 149–173.

Barge, J. K., & Fairhurst, G. T. (2008). Living leadership: A systemic constructionist approach. *Leadership Quarterly, 4*(3), 227–251.

Bolman, L. G., & Deal, T. E. (1991). *Reframing organizations: Artistry, choice and leadership.* San Fransisco, CA: Jossey-Bass.

Bordia, P., Hobman, E., Jones, E., Gallois, C., & Callan, V. J. (2004). Uncertainty during organizational change: Types, consequences, and management strategies. *Journal of Business and Psychology, 18*(4), 507–532.

Crossan, M. M., Lane, H. W., & White, R. E. (1999). An organizational learning framework: From intuition to institution. *Academy of Management Review, 24*(3), 522–537.

Fairhurst, G. T. (1993). Echoes of the vision: When the rest of the organization talks Total Quality. *Management Communication Quarterly, 6*, 331–371.

Fairhurst, G. T. (2008). Discursive leadership: A communication alternative to leadership psychology. *Management Communication Quarterly, 21*(4), 510–521.

Gallivan, M. J. (2001). Meaning to change: How diverse stakeholders interpret organizational communication about change initiatives. *IEEE Transactions on Professional Communication, 44*, 243–266.

Gersick, C. J. G. (1991). Revolutionary change theories: A multilevel exploration of the punctuated equilibrium paradigm. *The Academy of Management Review, 16*(1), 10–36.

Johnstone, D. B., Dye, N. S., & Johnson, R. (1998). Collaborative leadership for institutional change. *Liberal Education, 84*(2), 12-20.

Lewis, L. K. (1999). Disseminating information and soliciting input during planned organizational change: Implementers' targets, sources, and channels for communicating. *Management Communication Quarterly, 13*(1), 43–75.

Lewis, L. K. (2000). Communicating change: Four cases of quality programs. *The Journal of Business Communication, 37*(2), 128–155.

Lewis, L. K., Hamel, S. A., & Richardson, B. K. (2001). Communicating change to nonprofit stakeholders: Models and predictors of implementers' approaches. *Management Communication Quarterly, 15*, 5–41.

Lewis, L. K., & Russ, T. L. (2011). Soliciting and using input during organizational change initiatives: What are practitioners doing? *Management Communication Quarterly, 26*(2), 267–294.

Lewis, L. K., Schmisseur, A., Stephens, K., & Weir, K. (2006). Advice on communicating during organizational change: The content of popular press books. *Journal of Business Communication, 43*(2), 1–25.

Lewis, L. K., & Seibold, D. R. (1993). Innovation modification during intraorganizational adoption. *Academy of Management Review, 18*, 322–354.

Piderit, S. K. (2000). Rethinking resistance and recognizing ambivalence: A multidimensional view of attitudes toward an organizational change. *Academy of Management Review, 25*(4), 783–794.

Rogers, E. M. (1995). *Diffusion of innovations* (4th ed.). New York: Free Press. pp. 371–404.

Schneider, B. (1990). The climate for service: An application for the climate construct. In B. Schneider (Ed.), *Organizational climate and culture* (pp. 383–412). San Francisco, CA: Jossey-Bass Publishers.

Simsek, H., & Louis, K. S. (1994). Organizational change as paradigm shift: Analysis of the change process in a large, public university. *The Journal of Higher Education, 65*(6), 670–695.

Smulowitz, S. (2014). Planned organizational change in higher education: Dashboard indicators and stakeholder sensemaking—A case study (Unpublished doctoral dissertation). Rutgers, The State University of New Jersey, New Brunswick, NJ.

Timmerman, C. E. (2003). Media selection during the implementation of planned organizational change: A predictive framework based on implementation approach and phase. *Management Communication Quarterly, 16*(3), 301–340.

Weick, K. E. (1995). *Sensemaking in organizations.* Thousand Oaks, CA: Sage.

Zorn, T. (2002). The emotionality of information and communication technology implementation. *Journal of Communication Management, 7*(2), 160–171.

REFERENCES CH. 8

Barge, J. K., & Fairhurst, G. (2008). Living leadership: A systemic constructionist approach. *Leadership Quarterly, 4*(3), 227–251.

Berger, P. L., & Luckmann, T. (1967). *The social construction of reality: A treatise in the sociology of knowledge.* Garden City, NY: Doubleday.

Blumer, H. (1979). Symbolic interaction. In R. W. Budd & B. D. Ruben (Eds.), *Interdisciplinary approaches to human communication* (pp. 135–153). Rochelle Park, New Jersey: Hayden Book Company, Inc.

Burr, V. (2003). *Social constructionism* (2nd ed.). New York, NY: Routledge.

Conrad, C. (1978). A grounded theory of academic change. *Sociology of Education, 51*(2), 101–112.

Ford, J. D., & Ford, L. W. (1995). The role of conversations in producing intentional change in organizations. *The Academy of Management Review, 20*(3), 541–570. Quote p. 560.

Ford, J., & Ford, L. W. (2010). Stop blaming resistance to change and start using it. *Organizational Dynamics, 39*(1), 24–36.

Halloran, J. D. (1985). Information and communication: Information is the answer, but what is the question? In B. D. Ruben (Ed.), *Information & behavior: Vol. 1* (pp. 27–39). New Brunswick: Transaction Books.

Johnstone, D. B., Dye, N. S., & Johnson, R. (1998). Collaborative leadership for institutional change. *Liberal Education, 84*(2), 12-20.

Lewis, L. K. (2000). "Blindsided by that one" and "I saw that one coming": The relative anticipation and occurrence of communication problems and other problems in implementers' hindsight. *Journal of Applied Communication Research, 28*(1), 44–67.

Lewis, L. K. (2007). An organizational stakeholder model of change implementation communication. *Communication Theory, 17*, 176–204.

Lewis, L. K. (2011). *Organizational change: Creating change through strategic communication*. Malden, MA: Wiley-Blackwell.

Mohrman, S. A., Mohrman, A. M., & Ledford, G. E. (1989). Interventions that change organizations. In A. M. Mohrman, S. A. Mohrman, G. E. Ledford, E. E. Lawler & Associates (Eds.), *Large scale organizational change*. San Francisco, CA: Jossey-Bass Publishers, Inc.

Poole, M. S. (2009). Adaptive structuration theory. In E. Griffin (Ed.), *A first look at communication theory* (7th ed., pp. 235–246). New York: McGraw Hill.

Ruben, B. D. (1983). A system-theoretic view. In W. B. Gudykunst (Ed.), *Intercultural Communication Theory* (pp. 131–145). Beverly Hills, CA: Sage.

Ruben, B. D. (1979). General system theory. In R. W. Budd & B. D. Ruben (Eds.), *Interdisciplinary approaches to human communication* (pp. 95–118). Rochelle Park, New Jersey: Hayden Book Company, Inc.

Ruben, B. D., DeLisi, R., & Gigliotti, R. A. (2017). *A guide for leaders in higher education: Core concepts, competencies and tools*. Sterling, VA: Stylus Publishing.

Ruben, B. D., & Gigliotti, R. A. (2019). *Leadership, communication, and social influence: A theory of resonance, activation, and cultivation*. Bingley/West Yorkshire, UK: Emerald Publishing.

Ruben, B. D., & Kim, J. Y. (Eds.). (1975). *General systems and human communication theory*. Rochelle Park, NJ: Hayden Book Company, Inc.

Ruben, B. D., & Stewart, L. P. (2006). *Communication and human behavior* (5th ed.). Boston, MA: Pearson Education.

Shane, P. (1990). Why are so many people so unhappy? Habits of thought and resistance to diversity in legal Education. *Iowa Law Review, 75*, 1033–1056.

Smith, A. G. (1979). Anthropology. In R. W. Budd & B. D. Ruben (Eds.), *Interdisciplinary approaches to human communication* (pp. 57–70). Rochelle Park, New Jersey: Hayden Book Company, Inc.

Smulowitz, S. (2014). Planned organizational change in Higher Education: Dashboard indicators and stakeholder sensemaking—A case study (Unpublished doctoral dissertation). Rutgers, The State University of New Jersey, New Brunswick, NJ.

Thayer, L. (1979). Communication: Sine qua non of the behavioral sciences. In R. W. Budd & B. D. Ruben (Eds.), *Interdisciplinary approaches to human communication* (pp. 7–31). Rochelle Park, New Jersey: Hayden Book Company, Inc.

von Bertalanffy, L. (1950). An outline of general systems theory. *The British Journal for the Philosophy of Science, 1*(2), 134–165.

von Bertalanffy, L. (1975). General system theory. In R. W. Budd & B. D. Ruben (Eds.), *Interdisciplinary approaches to human communication* (pp. 95–118). Rochelle Park, NJ: Hayden Book Company, Inc.

Weick, K. E. (1979). *The social psychology of organizing* (2nd ed.). Reading, MA: Addison Wesley.

Weick, K. E. (1995). *Sensemaking in organizations*. Thousand Oaks, CA: Sage.

Weick, K. E. (2001). *Making sense of the organization*. Malden, MA: Blackwell Publishing.

REFERENCES CH. 9

Allen, M. M. C. (2014). Hirschman and voice. In A. Wilkinson, J. Donaghey, T. Dundon, & R. Freeman (Eds.), *The handbook of research on employee voice* (pp. 36–51). Cheltenham and New York: Edward Elgar Press.

Allen, N. J., & Meyer, J. P. (1990). The measurement and antecedents of affective, continuance and normative commitment to the organization. *Journal of Occupational Psychology, 63*, 1–18.

Edwards, P., Collinson, D., & Rocca, G. D. (1995). Workplace resistance in Western Europe: A preliminary overview and a research agenda. *European Journal of Industrial Relations, 1*(3), 283–316.

Fulmer, C. A., & Ostroff, C. (2017). Trust in direct leaders and top leaders: A trickle-up model. *Journal of Applied Psychology, 102*(4), 648.

Hamilton, G. G., & Feenstra, R. C. (1997). Varieties of hierarchies and markets: An introduction. In M. Orru, N. W. Biggart, & G. G. Hamilton (Eds.), *The economic organization of East Asian capitalism* (pp. 55–96). Thousand Oaks, CA: Sage.

Naus, F., van Iterson, A., & Roe, R. (2007). Organizational cynicism: Extending the exit, voice, loyalty, and neglect model of employees' responses to adverse conditions in the workplace. *Human Relations, 60*(5), 683–718.

Thomas, G. F., Zolin, R., & Hartman, J. L. (2009). The central role of communication in developing trust and its effect on employee involvement. *The Journal of Business Communication, 46*(3), 287–310.

U.S. Department of Education. (2006). *The Spellings Commission report*. Washington, DC: Department of Education.

Whitley, R. (2003). From the search for universal correlations to the institutional structuring of economic organization and change: The development and future of organization studies. *Organization, 10*(3), 481–501.

REFERENCES CH. 10

Achor, S. (2013). *Before happiness: The five hidden keys to achieving success, spreading happiness, and sustaining positive change.* New York, NY: Random House.

Barge, J. K., & Fairhurst, G. T. (2008). Living leadership: A systemic constructionist approach. *Leadership Quarterly, 4*(3), 227–251.

Coelho, P. (2014). *The alchemist.* New York, NY: HarperOne, Publishers.

Delgado, J. M. R. (1979). Neurophysiology. In R. W. Budd & B. D. Ruben (Eds.), *Interdisciplinary approaches to human communication* (pp. 119–134). Rochelle Park, NJ: Hayden Book Company, Inc.

Dervin, B. (1977). Useful theory for librarianship: Communication, not information. *Drexel Library Quarterly, 13*(3), 16–32.

Fairhurst, G. T. (2008). Discursive leadership: A communication alternative to leadership psychology. *Management Communication Quarterly, 21*(4), 510–521.

Gigliotti, R. A. (2019). An introduction to competencies and competency-based leadership. In R. A. Gigliotti (Ed.), *Competencies for effective leadership: A framework for assessment, education and research.* Bingley, UK: Emerald Publishing Limited.

Lyubormirsky, S. (2008). *The how of happiness: A new approach to getting the life you want.* New York, NY: The Penguin Press.

Northouse, P. (2016). *Leadership theory and practice* (7th ed.). Thousand Oaks, CA: Sage Publishing.

Perlmutter, D. D. (2017, Jan. 1). Administration 101: Deciding to lead. *The Chronicle of Higher Education.* https://www.chronicle.com/article/Administration-101-De ciding/238757.

Strobel, K. (n.d.). Kim Strobel happiness coach: Women rising. https://kimstrobel .com/.

REFERENCES CH. 11

Antonacopoulou, E. P., & Gabriel, Y. (2001). Emotion, learning and organizational change. *Journal of Organizational Change Management, 14*(5), 435–451.

Armenakis, A. A., Bernerth, J. B., Pitts, J. P., & Walker, H. J. (2007). Organizational change recipients' beliefs scale: Development of an assessment instrument. *The Journal of Applied Behavioral Science, 43*, 481–505.

Armenakis, A. A., & Harris, S. G. (2009). Reflections: Our journey of organizational change research and practice. *Journal of Change Management, 9*(2), 127–142.

Bartel, C. A., & Saavedra, R. (2009). The collective construction of work group moods. *Administrative Science Quarterly, 45*(2), 197–231.

Bartunek, J. M., Balogun, J., & Do, B. (2011). Considering planned change a new: Stretching large group interventions strategically, emotionally and meaningfully. *The Academy of Management Annals, 5*(1), 1–52.

Berger, P. L., & Luckmann, T. (1967). *The social construction of reality: A treatise in the sociology of knowledge.* Garden City, NY: Doubleday.

Burr, V. (2003). *Social constructionism* (2nd ed.). New York, NY: Routledge.

Gioia, D. A., & Chittipeddi, K. (1991). Sensemaking and sensegiving in strategic change initiation. *Strategic Management Journal, 12*(6), 433–448.

Huy, Q. N. (1999). Emotional capability, emotional intelligence, and radical change. *Academy of Management Review, 24*(2), 325–345.

Lerner, J. S., & Keltner, D. (2000). Beyond valence: Toward a model of emotion-specific influences on judgement and choice. *Cognition & Emotion, 14*(4), 473–493.

Rafferty, A. E., Jimmieson, N. L., & Armenakis, A. A. (2013). Change readiness: A multilevel review. *Journal of Management, 39*(1), 110–135.

Ruben, B. D. (1983). A system-theoretic view. In W. B. Gudykunst (Ed.), *Intercultural communication theory* (pp. 131–145). Beverly Hills, CA: Sage.

Ruben, B. D., DeLisi, R., & Gigliotti, R. A. (2017). *A guide for leaders in higher education: Core concepts, competencies and tools.* Sterling, VA: Stylus Publishing.

Saunders, M. N., Altinay, L., & Riordan, K. (2009). The management of post-merger cultural integration: Implications from the hotel doctoral dissertation). Rutgers, The State University of New Jersey, New Brunswick, NJ.

Steigenberger, N. (2015). Emotions in sensemaking: A change management perspective. *Journal of Organizational Change Management, 28*(3), 432–451.

Thayer, L. (1968). *Communication and communication systems.* Homewood, IL: Irwin.

Vaara, E. (2000). Constructions of cultural differences in post-merger change processes: A sensemaking perspective on Finnish-Swedish cases. *Management Communication Quarterly, 3*(3), 81–110.

von Bertalanffy, L. (1975). General systems theory. In R. W. Budd & B. D. Ruben (Eds.), *Interdisciplinary approaches to human communication* (pp. 95–118). Rochelle Park, NJ: Hayden Book Company, Inc.

Weick, K. E. (1979). *The social psychology of organizing* (2nd ed.). Reading, MA: Addison Wesley.

Weick, K. E. (1995). *Sensemaking in organizations.* Thousand Oaks, CA: Sage.

REFERENCES CH. 12

Armenakis, A. A., & Harris, S. G. (2002). Crafting a change message to create transformational readiness. *Journal of Organizational Change Management, 15*(2), 169–183.

Armenakis, A. A., Bernerth, J. B., Pitts, J. P., & Walker, H. J. (2007). Organizational change recipients' beliefs scale: Development of an assessment instrument. *The Journal of Applied Behavioral Science, 43*, 481–505.

Armenakis, A. A., Harris, S. G., & Mossholder, K. W. (1993). Creating readiness for organizational change. *Human Relations, 46*, 681–703.

Holt, D. T., Armenakis, A., Field, H. S., & Harris, S. G. (2007). Readiness for organizational change: The systematic development of a scale. *The Journal of Applied Behavioral Science, 43*(2), 232–255.

Holt, D. T., Armenakis, A., Harris, S. G., & Field, H. S. (2007). Toward a comprehensive definition of readiness for change: A review of research and instrumentation. *Research in Organizational Change and Development, 16,* 289–336.

Lewin, K. (1946). Action research and minority problems. *Journal of Social Issues, 2*(4), 34–46.

Lippitt, R., Watson, J., & Westley, B. (1958). *Dynamics of planned change.* New York, NY: Harcourt Brace.

Neely, A. (1999). The performance measurement revolution: Why now and what next? *International Journal of Operations and Production Management, 19*(2), 205–228.

Ruben, B. D. (2009). *Understanding, planning and leading organizational change: Core concepts and strategies.* Washington, DC: NACUBO.

Smulowitz, S. (2014). Planned organizational change in Higher Education: Dashboard indicators and stakeholder sensemaking—A case study (Unpublished doctoral dissertation). Rutgers, The State University of New Jersey, New Brunswick, NJ.

Tromp, S. A., & Ruben, B. D. (2004). *Strategic planning in higher education: A leader's guide. Planning and Improvement in Colleges and Universities* (2nd ed.). Washington, DC: NACUBO.

Weisbord, M. R. (1987). Toward third-wave managing and consulting. *Organizational Dynamics, 15*(3), 5–24.

REFERENCES CONCLUSION

Barge, J. K., & Fairhurst, G. T. (2008). Living leadership: A systemic constructionist approach. *Leadership Quarterly, 4*(3), 227–251.

Berger, P. L., & Luckmann, T. (1967). *The social construction of reality: A treatise in the sociology of knowledge.* Garden City, NY: Doubleday.

Burr, V. (2003). *Social constructionism* (2nd ed.). New York, NY: Routledge.

Fairhurst, G. T. (2008). Discursive leadership: A communication alternative to leadership psychology. *Management Communication Quarterly, 21*(4), 510–521.

Lewis, L. K. (2000). Communicating change: Four cases of quality programs. *The Journal of Business Communication, 37*(2), 128–155.

Lewis, L. K. (2007). An organizational stakeholder model of change implementation communication. *Communication Theory, 17,* 176–204. Quote p. 181.

Miller, J. G. (1965). Living systems: Basic concepts. *Behavioral Science, 10*(3), 193–237.

Ruben, B. D. (1983). A system-theoretic view. In W. B. Gudykunst (Ed.), *Intercultural communication theory* (pp. 131–145). Beverly Hills, CA: Sage.

Ruben, B. D., DeLisi, R., & Gigliotti, R. A. (2017). *A guide for leaders in higher education: Core concepts, competencies and tools.* Sterling, VA: Stylus Publishing.

Thayer, L. (1968). *Communication and communication systems.* Homewood, IL: Irwin.

von Bertalanffy, L. (1975). General systems theory. In R. W. Budd & B. D. Ruben (Eds.), *Interdisciplinary approaches to human communication* (pp. 95–118). Rochelle Park, NJ: Hayden Book Company, Inc.

Weick, K. E. (1979). *The social psychology of organizing* (2nd ed.). Reading, MA: Addison Wesley.

Weick, K. E. (1995). *Sensemaking in organizations.* Thousand Oaks, CA: Sage.

Weick, K. E. (2001). *Making sense of the organization.* Malden, MA: Blackwell Publishing.

Westley, B. H., & MacLean, M. S. (1970). A conceptual model for communications research. In K. K. Sereno & C. D. Mortensen (Eds.), *Foundations of communication theory* (pp. 103–107). New York, NY: Harper and Row Publishers.

Index

Note: Page references for figures are italicized.

accreditation programs and standards, 19–20
action stage of planned organizational change, 146
adaptive challenges, 55. *See also* technical challenges
adaptive leaders/leadership, *51*, 55
adjunct faculty, 69
Argyris, Chrys, 16, 17, 47
Armenakis, A. A., 17
Aristotle, 24, 26, 27
artifacts, 30–31
assessment, 147, *148*; subject matter experts, 132–33
assumptions, 122–23, *123*, *124*. *See also* self-discovery
authentic leaders/leadership, *50*, 53
awareness campaign/program, 101, 139–42; celebration, 142, *143*; formal progress updates, 141–42; kickoff, 139–40; smaller working teams, 140; town meetings, 141; weekly team activity report, 140–41

Balanced Scorecard, 18, 19
Beavin, J., 26, 27
behavioral approach to leadership, *49*, 52

#BlackLivesMatter movement, 67
Blake, Robert, 16
buy-in/commitment loop, 107, *108*, 113–14

celebration, 142
change agents. *See* leaders/leadership
channel, 24, 25
charismatic leadership, 48
clarity, 77–78. *See also* uncertainty
cocreate reality, 86, 96–98, 101, 120, 141
cognition, 130–31, 133
cognitive map, 29–30
commitment, 75–81, 85, 87–88, 99, 144, *145*, 146; buy-in, 107, *108*, 109–10, 113–14; voice and, 112–13
communication, 23–35, 154; cocreation of reality, 86, 96–98; environment, 98, 103, 113, 141; information and, 27–28, 95–103, 141; inner workings of, 28–35; intentional *vs.* unintentional, 100–103; kinetic flow, 25–26; leaders/leadership and, 95–103; as meaning view, 26–27; models, 23–27; nonverbal, 46, 100; one-way flow, 24–26; planned *vs.*

unplanned, 100–103; two-way model, 26; worldviews, 98–100
communication-as-meaning view, 26–27
communities, 68
competencies, leadership, 52, *54*, 125
consultants, 133
costs of higher education, 68
COVID-19 pandemic, 66–68

Dance, Fred, 26
Dashboards, 18–19, 144, 146, *148*
decision-making, organizational member in, 109–10
discrimination, 67
distributed leadership, 56

emotional healing, 53
emotions, 9, 86, 110, 131–32
empirical-rational strategy, 17
empowerment of organizational member, 87–88
environmental threats, 31
everyday leadership, *51*, 56
Excellence in Higher Education, 18–20
expertise, 124

faculty: adjunct, 69; consultants and, 133; full-time, tenure-track, 69. *See also* leaders/leadership
feedback, 25, 78–79, 101, 140
followers, leaders/leadership and, 46, 125
Freud, S., 56
full-time, tenure-track faculty, 69
funding. *See* grants and funding

grants and funding, 68

happy, happiness, 120–22, 132, 134, 138, 140
hard skills, 67, 68
Harris, S. G., 17
higher education: challenges faced by, 1–2, 66–69, 85; leaders in, 2; systems thinking, 70–72; traditional industry *vs.*, 70, 103

implementation, 137–48; and action, 146; and agreement, 142–43; and assessment, 147; and awareness, 139–42; and commitment, 144, *145*, 146; and integration, 146; and involvement, 143–44; and planning, 138–38
information exchange, 95, 96, 142. *See also* communication
information overload, 120–21
information processing and information strategies, 95, 96
in-person courses, 69
Inside Higher Education Survey of Chief Academic Officers, 67
integration stage of planned organizational change, 146
intentional *vs.* unintentional communication, 46, 100–103
involvement, 87–88, 143–44
ISO, 18

Jackson, D., 26, 27
job-related uncertainty, 77

Kaizen, 18
Katz, R. L., 24
kickoff, 139–40

Lasswell, H. D., 24
Lazarsfeld, P. F., 24
leader-member exchange theory, *50*, 52–53
Leadership Grid, 52
leadership styles, 124–26
leaders/leadership, 45–56, 153; adaptive, *51*, 55; as an important issue, 47–48; approaches and styles, 48–56, 124–25, 138; assumptions, 119, 122–25; authentic, *50*, 53; behavioral approach to, *49*, 52; change agent, 85–90, 96–97, 138, 140, 146; change effort process and, 88–90; charismatic, 48; clarity, 77–78; commitment, 75–81, 85,

88, 99, 109–10, 138, 144, *145*,
146; communication, 95–103, 113,
141; competencies, 52, *54*, 119,
125; components, 46–47; concept,
45–47; everyday, *51*, 56; expertise,
124; of failed change efforts, 10;
feedback, 78–79, 101, 140; followers
and, 125; leader-member exchange
theory, *50*, 52–53; mindset of, 48,
52; momentum, 79–80, 101; new
learning opportunity, 124; Path-Goal
Theory, *49*, 52; priorities, 79–80,
101; psychodynamic approach to,
51, 55–56; relational situations, 56;
resources, 80–81, 101, 138; self-
discovery, 119–26, 138; servant,
50, 53, 55; Situational Approach,
49, 52; skills, 48, *49*, 52, 125; task
situations, 56; team, *51*, 56; traits
and characteristics, 48, *49*, 125;
transformational, *50*, 53; uncertainty,
77–78, 141; urgency, 79–80, 101;
as vital and visible determinant, 10;
vision, 75–77
Lean, 18
Lewin, Kurt, 15, 16, 17, 20
Lightner, Candy, 32
Likert, Rensis, 16
Lippitt, R., 16, 20

MacLean, M. S., 25
Malcolm Baldridge National Quality
    Award Program (MBNQA), 18, 19
Managerial Grid. *See* Leadership Grid
The Managerial Grid (Blake and
    Mouton), 16, 52
Maslow's Hierarchy of Needs, 132
message, 24–26, 96, 130, 138–39, 142
#MeToo movement, 67, 111
Middle States Commission on Higher
    Education, 19
momentum, 79–80, 101
Mothers against Drunk Driving
    (MADD), 30, 32
Mouton, Jane, 16

negative emotions, 132
negative feedback, 31
neglect, 113
noise, 24
nonverbal communication, 46, 100
normative re-educative strategies, 17, 18

Open House, 71
open online courses, 68–69
organizational change, 7–8; buy-in/
    commitment loop, 107, *108*,
    113–14, 133; concept, 7; planned.
    See planned organizational change;
    unplanned, 7
Organizational Change Recipients'
    Beliefs Scale, 132, 143, 144
organizational member: buy-in/
    commitment loop, 107, 110–14, 134;
    communication and information
    processing, 97; cues for, 86, 101;
    decision-making and, 109–10;
    discovery, 2, 129–33; empowerment,
    87–88; informal discussions, 86;
    neglect, 113; outlets to talk and
    share, 85–87, 140–41; participation,
    87–88; social influence and, 86;
    social interactions, 96; voice, 110–
    13; worldviews, 98–100

participation, 9–10, 47, 87–88, 110,
    112, 133
Path-Goal Theory, *49*, 52
peer-review system, 112
perception, 29–30
performance measurement system,
    18–20
Performance Prism, 18, 19
Persona, 130, 133
planned organizational change, 7–8;
    action, 146; agreement about the
    need to change, 142–43; assessment,
    147, *148*; awareness, 139–42;
    barriers to, 10; buy-in, 107, 110, 133;
    change agent, 85–90, 96–97, 138,
    140; commitment, 75–81, 85, 144–

46; effect of, 8–10; implementation, 2, 137–48; integration, 146; involvement, 143–44; leadership of, 47; models of, 16–17; performance measurement system, 18–20; planning, 138–39; resistance to, 8–10, 90; resource list, 132, 134; steps to, 137–48; strategies for, 15–16; top-level strategy, 17–18

planned *vs.* unplanned communication, 46, 100–103

planning, for planned organizational change, 138–39

positive emotions, 131

power-coercive strategies, 17, 18

priorities, 79–80, 85, 88–90, 101, 139–40, 142

project management, 88–89

property tax exemption, 68

psychodynamic approach to leadership, *51*, 55–56

racism, 67

receiver, 24–26

regional accreditation programs, 20

resistance, 8–10, 90, 121; as behavior, 9; cognition, 9; emotional, 9; to open online courses, 68–69; participation for overcoming, 9–10

resources, 80–81, 89, 101, 138, 140

Ruben, B. D., 17, 20

self: sense of, 28–29; unconscious realities of, 31

self-awareness, 119–22

self-discovery, 2, 119–26, 138; assumptions, 122–23, *123*, *124*; leadership styles, 124–26; new learning opportunity, 124; self-awareness of worldviews, 119–22; managing perceptions, 122–26

self-reference, 32

self-reflexivity, 32

self-talk, 121

sender, 24–26

sensegiving, 131, 134, 139

sensemaking, 26, 86, 96–97, 101, 131, 134, 141

sense of self, 28–29

servant leaders/leadership, *50*, 53, 55

sexual assault, 67

sexual harassment, 67

Shannon, C. E., 24

shared emotions, 131–32

Situational Approach to leadership, *49*, 52

Six Sigma, 18

skills, leadership, 48, *49*

Skills Model, *49*, 52

social influence/social influencers, 86, 90, 111, 113, 120

social interactions, 96

socialization, 29; learning process of, 31

social systems, 32–35

Socio-Technical Systems Perspective, 16

soft skills, 67–68

source, 24, 25

Spellings Commission Report, 18, 66, 107

strategic uncertainty, 77

strategies, 15–16; decide and announce, 96; top-level, 17–18

structural uncertainty, 77

student debt, 68

subject matter experts, 132–33

SWOT, 138–39, 143

systems thinking, 27, 31, 70–72, 102–3

Tavistock Institute of Human Relations, 16, 56

tax exemption, 68

team leaders/leadership, *51*, 56

technical challenges, 55. *See also* adaptive challenges

telephone, 31

Thayer, L., 25

Three-Skills Approach, 48

top-level strategies, 17–18

Total Quality Management (TQM), 18

town meetings, 141
traits and characteristics, leadership, 48, *49*
transformational leadership, 50, 53
Trist, Eric, 16
trust, 89, 99, 101, 109, 113

uncertainty, 77–78, 87, 141. *See also* clarity
unconscious self, 31
unintentional *vs.* intentional communication, 100–103
unplanned *vs.* planned communication, 100–103
urgency, 79–80, 101, 139–40, 142

Venn diagram, 132

visible leadership commitment, 144; checklist, 145
vision, 10, 75–77, 85, 87, 89, 138–39
voice, 110–13, 133; power and, 110–11; social influencers and, 111
vulnerabilities, 99

Watson, J., 16, 20
Watzlawick, B., 26, 27
Weaver, W., 24
weekly team activity report, 140–41
Weisbord, M. R., 17, 20
Westley, B., 16, 20, 25
worldviews, 35, 46, 86, 96, 98–100, 131; cognitive map, 29, self-awareness of, 119–22, 125, 129–30, 133, 138

About the Author

Dr. Stacy Smulowitz, ABC, is executive director of the Eastern Communication Association, a tenured assistant professor at the University of Scranton and former director of alumni at Wilkes University. Her passion for leading change started in 1995 as she traveled the United States to change the culture of an organization and continues through today as she helps leaders in higher education to make successful planned organizational change so that their institution can become more effective.